Harlem vs. Columbia University

Harlem vs.

Black Student Power

URBANA, CHICAGO, AND SPRINGFIELD

Columbia University

in the Late 1960s

Stefan M. Bradley   3/15/15

To Sis Marguerite,
Please stay in the fight!

S. Brad

UNIVERSITY OF ILLINOIS PRESS

First Illinois paperback, 2012
© 2009 by the Board of Trustees
of the University of Illinois
All rights reserved
Manufactured in the United States of America

∞ This book is printed on acid-free paper.

Portions of this book were first published as "Gym Crow Must
Go! The 1968 Student Rebellion at Columbia University in
the City of New York," in "We Shall Independent Be": African
American Place-Making and the Struggle to Claim Space in the
United States, ed. Angel David Nieves and Leslie M. Alexander
(Boulder: University Press of Colorado, 2008); "'Gym Crow Must
Go!' Black Student Activism at Columbia University, 1967–1968,"
Journal of African American History 88 (Spring 2003): 163–81;
and "'This Is Harlem Heights': Black Student Power and the 1968
Columbia University Rebellion," Afro-Americans in New York
Life and History 32 (January 2008): 99–122, and are included here
with permission.

The Library of Congress cataloged the cloth edition as follows:
Bradley, Stefan M.
Harlem vs. Columbia University: Black student power in the late
1960s / Stefan M. Bradley.
p.   cm.
Includes bibliographical references and index.
ISBN 978-0-252-03452-7 (cloth: alk. paper)
1. Columbia University—Student strike, 1968.
2. African American student movements—New York (State)—
New York—History. 3. Black power—New York (State)—
New York—History. 4. Morningside Park (New York, N.Y.)—
History. I. Title.
LD1250.B73   2009
378.747'1—dc22   2008037938

Paperback ISBN 978-0-252-07886-6

Contents

Prologue

Years ago, an archivist asked me what attracted me to a topic that was very much New York local history. She tactfully noted that I had not attended an Ivy League university and that I certainly was not from New York (I talked painfully slow for many of the New Yorkers I ran across). I explained to her that what happened in New York City, which many considered the capital of the world, had an impact on the rest of the nation and the world. What was to New Yorkers a local controversy over a park became a national news item and a symbol of the conflict that occurs between institutions and minority communities to the rest of the country. That was enough of a reason for an outsider like myself to take interest in what the archivist characterized as local history.

I grew up the son of southerners in the Evergreen State of Washington. We proudly breathe easy and enjoy our space. In Washington, trees are abundant and it is truly green everywhere. I suppose we northwesterners sometimes take for granted the fact that not everyone can enjoy these natural luxuries. With that mindset, in 1997 I visited New York for the first time. I was amazed at how fast-paced the Borough of Manhattan was, and I marveled at the skyscrapers and bright lights on the buildings. I was somewhat unsettled, however, that so many people were bumping into me and that I was bumping into so many people.

I stayed with the son of one of my former professors in the basement of an apartment building near 110th Street and Broadway. Living in that apartment was my host, his wife, and a new baby. I found this to be very strange. It was not strange that a young family would be living in an apartment, but that this family was living in a one-bedroom apartment where the pipes were exposed, there were no windows, and there was very little space at all. For such cramped living quarters, I found out that my host family paid well over $1,000 a month. That was mind-boggling; I could not fathom paying so much for so little, but I suppose it was necessary to survive.

As I began my research at Columbia, I walked to the university. On the way, I saw all types of people, which was exciting. I also did research at the Schomburg Center on 135th and Lenox (Malcolm X Boulevard) in Harlem. I had to walk there as well. While doing all of this walking, I noticed several things. First I noticed that my feet hurt; New Yorkers walk a lot. Second, I observed that, in that part of the city, everything seemed very gray, and it was at times hard to see the sun. The most poignant image I took in was that of children playing football on the sidewalk. As they were playing rather roughly, I thought that maybe concrete was not the best venue for such a game.

Then it all occurred to me at once and I stopped walking. The 1968 controversy at Columbia was connected to all of my observations. Space in New York comes at a high price. There are skyscrapers because there is little horizontal space left. Because there were so many different kinds of people in the city, people were destined to bump into each other literally and figuratively in search of space of their own. Finally, green space—places where children could play tackle football—was rare and could be found almost exclusively in parks. That was what made Morningside Park so important to both Columbia and the residents of Harlem. In a place where concrete reigns and life moves so quickly, recreational space was as much a commodity as was living space. Also, the impossibility of finding and keeping inexpensive living arrangements was why bad blood ran between Columbia and the Harlem community. The racial and economic disparities between those who lived on the Upper West Side of Manhattan in the 1960s added to the recipe of confrontation. In retrospect, the fact that this stew of city life boiled over in 1968 seemed almost predictable.

I must extend my deepest gratitude to those who made this work possible. I received a great deal of financial support from the little school that could, Southern Illinois University Edwardsville. Although I have since moved on, the encouragement I received from friends like Shirley Portwood, Anthony Cheeseboro, Rudy Wilson, Earleen Patterson, and Narbeth Emmanuel sustained me. Thanks also to my new academic family at Saint Louis University for recognizing the value of the project. My students have always been great cheerleaders.

Thank you to all of the archivists at Columbia, Teachers College, Barnard, and the Schomburg Center for their patience and assistance. Also, thanks to the countless librarians who helped me access materials that I did not even know existed. I am also thankful to those who allowed me to interview them. Ray Brown, Bill Sales, Cicero Wilson, Thulani Davis, Arnim Johnson, Zach Husser, Alford Dempsey, Cheryl Leggon, Christine Clark-Evans, the Reverend Samuel Brown, Daniel Douglas, Christiane Collins, Wm. Theodore de Bary, Thomas Kennedy, Bob Feldman, Mark Rudd, and Eric Foner took the time to help this aspiring historian along, and it meant so much.

I am also extremely grateful to those who read my work and provided further sources. My good friend and personal editor Marquinez Savala did well to go over my work sentence by sentence. I greatly appreciate the press editors who were able to help my duckling become a swan. Both my advisor, Carol Anderson, and my mentor, Robert Weems, offered commentary as well as encouragement. Current colleagues and several other superstar scholars have generously shared their thoughts on the work as well. Felix Armfield (thanks for the hook-up), Paul Cronin (thanks for the images), Kelton Edmonds, Monroe Fordham, V. P. Franklin, Robert Harris, Gerald Horne, Robin Kelley, Manning Marable, Joi Moore, Leonard Moore, Howard Rambsy, Sonya Ramsey, Ronald Roach, Lee Ann Whites, and countless others have done more than their share to move this project along.

Finally, from the deepest part of my heart, I give thanks for my mother and father, my two older brothers and younger sister (and all their mischievous children), my Weezie (a.k.a. Mrs. Bradley), and all of the family and friends who provided me with moral support throughout this whole endeavor. Their encouragement and love made this work a reality for me. This book is dedicated to the family survivors, Annie Lee, Alphonso, and Timothy Bradley.

Harlem vs. Columbia University

Introduction

If they build the first story, blow it up.
If they sneak back at night and build three stories,
burn it down. And if they get nine stories built,
it's yours. Take it over, and maybe we'll
let them in on the weekends.

—H. Rap Brown, February 1967

Race and power are two key elements in the narrative of American history, and they are even more important to the story of Columbia University's student revolt that started in April 1968 and continued into the fall of 1969. The predominantly white Ivy League school, in the Morningside Heights neighborhood of New York, functioned, as did many white institutions in the 1960s, as one that would impose its will on the seemingly defenseless black communities of Morningside Heights and neighboring Harlem by building a ten-story gymnasium in the precious recreational space of Morningside Park.

In the 1950s, university officials planned to build a new gymnasium in the park for several reasons. First, the university officials had already constructed softball fields in the park earlier in the decade, so they wanted a field house to go along with the ball fields. Second, as part of the federal, state, and city renewal movement of the 1950s and 1960s, officials believed that they had the right to use whatever land the university could afford to buy in order to improve the aesthetics and appeal of the school to current and potential students. Third, the university assumed that the neighboring communities, mostly black and Puerto Rican, did not have the power to stop Columbia. This last belief was based on several premises, including paternalism, white privilege, and class privilege.

Despite its claims of wanting to cooperate with the Harlem and Morningside Heights communities on matters such as the gymnasium, the university was using its power to expand into black neighborhoods that could rarely resist a large, white institution's efforts to encroach onto land that they considered their own. Because of Columbia's power and prestige in American society, many university officials did not see the need to respect the idea of ownership that black people in the nearby neighborhoods believed was so important to their survival and advancement in the United States.

Those who held top positions at Columbia also led the world. Nicholas Butler, president of Columbia from 1902 to 1945, had received the Nobel Peace Prize and was president of the Carnegie Endowment for International Peace. At one point, Butler had even received nominations to become the vice president of the United States. During Butler's tenure as president, Columbia expanded greatly and provided the venue for such endeavors as the Manhattan Project. Such leadership was apparently common at the school on the Heights. After he orchestrated the victorious campaigns of the Allies in World War II, General Dwight D. Eisenhower became the president of Columbia University and served in that capacity until 1953. He left Columbia to take his post as president of the United States. Grayson Kirk, who was president of Columbia from 1953 through the controversy of the 1960s, had served with the Department of State and had helped to broker the United Nations Charter. The trustees of Columbia were equally notable and even more powerful. Members of the university's Board of Trustees were stalwarts in the U.S. economy, owned or operated the nation's most lucrative companies, and oversaw the university's governance and assets. They held top positions at CBS, National City Bank, and the New York Times, as they worked to economically enrich the university.[1] For as powerful as all these men were in the world, they were just as powerful in the neighborhoods of Morningside Heights and Harlem. Their influence led to Columbia's expansion.

The fact that this story involved the Harlem community makes it that much more important to American and African American history. Scholar Harold Cruse, author of The Crisis of the Negro Intellectual, made a very keen observation about Harlem. He claimed that "Harlem has, in this century, become the most strategic community of black America."[2] Furthermore, he asserted, "Harlem is the black world's key community for historical, political, economic, cultural, and/or ethnic reasons." As it was, Columbia University's close proximity to this historically significant black community linked the school to the narrative of black America.

Taking that into account, this work attempts to draw out some of the important factors that contributed to the 1968–69 uprisings on the Morningside Heights campus. Particularly, it focuses on issues of landownership and spatial control as they relate to power in the United States. This work also speaks to issues of social protest movements because the Civil Rights, Black Power, New Left, and student protest movements all collided on Columbia University's campus in 1968 and 1969. The role of higher education is important to this story, as some students attempted to effect change to the university's curriculum during the latter part of the protest. Finally, issues of whiteness in relation to blackness, especially in regard to privilege and power, are integral to this work. All of those issues combined deal with race and power and how they affect American society, and in this case, how they changed the university on the Heights.

Although the focus of this work is mainly on Columbia University in the late 1960s, it attempts to answer several questions about larger society. By using Columbia as a case model, the work addresses the following questions:

* Why was it possible for white institutions to take land and power from minority populations, particularly black people, without consulting those populations?
* What were the immediate and long-term effects of the confrontation method that the student protesters had adopted from the Civil Rights movement of the mid-1960s?
* In the late 1960s, why did black and white student protesters across the nation split? Were their goals inherently different, or were the racial and class differences too deep to avoid separation? Also, how did they use each other to advance their goals?
* Why did American institutions, like universities, choose to capitulate to the demands of student demonstrators in the 1960s? Did university officials find that the students were justified in the various demands they made and the methods they used, or were the demonstrators so disruptive that university officials chose to satisfy the students' demands to keep the peace on college campuses?

Structurally, this work breaks down into two distinguishable parts and eight chapters. As Columbia affected black people on and off campus, this story becomes one about both students and the neighboring black community. The first part of the work explores Columbia's relationship with people and land in the City of New York, and the second part deals with the role of students in changing Columbia. Chapter 1 addresses issues of land, ownership, and the university while providing a short background on the development of Harlem and Morningside Heights.

The university acted as not only an institution of higher education but also a landowner and landlord in the surrounding area. Some of the university officials' ideas about landownership and property rights were tied to the apparent race and class privilege that the university held over the neighboring black communities. As the ideas of landownership held by residents of Harlem and Morningside Heights conflicted with those of the Ivy League school, chapter 1 also explains some of the rising hostility between the university and the surrounding neighborhoods. The second chapter deals with Morningside Park as a recreational space for both Harlem and Columbia. It also delves into the community's reaction to Columbia's plan for the gymnasium.

Chapter 3 covers the rise of the New Left and Black Power movements and their expansion onto the campuses of American universities. In the late 1960s, groups like Students for a Democratic Society (SDS) made their push for student power and were frequently successful in restructuring their institutes of higher learning so that students could take part in the decision-making processes of their universities. Similarly, the influence of Black Power on students at universities such as Columbia became apparent in the initial 1968 Columbia protest when members of the Students' Afro-American Society chose to act on behalf of the community. Chapter 3 also describes the integrated protest efforts of the black and white demonstrators to change the university. Later, the black and white student demonstrators separated to achieve their goals. As chapter 4 reveals, this resulted in Black Student Power, which involved black students on predominantly white campuses viewing themselves as Black Power activists, defining their own organizations, leading their own campus campaigns, and achieving their own victories. The chapter shows how black student protesters attained many goals by attaching themselves to the larger Black Freedom movement. Chapter 5 highlights the supportive role of SDS and its campaign to radicalize the student body.

Chapters 6 through 8 illustrate the victories that the Harlem and Morningside Heights communities and student protesters gained against the university, as well as the implications of those power struggles. Chapter 6 shows how, at Columbia, the strategies and goals of Black Student Power continued into the spring of 1969 as the black student group, with the support of SDS, called for changes in admissions policies. Chapter 7 discusses how Columbia University was not the only Ivy League university to be impacted by Black Power. Chapter 8 details the permanent changes that the university made to satisfy the community and student protesters and considers issues of higher education as well as university/community relations. These changes revealed some of the positive aspects of improving communication between these various groups.

From the spring of 1968 to the fall of 1969, hundreds of students participated in several strategic rebellions on the small Morningside Heights campus of

Columbia University. In April 1968, following the lead of many neighboring Harlem and Morningside Heights community members, student protesters from the university attempted to halt the construction of a gymnasium in Morningside Park, asserting that Columbia University, as an imposing white institution, was using its affluence, influence, and power to build the structure against the will of the neighboring black community. Besides the primary issue of the gym in the park, the protesters were also motivated by other factors. Those included the suspension of several students for a demonstration held earlier in the year, the school's contract with the U.S. Defense Department during the Vietnam War, and the desire for more of a voice in the decision-making processes of the university. Students—both black and white—focused on the issue of the new gym to draw the attention of the world to what they felt were Columbia's racist acts concerning the university's expansion into the nearby black community and its unfair policies regarding student participation in university affairs.

With buildings, concrete, and asphalt providing the aesthetic background for much of Manhattan and Columbia, local residents more than welcomed the beauty of a green park. As industry burgeoned in cities like New York in the late 1800s and early 1900s, city officials began to note the need to section off green areas as enclaves from the meanness that they felt came along with urbanization. In New York, officials placed landscape architects Frederick Law Olmsted and Calvert Vaux in charge of designing several of the major parks in the city, including Central, Riverside, Prospect, and Morningside parks. These parks were supposed to help foster the mentality that the industrial city could coexist with nature.[3] As the years passed, however, the city grew but the amount of available park space did not. Often, the city, universities, high schools, and community residents were in competition for the same parkland, and that was indeed the case in 1968. That year, competition for the sacred green parcels of land came to a head over Columbia University's attempt to build a large gymnasium in Morningside Park.

Landownership, including ownership of parks, has long been an important aspect of black political, social, and economic life. More important, one of the truest forms of freedom in the United States has been the ownership of land. It has defined citizenship, voting rights, and economic independence. Some historians have argued that many American patriots fought the War of Independence to maintain ownership of their land assets.[4] Land and ownership have been particularly important to African Americans who could note their transition from once being owned to becoming those who eventually owned. One of the major criticisms of Reconstruction was that, because of the prejudice of white local and state officials, black Americans did not have access to the land that they had for so long worked.[5]

That fact further rankled as segregation and discrimination restricted black citizens from purchasing their own part of America during the years of Jim Crow. During those years, many white Americans in the North and South treated black people as second-class citizens. Some of these black citizens recognized that, without the ownership of land, they had no real claim to the power that fuels a nation.[6] Black Americans argued that they should receive better treatment because of the blood and sweat that they had given to America as slaves and laborers. They knew that in the grand scheme of things, those who own land have the power to effect social change. In the twentieth century the economic status of some groups of black people improved and they were able to purchase land, but in segregated areas such as the south side of Chicago and Harlem in New York, as well as countless areas in the South, landownership was not always the norm.

This situation led many of the black Americans who actually owned land to believe that they were undoubtedly entitled to the rights of citizenship that white America had denied them up until that point. Jim Crow, in some ways, also fostered a sense of ownership in the areas to which these black citizens were segregated. Already bothered by the fact that they could not choose where to live, black residents in places like Harlem protested when white institutions attempted to encroach into their neighborhoods by purchasing land and buildings. This work documents what happened when these white institutions encroached too far onto land and property that black people believed belonged to them.

Many university students learned of the controversy over the gym through community groups and student organizations. Two campus-based groups in particular—the Students' Afro-American Society (SAS) and the Columbia branch of the nationwide student organization SDS, led by Mark Rudd, strongly opposed the raising of the gym, arguing that Columbia acted on racist motives. These groups believed that the university did not need to build a new gymnasium in the neighboring black community's park, where the residents were already short of parkland.

Even though SAS and SDS shared the goal of halting construction of the gym, they held different agendas in general. The main goal of SDS during the protest was the radicalization of the mostly white population of the school. For the black students of SAS, halting construction on the gymnasium was their primary issue throughout the 1968 protest. This was because SAS privileged the concerns of black people as a whole, whether students or community members, over the interests of the relatively small number of people on college campuses. The fact that SDS used the gymnasium, an issue that had direct effects on the black community in the city, as a means to move its goal (the radicalization of students) eventually contributed to the break along racial lines of the protesting groups.

In spite of these differences, by the end of the protest in April 1968, both groups succeeded in achieving their goals of halting construction of the gym and radicalizing the majority of the student body. They did not do so, however, by using the racially integrated struggle approach that civil rights leaders such as Martin Luther King Jr. advocated. Instead, the relationship of the university chapter of the mostly white SDS and the black SAS illustrated some of the trends that were occurring in the national student movement by first separating along racial lines and then employing different tactics and methods to reach their goals.

The debate surrounding the racial integration of reform and protest movements dates back to before the Civil War but is extremely relevant to the demonstrations that took place at Columbia in 1968–69. Leaders and reformers have taken various stances on the debate and approaches to the problems of racism, discrimination, and injustice. Before the start of the Civil War, both black and white reformers dealt with the prospect of integration in the abolitionist movement. As historian Charles Wesley pointed out, some white abolitionist organizations attempted to limit the amount of black participation in the movement.[7] In a similar vein, some black people who attempted to avoid the racism and exclusion they had experienced in predominantly white antislavery organizations started their own abolitionist groups. Members of these black abolitionist groups, such as J. Mercer Langston and Frederick Douglass, became disillusioned with the acts of renowned abolitionists such as William Lloyd Garrison and the Tappan brothers.[8] Many black abolitionists found that they had little, if any, power in decision making within the integrated abolitionist movement.[9]

During the twentieth century, the debate surrounding racially integrated reform manifested itself in the words of Malcolm X, who detested the integrated Civil Rights movement of the early 1960s.[10] He asserted that the efforts of black activists would, in the end, be unacknowledged and unsuccessful. His rationale was that if black leaders allied themselves with white leaders, soon the white leaders would take over the protest movement because it was white people who retained most of the economic and political power, a situation reflecting the national abolitionist movement. Therefore he thought it essential that in matters directly concerning black people, only black leaders should make decisions.[11] Otherwise, he warned, white liberal leaders might misrepresent the original goals of black participants in the movement.

Another example of the fissure between those who would and would not implement integrationist strategies in the struggle against racism was the 1966 split between the Southern Christian Leadership Conference (SCLC) and the Student Non-Violent Coordinating Committee (SNCC). In the late 1950s, Martin Luther King Jr. organized the SCLC as an umbrella organization that could train people for nonviolent direct-action protest. Under King's leadership, SCLC included both black and white members because he believed that the two groups could solve America's racial problems together.[12] Young people, heeding the counsel of SCLC official Ella Baker, formed SNCC as an offshoot of SCLC. In 1966, after a march led by the two groups and James Meredith, the first black student to attend the University of Mississippi, some of the members of SNCC began to question the effectiveness of the nonviolent approach to protest as they watched the violence against blacks increase and the possibilities of change remain stagnant.[13]

Using knowledge they gained from leaders such as Malcolm X regarding black separatism, SNCC officials Stokely Carmichael and H. Rap Brown claimed that the black SCLC leaders were too accommodating of the strategies of white members and allies. Furthermore, the increasingly militant leadership of SNCC believed that while the war against racism was as bitter as ever in the South, the campaign should be directed to the North, where racism also thrived. With that, SNCC bolted from association with SCLC and pushed for what it called "Black Power."[14] The leadership advocated a separation from whites as well as black socioeconomic self-reliance, reminiscent of Malcolm X's viewpoints. Soon, SNCC purged itself of its white members and brought its struggle northward.[15] This split affected the student movement in that white students, who had worked alongside black student protesters, were being asked to leave organizations like SNCC and start their own groups, provided the white students were still interested in creating a society of racial equality. Many of those students went on to create the national organization SDS.

The debate over which approach to take spilled onto the Morningside Heights campus of Columbia University in 1968. The separation tactics that Malcolm X and later Black Power leaders advocated worked to advance the protest as the black students of SAS eventually asked the white radicals of SDS to start their own demonstration so that the black group could focus on its own issue: the university's attempt to build the gym in Morningside Park.[16] In this rare case in American history, black activists succeeded in taking something back from a white establishment. Although the Harlem community still complained about the alleged racist acts of the university, it could boast of one small, tangible victory: 2.1 acres of Morningside Park.[17] With black students acting as representatives of the nearby black neighborhoods, the community received a more respected status in that relationship. By separating from the white protesters early on, the black demonstrators made their race an issue that the university had to address. Using the black communities of Harlem and Morningside Heights as its base of support to accomplish its goal, SAS played on the administrators' fear of a race riot spilling onto campus. That fear was all the more real as the spring protest of 1968 took place just weeks after the assassination of Martin Luther King Jr., which incited riots in the neighborhoods that surrounded the school.[18]

In an alliance with the black community of Harlem, student and community activists would attain Black Power in its most essential form. For the black students and community members, what occurred during the 1968 protest was truly amazing. Two groups managed to overcome class divisions to ally themselves along racial lines. As members of the black intelligentsia and the working class, they were able to manifest power by using their race to invoke fear and reconsideration in a powerful white institution, and this was extremely rare for black people in the United States.

For white America, power had manifested itself in the same way since the founding of the country. After Nathaniel Bacon's Rebellion in 1676, white people were able to ally themselves along racial lines to assert their place in society.[19] The same occurred when the Ku Klux Klan mustered members from the ranks of both politicians and sharecroppers to disfranchise newly freed black Americans during Reconstruction and even into the twentieth century.[20] This carried on during the Jim Crow era and even into modern politics, when presidential candidate Richard Nixon used his "southern strategy" to stabilize a white southern constituency at the expense of black progress.[21] In 1968–69 black students and working-class black community members used the same tactic to achieve Black Power, to keep the gym out of the park, and to force Columbia to treat the black community with respect. If Black Power were ever to be fully achieved in this country, at least politically, it would take an alliance of what sociologist E. Franklin Frazier called the "black bourgeoisie" and the black proletariat.[22] This alliance manifested itself in the rebellions of 1968–69.

In the years leading up to the spring 1968 protest, the enrollment of black students at Columbia University was low. Although Columbia and the other Ivy League schools attempted to recruit black students with the help of the National Scholarship Service and Fund for Negro Students (NSSFNS), not many students of color enrolled. To deal with this, during the mid-1960s Columbia participated in the Association of College Admissions Counselors' Ivy Talent Searching Program to attract black students.[23]

Director of Admissions Henry Coleman explained the institution's desire for more black students. "The whole future for the Negro people is tied up in education, and the universities and colleges can, by their actions, help the nation as a whole," he claimed.[24] Columbia, then, would be doing its part to aid society by admitting those who needed education most. Furthermore, Coleman believed that "education is a process in preparation for life, and it would be unrealistic in today's world to ignore the reality of an integrated society." Considering Columbia's proximity to a black neighborhood and the number of black students that were on campus at the time, it seemed as though Columbia had thus far done well to ignore that reality.

As it was, the number of black students at Columbia did not increase greatly. In fact in Columbia's College of Arts and Sciences, there were fewer than fifty black students out of approximately 2,500 in the 1964–65 academic year.[25] One reason for the low enrollment number was that Ivy League universities competed fiercely to recruit the brightest black students across the nation. Often, Harvard University won the competition for the students who desired an Ivy League education. Before Columbia formed its partnership with the NSSFNS to launch the talent search, Harvard was already allocating special funds to scholarships for black students.[26] That fact, in combination with Harvard's history of esteemed black alumni, influenced students of color to apply and attend. According to Columbia's student newspaper, another reason that Columbia's numbers were so low was that admissions officers visited schools in the South (where many black students still attended illegally segregated schools) but did not stop at primarily black schools. The same situation was true of admissions counselors and mostly black secondary schools in New York City. The paper indicated that Columbia had not previously sought the assistance of current university students in recruiting high school students, nor did the university hold conferences or interest meetings that would allow potential black students to become aware of the possibility of attending Columbia.[27] Doing so might have improved the Ivy League institution's opportunity to boost its black enrollment.

Black students who chose to attend Columbia faced certain trials while on campus. For instance, they were regularly stopped by the security guards (sometimes black) to have their identifications checked while most white students were not stopped. Then, there were the uncomfortable feelings that black students would have at university events when someone would tell a joke about the white student who had mistakenly taken the wrong subway car and emerged out of the subway station at 116th and Lenox (Harlem) instead of 116th and Broadway (outside of Columbia's campus). Some black students remembered the confrontations that occurred between them and white male students at mixers when the black students danced with white Barnard College women. During the 1960s, black people frequently felt out of place on Columbia's campus.

Under these circumstances, in 1964 a small number of concerned black students organized into a discussion group, which later became the Students' Afro-American Society. Hilton Clark (son of Mamie Clark and famed psychologist Kenneth Clark, who were Columbia alumni) initially founded the group as a national organization. Before the spring rebellion of 1968, the society's protest activity was fairly moderate.[28] One of the group's main goals was the creation of a sense of identity for the small number of black students in American universities, particularly Columbia.

In a *New York Times* article, Clark explained that "there is a great deal of apathy among educated or so-called Ivy League Negroes to our race's continuing struggle."[29] To that end, he noted: "They [black Ivy League students] are losing identification with the masses of Negroes who are far below them educationally and economically." Clark reasoned that "the Northern Negro, perhaps well-to-do with a prep-school education, has experienced only the more subtle forms of discrimination and begins to get used to them. . . . He feels he has little in common with the great majority of his race." Extending his hypothesis, he included the southern black student: "On the other hand, the Southern Negro, who is probably poorer and may even have come from segregated schools, finds things so much better here that he doesn't see the subtle forms of discrimination. He begins to lose interest in the struggle." This, he concluded, led to apathy and a lack of identity among black students as a whole. In his view, SAS would become "an experiment to try and make the Negro at Columbia aware of the problems, get him talking about it with others in a similar situation and hopefully have the individual come up with some answers for himself." SAS, he predicted, would encourage its members to think "about their identity with other Negroes."[30]

Before the 1968 protest, the members of SAS protested for a change in the structure of conservative Columbia University. They specifically fought for the employment of more black faculty members, the implementation of black curricula, and the recruitment and admission of a larger number of black students.

As the 1967–68 school year approached and Black Power roared around the nation, the leadership of the nearly 150-member group became increasingly more militant, and the goals of the group expanded to include taking up the struggle of black people in neighboring Harlem against the towering Columbia University. Newly enrolled students like Leon Denmark, Mark Durham, Ralph Metcalfe Jr. (son of the 1936 Olympian), Larry Frazier, and Cicero Wilson brought with them a Black Nationalist perspective. With their desire to gain power in the United States by using white institutions for both knowledge and employment, SAS reflected its vision of Black Power.

An anonymous observer of these black student activists reported to the Fact-Finding Commission (a university-appointed committee formed to assess the causes of the rebellion, also known as the Cox Commission) that the purpose of black students' participation in the protest "was to dramatize the unresponsiveness of the university primarily to them," instead of the university's neglect and mistreatment of the community of Harlem.[31] Yet by the spring of 1968, the issue that SAS had wanted to dramatize was the construction of a "racist" gym in Morningside Park, not its own bid for power, claimed Professor of Sociology Immanuel Wallerstein.[32] In the view of the black student protesters, they struggled for more than their own advancement. Their larger concern was for the interests of their race, which was integral to the Black Power philosophy. Because of the commonality of their race, the black students and black community members shared a bond in their battle against racism.

As Professor Wallerstein indicated, "The black students acted as representatives for Harlem within Columbia."[33] Unlike many other young black people in predominantly white schools in the 1960s, black students at Columbia found themselves surrounded by a black community. Simply because of this proximity, the black students at the school had the opportunity to work closely with, and to affect directly, the surrounding community. Ray Brown, a senior majoring in history in 1968, stated that "the black students are specifically opposed to Columbia University's use of its position of political strength to take advantage of the powerlessness of the black community."[34] The issue of the gymnasium in the park gave these young black students the chance to become activists for black equality.

After witnessing the serious and driven attitudes of black students at Columbia during the spring 1968 protest, Archibald Cox, a member of the university's Fact-Finding Commission, observed that the "Negro students on campuses, large and small, throughout the country have made unprecedented efforts to bring about changes in campus life[,] increasing their participation and enhancing respect for their identity."[35] According to Lerone Bennett Jr., a writer for *Ebony* magazine, the Cox Commission's report correctly assessed the mood of many black students across the country. In an article entitled "Confrontation on the Campus," Bennett wrote about the phenomenon of black students revolting against universities, black and white alike, to attain their goals. Like black student demonstrators at Columbia, black students elsewhere were "struggling, often physically, for the ultimate in power—the power to control the cultural apparatus which defines reality and shapes and maims minds."[36]

Institutions of higher learning were bastions of the "cultural apparatus" to which Bennett referred. The black militants of SAS, in spite of their claim during the protest not to want student power, sought the power to change their university in relation to the surrounding community. By stopping the construction of the gymnasium in Morningside Park, they would undoubtedly change the structure of Columbia University, and hopefully the way their school treated its neighbors.

After consulting with various members of the Harlem community, the Students' Afro-American Society saw the proposed gym in the park as a symbol of racism and a struggle for control over land in the adjacent neighborhoods. Many Harlem residents believed that, by constructing the gym in Morningside Park, the university was trying to take even more land from the community, and they were correct. Not only did Columbia own many buildings and much land in Harlem, but it had also already leased several acres of land in the park. The proposed ten-story gymnasium allocated the community only a small percentage of actual floor space and forced non-Columbia affiliates to enter through a different set of doors.[37] During the protest, the black demonstrators cleverly referred to the proposed structure as "Gym Crow."[38]

Along with the hundred or so black demonstrators on campus, the white radicals of Students for a Democratic Society and their followers also protested what they considered to be the unfair and repressive nature of the university. Thomas Kennedy, who was a white graduate student in the department of East Asian languages and cultures, remembered that "the people that took charge of [the protest] were a group known as SDS."[39] In 1960, white leftist Robert Alan "Al" Haber and several others founded the group in Michigan. Two years later, Thomas Hayden, also a white leftist, took the reins of leadership and submitted his Port Huron Statement that denounced racism, repudiated war escalation, and called for the deliverance of decision-making power to ordinary citizens (including young people and students). According to Hayden, its main goal was "the development of a political means toward the creation of a radical society."[40] To achieve this goal, SDS sought to restructure society by restructuring the university. Alan Adelson, author and former SDS member, recalled SDS "spent long hours discussing the university's role in society."[41] Members of the group found that, "despite its pretenses of accumulating knowledge and inspiring scholarship," the university itself was "an integral part of the system's corruption."

The challenge for SDS members at Columbia was to convince the generally politically apathetic student population that there was a need for change in society and particularly at the university. That task became difficult when students believed that the institutions and environments that needed change had little to do with them on the safe Morningside Heights campus. Issues such as poverty, racism, and social inequality did not rest heavily on the students, who could afford to worry about what to eat, where to eat, and who to pay for serving them their meal.

This understanding had much to do with their class and worldview. As Columbia University psychiatry lecturer Robert Liebert has noted, many of the students at the university were not from the underclass and had benefited from a relative economic advantage over many citizens in the country.[42] To end the apathy that often comes along with the privilege of affluence, white radicals at Columbia had to identify issues that affected the students personally. SDS needed, in Adelson's words, "something very concrete that they [Columbia students] can't ignore; and, if at all possible, something that will finally produce moral indignation in people."[43]

One of the issues they used to arouse such moral indignation was the proposed gymnasium. SDS presented the gymnasium issue to the largely class-privileged, apathetic white student body as one of racism. This was particularly effective, as well as timely, because of the April 4 death of the Reverend Martin Luther King Jr., who was a respected and recognizable figure for many of the students. The students could see how King's death affected the black residents of Harlem, which was just below the university, and they believed that they could do something to end racism by protesting the gymnasium. Along with the gym, the other main objects of the Columbia chapter's protest were the Institute for Defense Analyses (IDA), which tied the university to the Vietnam War effort, the Naval Reserve Officers Training Corps (NROTC), and Central Intelligence Agency (CIA) contracts.[44] Many of the students believed that their university should not be a laboratory for war experiments that the military would use in its efforts against North Vietnam. In the view of these protesters, these issues were all part of the imperialist and racist behavior of American elites and the government. Demonstrator Mark Rudd explained that SDS's role was "changing people's understanding of society, getting them to understand the forces at work to create a university the way it is."[45]

To be most effective, SDS needed a demonstration that would have an impact on not just Columbia's campus but college campuses everywhere. Rudd remembered that the protest would be a "straight political act to gain power—to gain *some* power."[46] As it turned out, the protest that actually occurred around the gym in Morningside Heights involved black student militants, moderate members of the student body, and indignant community members. SDS and the rest of those involved did gain some power; however, they did so separately.

It would be too simple to state that during the 1968–69 Columbia University protests the black students of SAS achieved their goal of stopping the construction of the gym single-handedly. In fact, the black protesters needed the white student protesters of SDS just as the white radicals needed the black militants to advance their goals. While the black demonstrators had some ability to draw the attention of university officials, the larger number of white radical protesters added louder resonance to the voices of the black students who protested on behalf of the community. In turn, the black student demonstrators' insistence on separating themselves from the white protesters helped the radical white students to focus on their own agenda and goals. With help from the black protesters, SDS radicalized much of the general student body and eventually shut the university down for six weeks.

As many of the student protesters viewed it, the 1968 protest was over power. Although all participants in the controversy—the university administration and faculty, the Harlem and Morningside Heights communities, and black and white students—held power, it clearly was not equally distributed. The black student protesters knew that what little power they had in relation to the university was not enough to influence the type of change they sought to make. With that in mind, they turned to the nearby black neighborhoods of Harlem and Morningside Heights, whose members were willing to support black student militancy when that militancy was directed against the gymnasium. Indeed, it was the gym that symbolized for SAS the continuing struggle for ownership and control of the black community. It also symbolized the potential for SAS members to change the university's relationship with the city that surrounded it. The white student radicals also knew that they had power, but not enough to change the structure of Columbia University. They, like the black student protesters, needed a larger body of advocacy to accomplish their goal of student power, and during the 1968 protest they turned to the mostly white, moderate student body, which they eventually helped to radicalize.

Several historians have written about the Columbia student revolt of 1968. Interestingly, most of the authors completed their work very near the time of the rebellions. My work, therefore, benefits from the advantage of thirty-some years of hindsight and, more important, access to large caches of archival material. One author, Roger Kahn, documented the student rebellions at the time and attributed the protest to the rise of the New Left and its influence on the university's campus. He claimed that radicalism was the main impetus of the uprising. Students, mostly radical and white, wanted to confront what they believed was the "militarization" of their university. By militarization, Kahn referred to the fact that during the 1960s Columbia University, along with an increasing number of American universities, was taking part in the effort to prepare the United States for a potential third world war with the Soviet Union.

Columbia did indeed have ties with the U.S. Defense Department, which provoked many students to protest against their school. Historians have dealt directly with the subject of militarization and its effects on American society during the cold war years.[47] They have asserted that the nation was using many institutions, such as its universities, to build up the military-industrial complex that President Eisenhower (who incidentally was a previous president of Columbia University) had warned against in his farewell address. Kahn maintained that this militarization of the university, combined with Columbia's racist policies toward the adjacent neighborhoods and the conservative hierarchy that had existed for years at the school, gave the students enough reason to rebel.[48]

Concerned students like those at Columbia University attempted to address their colleges and universities through the use of direct-action confrontation, a method that was becoming popular after the University of California–Berkeley's Free Speech Movement of 1964. At Berkeley, concerned leftist students made demands of their university for more student power. Much like Kahn, Jerry Avorn, a writer for the student newspaper *Columbia Daily Spectator* during the 1968 protest, saw the Columbia controversy as a revolution of the students against an institution that, as he suggested, epitomized society's repressive authoritarian nature. Avorn claimed that these students questioned America's traditional ability to choose between order and law and morality, and they chose to react to the insensitivity of the administration to students and to the neighboring community.[49] Robert Liebert, who taught psychiatry at the university, took a similar view by stating that the strife of the nation manifested itself in microcosm on Columbia's campus. Much as SAS and SDS claimed, issues concerning the Vietnam War, racism, and the generational gap of the 1960s did indeed affect not just the larger society, but also the smaller ones of American universities.[50]

At least two authors take a different position on the issue of Columbia's controversy. Daniel Bell, who was a sociology professor at the university during the time of the protest, disagreed with Liebert's assertion that the university was a microcosm of the United States.[51] He stated that the student radicals at Columbia, particularly those in SDS, chose to take out their frustrations with society on the college campus because a university is basically defenseless, which would have meant less-negative consequences for negative actions for the group in general. Had the radical students taken their demonstration off campus, Bell claimed, the repercussions would have been much greater than they actually were. Another author, Joanne Grant, claimed that the students who participated in the protest were attempting to move away from the "ivory tower" image of the university to one that was more of a "moral force" in society; that is, one that dealt with all the problems that Kahn, Avorn, and Liebert had mentioned.[52]

None of the authors features race as a leading factor in the cause of the student protest at Columbia and across the nation, but instead they point to factors such as the Vietnam War and the rise of the youth culture and the New Left as driving forces. It is my position that race was, indeed, a driving force in the way the prestigious white university related to the mostly black and Puerto Rican Morningside Heights and Harlem communities, and in its reaction to the student protests. Moreover, race was a primary factor in the split of the demonstrating students that lasted throughout the protest.

As the authors quoted above have indicated, along with the gymnasium, there were two other catalysts that ignited protest between 1968 and 1969. The Vietnam War was one of these. U.S. intervention in South Vietnam was a source of great controversy. As the nation questioned its leadership's choice to intervene, many young people called for an immediate removal of troops. Concerned with the morality of the war, as well as the safety of the lives of themselves and their peers, many college-aged students called for an end to the war. This call became increasingly louder in the late 1960s, especially as President Richard Nixon began to end the college deferments that were available to students before 1968.

One other form of pressure that caused the Morningside Heights campus to erupt was the movement of the New Left onto American campuses. By the 1960s the U.S. population reflected the fact that there were more people under the age of twenty-five than there were over it. Many of these young Americans believed that they had an obligation to change society for the better. One of the ways they chose to do so was through the university and through organizations like SDS, which glamorized many leftist ideals on campuses with the use of participatory democracy. These groups wanted a larger say in society, which meant that their advocates attending American universities wanted to change the hierarchical structures of those institutions.

As the students formulated their campaign for power and against the Vietnam War, resentment toward Columbia University arose in the black neighborhoods of Harlem and Morningside Heights. The school had fostered rocky relations with the residents of those areas long before the protest. Because of this, the residents' ill feelings toward the university went deeper than just the proposal for the gymnasium in the park and the school's recent treatment of people in the surrounding area. Columbia University, like many white institutions throughout the United States, was guilty of treating black and other minority citizens poorly in order to advance the goals of the institution, which in this case involved expanding its ownership of land and buildings.

Columbia University's attempt to take the land and property of black people in Harlem and Morningside Heights was just part of a long story of white authorities disrespecting people in those neighborhoods. Indignant feelings of community members about the school were influenced in part by national and international events that affected blacks in America. During the 1960s Harlem and many other black communities in America experienced civil unrest. In 1960 in Greensboro, North Carolina, several black students from North Carolina A&T attempted to integrate the city through lunch-counter sit-ins. Three years later, Lee Harvey Oswald was charged with assassinating President John F. Kennedy, whose constituency included many African Americans. The Black Muslim movement thrived, and civil rights leader Martin Luther King Jr. articulated his dream of racial harmony. Although Congress had passed the Civil Rights Act of 1964, the long, hot summer of that year saw yet another riot in Harlem after an off-duty police officer killed a black youth. The next year, as King marched in the South, several Black Muslim men (in a possible conspiracy) assassinated Malcolm X in Harlem, and, that summer, fueled by police brutality, the Watts section of Los Angeles exploded with racial violence.

After the mid-1960s the government increasingly called many young black men from their communities to fight in the Vietnam War, and those not drafted struggled to find employment. By 1968 Black Power, which advocated separation along racial lines, had reached its pinnacle, and unrest among many black people intensified. Certainly, the April 4 murder of King further unsettled many black communities. In Harlem people poured into the streets, rioting and grieving the murder of their leader. Many black people blamed the callousness of white America for these unfortunate incidents, and those black residents who lived next to the Ivy League school on Morningside Heights saw the institution as a representative of white oppression. Consequently, they made it a target of their frustration.

Many of the issues that frustrated Harlem residents in the years leading up to 1968 also concerned the students on campus. The factors that led many of the students to protest in the spring of 1968 continued to motivate demonstrators well into the fall of the next year. Nearly a year after the beginning of the crisis in 1968, the black members of SAS protested again. Feeding off the momentum they had gained from the protest efforts against the gymnasium the year before, they pushed the university to restructure its curriculum to include an independent black studies major and also to allow for the acceptance into the university of more black and Puerto Rican students from local high schools. Again, race played a role in the protest as the black demonstrators made sure to use the support of the surrounding black neighborhoods and SAS members held separate demonstrations from those of the mostly white members of SDS. In 1969 the university satisfied more of the black student group's demands, showing again the benefits of racial separation in student protests. Because the student protesters had been victorious in the efforts to halt the construction of the university's proposed gymnasium in 1968, they were able to carry on the next year.

During the spring 1968 protest, the gym issue provided the critical adhesive between Columbia's SDS and SAS, which had not maintained especially close relations prior to that time.[53] As Ray Brown of SAS put it, "Our position on other issues, specifically that of student power, is simply this: our immediate concern is not with the restructuring of Columbia University" or society.[54] To be sure, in the spring of 1968 SAS may not have stated as one of its goals the restructuring of the university, but that was indeed what it had sought in its earlier protests for an increase in black faculty members and courses. The same was true of its later proposals for a black studies major and increased black and Puerto Rican admissions into the university. For 1968, though, the proposed gym in the park was its primary target, and by employing tactics of racial separation from the white protesters of SDS and gaining the support of the black communities in Morningside Heights and Harlem, it gained a victory against institutional white America on behalf of the local community.

The protest efforts of the black and white students of Columbia University in 1968–69 provided examples to other Ivy League students who intended to change their universities. The characteristics of the Columbia protests, such as separation along racial lines, participatory democracy, and the occupation of buildings, reappeared in 1969 demonstrations at Harvard, Yale, Penn, and Cornell universities. There, too, key components of their gains concerned race and power, and the student protesters used them to their advantage. In effect, the protests that took place at Columbia University eventually contributed to the restructuring of several more of America's top universities and the functions of higher education as they concerned students and the black community.

1

Why I Hate You

Community Resentment of Columbia

The debate over what to do about the possibility of further institutional expansion highlights the competition that occurred between the city, the university, and the local Harlem and Morningside Heights communities for space. The role of city officials is also important to the background of the drama concerning Columbia's plans for expansion because the community's issues with the power structure became much more than just complaints—they became political debates with municipal consequences. This chapter offers a short history of black residents in New York City, Harlem, and Morningside Heights and points out the grievances of the different characters who initiated the protest against the university's expansion policies and eventually the proposal for a gym in Morningside Park. Particularly important to this chapter are the efforts of the residents of the neighborhoods that surround the Ivy League institution and what they reveal about the assertion of power against an overbearing opponent.

A major theme regarding the controversy between Columbia and the neighboring community involved the control of local residents over their living and recreational space, and that theme receives attention in this chapter. Specifically, this chapter covers Columbia University's power as a landlord and its relationship with the city. The neighborhoods adjacent to Columbia watched the university's encroachment into Morningside Heights and Harlem and saw that with each purchase of land or buildings, the situation became more hopeless. When Columbia attempted to take even more land in a park that Harlem residents considered their own, the community reacted to check these "imperialist" ambitions.[1]

While black resentment of white America had accompanied the first slave ship that arrived in the English colonies, Harlem's resentment of Columbia University developed mostly in the 1950s and 1960s. Located amid the nation's largest urban population, Columbia's main campus is adjacent to the lower west side of Harlem. Riverside Park is on the western side of the university, and on the eastern side is Morningside Park, which constituted the only barrier between the richly endowed, elite educational center and Harlem, where many working-class and poor blacks and Puerto Ricans resided.[2] Originally, the university had not been located on Morningside Heights. As early as 1775 the institution, then known as King's College, sat on the land of Trinity Episcopal Church, in the southern part of Manhattan Island. In 1897 it moved to what was known as Morningside Heights because, according to George Nash, author of *The University and the City,* Columbia University was attempting to "escape" the encroachment of the city onto the campus.[3]

The Morningside Heights section of Manhattan stretches north from 110th Street to 125th Street and west from Morningside Park to the Hudson River. Morningside Park, designed by Frederick Law Olmsted and Calvert Vaux in the early 1870s, is very strange in shape. There are cliffs and ledges within the park itself, with very few flat areas for practical use. Many years later, an article about a park patron claimed, however, that those ledges and cliffs "served as a poor-kid's jungle gym."[4] The patron claimed that the summertime was the best time to use the park because the children could climb under one of the protruding rock shelves and relax in the shade. Olmsted commented on its terrain in an 1873 report: "The only surfaces within it not sharply inclined, are two small patches lying widely apart, against the northeast and southeast corners respectively."[5] Harlem begins from the flats of the park and extends eastward and northward in direction. Above the park, on the Heights, is the Ivy League center of higher education, Columbia University, and below and adjacent to the park are the poorer neighborhoods of Harlem. Morningside Park provides the buffer zone between the two very different environments.

Black people in New York City and particularly Harlem have roots that run deep in history. After the Civil War, black migrants found some opportunity in New York as the city became an industrial metropolis. Ethnic groups like the Italians and Russians moved en masse to the city from Europe to fill industrial positions. Many Jewish people moved to the lower east side of Manhattan, and the Italian immigrants settled in similar patterns, creating areas like "Little Italy" on 110th Street.[6] Typically, newer immigrants moved to areas where land was cheaper and then, after amassing enough capital, left for the growing suburbs at the turn of the century. By 1900 there were 60,000 black residents in New York City, with 36,000 of them living in Manhattan. Until that point, black New Yorkers mostly occupied positions in the service industries, such as barbering, waiting, and catering. Some worked as skilled artisans. Some ten years later, blacks migrated mostly from the South to account for almost 92,000 of the city's population.[7]

Harlem, which occupies the northern part of Manhattan, provided a home for most of these black migrants. Originally part of the Dutch colony of New Amsterdam, Nieuw Haarlem village was established in 1658. Soon after, the English took control of the colony, renaming it New York and changing Nieuw Haarlem to Harlem. Between 1830 and the 1880s, Harlem became a suburb of the city, where mainly Jewish and Italian people resided. Black people did not become the majority population in Harlem until after the turn of the century, when the dynamics of U.S. immigration changed.

In 1917, as the United States became actively involved in the First World War, the nation closed its borders to most European immigrants. During and after the war, many black workers, seeking to fill the jobs that European immigrants had occupied until that point, came to the major U.S. metropolises of the North in search of opportunity and to escape the social hardships of the South. Historians have discussed why black migrants from the South would choose places like Harlem to settle.

These scholars considered the role of "push and pull factors." Some of the push factors were the droughts, floods, and boll weevil epidemics that were occurring just before and during the First World War. Another push factor was that racial violence was as intense as ever in the South, and black people chose to resist by leaving. Among the factors that pulled the black southerners northward were more opportunity for free education, shorter work days, higher wages, political autonomy, and, hopefully, less racism.[8] This phenomenon, known as the "Great Migration," contributed to the booming increase of New York City's black population to 327,000 by 1930.[9]

Considering these push and pull factors, Harlem, and later Morningside Heights, became places where many black southerners eventually settled. Believing that they had escaped voting restrictions, broken-down schools, separate-but-unequal facilities, and blatant racial injustice, not to mention inconsistent crop conditions, many southern blacks looked at life in New York City as an improvement over that in the South. In many ways, the city did constitute an improvement, with its indoor toilets, free schooling, and more consistent work opportunities. At least that was what many black migrants believed. But the jobs that southern black workers left their homes to find did not always materialize.

In the early 1900s most white employers were wary of employing unskilled black workers. Moreover, employers did not believe that blacks could master the skills necessary for various higher-paying industrial jobs and therefore would not train them. Some historians have attributed employers' attitudes concerning black workers to their ideas about whiteness.[10] For the employers it was not just logical that only whites could be capable enough to work as skilled laborers, but necessary for the creation of their identity to believe so. These employers continued to hire white workers in spite of the fact that many black migrants were actually skilled in a variety of industrial crafts. In any event, white employers based their beliefs on their perception that blackness somehow meant "otherness," and that the "others" (black laborers) could not be trusted with the opportunity to do "white work." In turn, employers acted on that rationale.

So the reality of racial discrimination stifled many southern black migrants' dreams of getting ahead financially in New York. Public education was free, but schools seldom offered black youth the type of education that was available to white children. Also, as more black migrants took up residence in the neighborhoods nearest the various factories and job sites, many white city dwellers began to fear the change that was occurring in the racial makeup of their environment. There was, as a consequence, a resurgence of the Ku Klux Klan in northern cities. Although most northern whites did not go so far as to join the Klan, racial intolerance was evident in the riots and melees that occurred in northern industrial cities between 1915 and 1921.[11] For southern black migrants, their "Great Migration" to New York and other northern cities did not provide the great improvement they sought.

Many black people who moved north soon realized that the "slum" was present in the North as well as the South.[12] Upon arriving in New York, they did what most migrant groups did and moved among their own people. Unlike the Jews or Italians, who could, if they desired, leave their ethnic neighborhoods after a generation or so, segregation limited the areas to which blacks could move for decades. So, much like the south side of Chicago, Harlem became a place where blacks had to remain, in spite of their economic condition. When segregation forced them to stay in Harlem, some prospered but a great many suffered the effects of the urban ghetto. Kenneth Clark, black psychologist and graduate of Columbia, described the ghetto: "The dark ghettos are social, political, educational, and, above all, economic colonies."[13] Harlem was no exception. Under these conditions, resentment and hostility against white America arose. Turning that frustration into fuel for their own artistic and creative projects, black writers and artists created a new era for Harlem.

During the Harlem Renaissance of the 1920s and early 1930s, Harlem thrived as a center for black talent and thought.[14] Views of the Harlem Renaissance have been important to the history of Harlem as a black enclave. Nathaniel Huggins has analyzed the way that the artists of the Renaissance served two purposes. The first was that by considering themselves "New Negroes," the artists enhanced a deeper level of race consciousness among blacks in America. Huggins also suggests that the Harlem Renaissance marked a repudiation of traditional Victorian values in the way of art, music, and writing. West Indian author Tony Martin explains how the literary movement that Marcus Garvey sponsored in his *Negro World* before and during the Harlem Renaissance pushed the envelope even further by "placing race first" and by not allowing white sponsors or supporters to steer the new movement.

While black leaders like Marcus Garvey suggested that black people return to Africa and start anew, others took more ownership of the United States by using art to express themselves and change the view of racist whites. Writers like Claude McKay, author of *Harlem Shadows* (1922), wrote of their experiences as blacks in Harlem and America. Also contributing to the Harlem Renaissance was poet Langston Hughes, who wrote the black pride–filled "The Negro Speaks of Rivers" and his observations of the economic advancements of Jewish people, "Fine Clothes to the Jew." These and many other authors and artists represented the "New Negro" of Harlem in the early twentieth century.

Before the Second World War, very few, if any, black families lived in the neighborhood of Morningside Heights. Early on, many Columbia faculty members resided in the comely apartments on Riverside Drive and Claremont Avenue. During the war, as part of the second "Great Migration," black people began moving into many of the once exclusively white neighborhoods of Morningside Heights. The rate of increase of black and Puerto Rican residents caused concern among some university officials.

Concurrently, the construction of the elevated transit lines out of 120th Street brought property values down and contributed to the deterioration of the area. As Melvin Webber put it in the book *Urban Planning and Social Policy*, "Highway and transit facilities . . . are now treated as both servers and shapers of the larger land-use and accessibility relationships." This statement spoke directly to the fact that city planners were most interested in getting those who worked in the city but lived in the suburbs directly in contact with the city through transportation. Unfortunately for many of the black residents and other minorities who had moved closer to the jobs in the city, this meant that the lines of transportation would cut through their neighborhoods.[15]

By the Second World War, the black population in Harlem had skyrocketed, creating a somewhat homogeneous community that dealt daily with racism and segregation. Regarding Harlem, historian Roi Ottley wrote that "it is the fountainhead of mass movements. From it flows the progressive vitality of Negro life."[16] That statement described the history of social protest in Harlem. Residents of Harlem rioted in 1935 in part because of the economic effects of the Great Depression and partly because of the frustration of blacks with local white shop owners. Protesters pointed out that while mostly black people lived in Harlem, white people owned a majority of the businesses there, leaving the residents feeling economically exploited.[17] Rioters destroyed the shops of those white owners who would sell to black people but would not hire them as clerks.

Part of Harlem's frustration dealt with foreign affairs. In 1935 Mussolini's Italian forces invaded Ethiopia, a black nation in Africa that held a high symbolic significance for blacks across the Diaspora. If Ethiopia fell to its European opposition, then many blacks in America and around the world feared that white Europeans would understand the victory over the independent black nation as certification of white supremacy. In response to this concern, black activists in New York formed the International Council of Friends of Ethiopia to protest the invasion.[18] Working with other groups, such as the Ethiopian Research Council of Washington, D.C., and the Provisional Committee for the Defense of Ethiopia, the council brought a case to the recently created League of Nations urging that the League block Italy's efforts in Africa. In places like Harlem, pro-Ethiopian sentiments ran deep, as Harlem was the home to many pan-African Garveyites, civil rights organizations, and churches. Leaders like the Reverend Adam Clayton Powell Jr. emerged to fuel the fight against fascism in Africa. Italy's invasion of Ethiopia touched the black community of Harlem in ways that transcended class and educational backgrounds.[19] Black people in New York and other major cities in America viewed Mussolini's actions in very racialized terms and as an outright attempt to further entrench the oppression of black people everywhere.

One mass protest in particular, the Harlem Riot of 1943, signified a difference between the way blacks in Harlem viewed themselves and how white Americans viewed them. In the midst of the Second World War, black residents in Harlem questioned the country's allegiance toward democracy for all when a white police officer shot a black uniformed soldier in a local hotel. The soldier, who had allegedly engaged the officer in a scuffle after the officer placed an elderly woman under arrest for disturbing the peace, attempted to run from the altercation. When news of both the arrest and the shooting traveled, Harlem residents filled the streets to vent their frustration with housing and employment discrimination as well as with police brutality. By the end of the riot, six black people had died and police had arrested over five hundred.[20] This disturbing scene set the stage for many others in the decades to come. It also showed that race relations would continue to be unstable, unless discrimination faded.

Columbia University sat very near this burgeoning black community. Between 1950 and 1960, the black population in Morningside Heights alone grew by 700 percent, from 470 to 3,133. In 1950 more than 90 percent of Morningside Heights's population was white; ten years later the percentage of white residents had declined to 79.[21] That decade also saw an increase in the number of Puerto Rican residents, from 1,650 to 3,014. Many Puerto Ricans arrived en masse in New York in the late 1940s and early 1950s.[22] Most settled in East Harlem, but many others moved to Morningside Heights. Like black migrants, Puerto Ricans faced slum living, poverty, and powerlessness. By the 1960s, 19 percent of Puerto Ricans and 17 percent of black people were on some sort of governmental relief.[23] The census showed that the average number of completed years in school in 1964 was 9.2 years for black people and 7.6 for Puerto Ricans.[24] Socially, things changed rapidly, and the living conditions in Harlem and Morningside Heights deteriorated considerably. As the black and Puerto Rican populations increased, corporate and municipal support in the area declined, and many parts of the community turned into ghettos, bringing a mix of problems.

One of the major problems in the black and Puerto Rican enclave of Harlem was an influx of drugs, particularly heroin. Claude Brown, the author of *Manchild in the Promised Land,* lamented the effects of heroin on Harlem in the postwar era. "It was a plague. You couldn't close all the doors and all the windows and keep [it] out. It was getting to everybody," he stated.[25] According to sociologists Douglas Massey and Nancy Denton, with the drugs came blatant vice, and the authorities, rather than moving to eradicate the presence of the poison, only attempted to contain it in black enclaves.[26] Contributing to the making of a ghetto, the drug business displaced many legitimate business entities in Harlem. With the assistance of a Ford Foundation grant, Columbia's Institute of Urban Environment attempted to help the situation by offering a weekend conference for the youth of Harlem.[27] It would take more to deal with the very serious issues of poverty, housing, and drugs.

These problems, along with the rapid growth of the black population in these areas, eventually led to the rise of single-room occupancy (SRO) buildings, which further destabilized the neighborhoods in those areas where many of the minorities lived during the 1960s. SROs were originally apartment buildings, but because of the weakness of the market, they were separated and rented out as rooms.[28] Initially, students used these SROs as dwellings; later, however, poorer and older people took over the residences because of the inexpensive rent. Rent for a room was typically less than $60 per month.[29] Some of the tenants were those who had troubles with the law, such as prostitutes and various roguish types. A report from the President's Committee on Urban-Minority Problems described the residents of SROs: "It is estimated that there are in New York City at least 30,000 SRO residents (not counting transients in smaller buildings) of whom perhaps 70% are Negro and 10% are Puerto Rican."[30] Regarding SRO dwellers, the report revealed that "those who live in SRO's are usually dependent and unattached individuals, often recent migrants from rural areas. Many are welfare recipients, aged or chronically ill, addicted to narcotics or, in even larger numbers to alcohol. Others are just the loneliest in the city's lonely crowd." One report indicated that the "average [income of SRO residents in the study area] is only $2,300 per year, compared to $5,800 for those who live in the apartment buildings." In 1960 the average SRO dweller made $3,000 or less.

Harlem, once the home of a renaissance, was rapidly withering. Within this declining economy, land values became even cheaper. This cheapness of land provided an impetus for Columbia University to expand its domains and usurp parts of the city.

The university attempted to deal with the problem of the ghetto by taking it over before it overran the Morningside Heights campus. In an earlier statement, George Nash made a comment concerning Columbia University's attempt to "escape" the city. One might have asked what exactly about New York the university was trying to escape. It would of course have been impossible for Columbia literally to escape the growth of the city onto the lands surrounding the university. What the Ivy League school wanted to escape was certain segments of the city, especially those filled with crime and vice (and quite possibly a large number of nonwhite people).

Along these lines, Jacques Barzun, Columbia University provost in 1967, believed that the neighborhoods that surrounded the university on the Heights and in Harlem were "uninviting, abnormal, sinister, and dangerous."[31] Barzun complained that "I have seen the streets become unsafe at night. . . . Gangs have attacked some of my colleagues, muggers have assaulted their wives, snatched their purses, and held up students."[32] Worrying about the well-being of his colleagues, Barzun exclaimed: "They must not be subjected to an environment that requires the perpetual qui vive of a paratrooper in enemy country."

The Faculty Civil Rights Group of Columbia University, which did a study on the university's policy in regard to the Morningside Heights neighborhood, quoted one of the university planners, Stanley Salmen, as stating: "We are looking for a community where the faculty can talk to people like themselves. We don't want a dirty group."[33] As there was only one full-time black faculty member at Columbia by the mid-1960s, it is clear what the planner meant by "people like themselves." It is also clear, given the population of mostly black and Puerto Rican residents of Harlem and Morningside Heights, that he was referring to the nonwhite dwellers of the surrounding community as the elements of the "dirty group." Whiteness and white privilege for faculty members like Barzun had made it possible for him to see whiteness as somehow culturally clean or natural and blackness as otherness.[34] In essence, the statement implied that the arrival of so many black and Puerto Ricans "dirtied up" the once clean (white) group of Morningside Heights residents. Consequently, it became one of the objectives of the university to clean up the "sinister" and "dirty" area surrounding the school.

In 1968 Roger Kahn, a critic of Columbia and an observer throughout the Morningside Park controversy, claimed that the university represented one of "the largest and most aggressive landlords on earth," and that more than half of its assets ($280 million) were in land, buildings, and mortgages.[35] Unfortunately for its dislocated residents, Harlem provided a prime location for many of Columbia's ventures. The *New York Times* recorded that "resentment, some of it justified, has built up over the years at Columbia's acquisition of many buildings on Morningside Heights."[36] Dr. Robert S. Liebert, instructor of psychiatry at Columbia, noted that in the 1960s alone, the university purchased 150 housing units used mostly by blacks and Puerto Ricans. A report of the Columbia College Citizens Council indicated that the university facilitated the displacement of 9,600 people, approximately 85 percent of whom were black or Puerto Rican.[37] In doing so, the university actually reversed the population trend of the 1960s, thus engineering the racial anatomy of the neighborhood. The report of the council recorded university planner Stanley Salmen as stating that "there are now only two houses on Morningside Heights which threaten the welfare of the neighborhood." It appeared that those houses were not nearly as threatening as the swiftly expanding Columbia.

Each time the school acquired a housing facility for the sake of expansion, many tenants lost their homes. A byline in the communist publication the *Worker* (which succeeded the *Daily Worker*) read "Columbia Crushing Tenants" and showed a picture of Columbia University's president, Grayson Kirk, above the caption, "Kirk—Ruthless Landlord."[38] The paper affirmed Liebert's contention by claiming that a majority of the people the university's housing policies affected were black and Puerto Rican, as well as poor whites who resided within the Morningside Heights district. Holding that the trustees were the invaders, the *Worker* alleged that "Columbia made war on its Harlem neighbors" without regard for their need for shelter and homes.[39] Kahn agreed and added that, "in . . . human terms, the story becomes an assault of Columbia, the immense institution, on underprivileged human beings living in Manhattan's SROs."[40] The SRO buildings represented the essence of the New York slum. Expressing his disdain for the university's treatment of the tenants, Kahn suggested that "eight derelicts pay more rent than a single family," and by most accounts he was correct.[41]

In spite of the criticism that some made against the university, the Ivy League school on Morningside Heights, similar to all universities, had the need to expand. Roger Starr, who in 1968 was the executive director of the Citizens Housing and Planning Council of New York, cited two reasons for the university to expand. The first was, of course, the need for buildings to house new additions to various graduate programs (business schools, law schools, etc.). The second was Columbia's perceived need to keep its attractiveness to potential students and faculty members by ridding the immediate areas of crime and those who would commit licentious acts. By buying buildings in the deteriorated neighborhoods in Harlem and Morningside Heights, ousting the tenants, restoring the edifices, and then marketing to a different sort of tenant, the university could justify its expansion policies as doing those neighborhoods a favor. That the university would plan to shape the surrounding neighborhoods in such a way seemed at best pathological and at worst cold.

Columbia officials justified the closing of tenant housing by claiming that the university sought to eradicate the crime that occurred in the surrounding neighborhood. The report of Columbia's own Citizenship Council exposed that concept as a fallacy. By 1964 "the crime rate in the neighborhood was not any higher than the crime rate of neighborhoods surrounding other Ivy League Schools."[42] In fact, according to the school's student newspaper, "between 1954 and 1964, the crime rate in the area had actually declined by about 50%; police statistics for the period show that in 1954, 11,000 incidents of crime were reported in the Columbia area, while in 1964, only 5,000 incidents were reported."[43] Furthermore, most of the crimes involved people in the SROs violating other residents of SROs and certainly not faculty members.

After the rise of the ghetto in the 1940s and 1950s, the concept of urban renewal became a national goal for many in the 1960s. The idea was that in order to alleviate the unsightliness, vice, and waste of the ghetto, institutions and businesses would invest in the inexpensive land and property of the ghettos to revitalize the economy. Columbia, along with other institutions across the country, would do so in coordination with federal, state, municipal, and private agencies. In this way, the cities would benefit from improvements and institutions would benefit from new markets and potential profits. Superficially, the concept of urban renewal seemed like a positive act; however, the underside of it was the displacement of residents who might not be able to afford to move anywhere else but other slums. Furthermore, neighborhood residents more than likely would not own the businesses and institutions in their communities. For institutions like Columbia University, the removal of tenants was more of an impediment to progress than a problem that needed resolution.[44] The perceived choice for large, white institutions like the university was either to expand or to be expanded upon. Columbia chose to expand.

Realizing its need for more campus buildings, the university began to evict tenants from the SROs that it owned. Between 1957 and 1968 Columbia decreased its number of SROs by nearly 70 percent, from 466 to 146 units, to build new campus buildings.[45] The university's method of approach to this project, as well as the residents' loss of fairly inexpensive living quarters, contributed much to the black community's resentment. Furthermore, many of the SRO tenants did not have direct access to lawyers or people of authority. Some members of the SRO population, because they had often faced legal scrapes, avoided confrontations with landlords or managers that might involve legal sanctions. Although Columbia helped to relocate some tenants, only a few were actually so fortunate. Many claimed that the school simply "ran them out."[46]

Yvelle Walker, a resident of a university-owned SRO referred to as the "Oxford Hotel," told Roger Kahn of her experience. Columbia, she said, forced her out of her home. She claimed that she was told that the school would soon turn her building into offices for Columbia, and that she must leave hastily. She thought that because she was frequently late with her rent, the story of razing the building was being used to evict her. When she went to pay her rent, the agent refused it and instead offered her twenty-five dollars to defray costs of finding a new home. She refused, and after a week she again tried to pay her rent but again met continued resistance. Finally, Walker arrived at her home one night to find that someone had filled the lock of her door with a thick, sticky substance resembling wax, which made it impossible to insert her key into the keyhole. Frustrated, she promptly left the Oxford Hotel.[47]

Walker was not alone in her housing situation. Douglas Davidove, Assadour Tanitian, Teymour Darkhosh, and Michael Stama te Latos all lived in a Columbia-owned SRO. Objecting to the expansion of the university, they circulated throughout the Morningside Heights neighborhood a document entitled "What Do the Tenants of the Occupied Buildings Say?" In it, they complained that Columbia University neglected its duties as a landlord. In their particular building, they asserted, there was only partial heat during the winters of 1965–66 and 1966–67, and no heat at all in 1967–68. They also complained of "shockingly unsanitary conditions," including impure hot and cold water in some apartments, and fire hazards in other already vacated units. These four concerned community members also raised the issue of the safety of their building. Even though there were several burglaries in the building, their landlord never repaired the broken front door lock. The four tenants contended that these were "typical examples of Columbia's tenant-removal tactics—buildings . . . allowed to deteriorate until the occupants find conditions intolerable." The publication concluded by urging tenants to "lend their support to . . . halt Columbia's harassment and mistreatment of the community."[48]

On January 4, 1965, the City Commission on Human Rights issued a statement that served notice of the city's awareness of Columbia's tactics and motivation for removal. It indicated that whether or not the university intended to do so, it was systematically displacing a majority of minority tenants at an alarming rate. The chair of the commission, Stanley Lowell, sent a letter to then Columbia vice president Lawrence Chamberlain stating that "there is no question that the ethnic composition of the Columbia area has changed and that university expansion has been responsible."[49] Not wholly indicting Columbia of racism, Lowell noted that "it's simply a matter . . . of Columbia following the logic of its expansion policy, and reaching out for the vulnerable spots." The vulnerable spots happened to be those where black and Puerto Rican tenants lived—where people could not afford lawyers or did not want to go to authorities because the authorities reminded them of Columbia officials. The commission strongly suggested that Columbia offer programs for social rehabilitation, make available alternate living quarters through relocation, and loosen its dependence on wholesale tenant removal. Lowell and the commission wanted the university to "undertake positive efforts to maintain the multiracial character of the area."

Even the university's student news organ took note of the strained relationship between the school and many of its neighbors. "Charges of racial bias against Columbia may be taken up by the City Commission on Human Rights at a full meeting of the fourteen-member body on Thursday," reported the student-run *Columbia Daily Spectator* in February 1965.[50] "Margaret L.

Cox, Democratic district leader of the 13th A.D. West, . . . has charged that the University discriminates against Negroes and Puerto Ricans through its expansion policies." In the December 2, 1966, issue of the *Spectator*, the title of an article read: "City Investigation Reveals Violations in Columbia SRO." The paper reported that one SRO, Cohar Hall, had "a number of code violations." These infractions spurred Morningsiders United, a neighborhood group, to accuse the university of "forcing tenants to leave by not making repairs."[51] Keeping track of this particular SRO building, several months later the *Spectator* printed tenant leader Justus Poole's allegation that "all but four tenants have left [Cohar Hall] . . . because they were 'harassed and sued by Columbia.'" As in the case of Walker in the Oxford Hotel, Columbia representatives also allegedly offered these tenants stipends to move.[52]

Columbia's actions in terms of the removal and treatment of residents led a contingent of community members to protest. The *New York Amsterdam News* reported that "uptown groups [are] planning a series of protest meetings against Columbia University's planned expansion program until the university agrees to do more to aid Harlem."[53] Under the leadership of the Morningside Tenants Committee, fifty protesters showed up at the university president's home near Morningside Park donning black clothes, claiming to mourn the death of several demolished tenant buildings on Amsterdam Avenue and West 113th Street. Several other community organizations showed support for the demonstration, including the Metropolitan Council on Housing, the Riverside Democratic Club, and Morningsiders United.[54]

It was apparent that the rich, predominantly white university had not fostered the most positive relationship with its Morningside Heights and Harlem neighbors. In his testimony to the Cox Commission, established by the university in April 1968, the vice chair of the Board of Trustees and chair of the University Gymnasium Committee, Harold McGuire, explained: "Columbia wants to be a friend . . . of the community, . . . [but] we must do it in such a fashion as to be dealing not as Lady Bountiful, but as one who is genuinely interested in and wishes to co-operate with the community."[55] After hearing testimony from university officials, the Cox Commission asserted that by buying buildings and removing residents from SROs, Columbia was trying to find a way to get rid of the "undesirables" of society. As evidence, the commission presented a Columbia publication that read: "Morningside Heights has been cleaned up. . . . All but two of the worst SRO houses have been eliminated, and nobody really regrets their passing."[56]

Certainly somebody regretted their passing. Aware of this, McGuire reasoned: "I can't blame them [those evicted]. I am not being at all critical of them. All I'm saying is that since they wish to stay, and since the only manner in which the university can expand is to acquire additional property . . . there is this inevitable and necessary conflict of interest."[57]

Subsequently, Archibald Cox, an arbitrator from Harvard Law School and chair of the Fact-Finding Commission, concluded that Columbia University had erred in several ways with regard to expansion. To begin with, Cox reported Columbia was guilty of not notifying its neighbors of its intended expansion plans. Second, Cox charged the university with "unduly harassing tenants in order to evict them, and with icy indifference to the problems of relocation."[58] For these reasons alone, many people who lived near or had once lived near the university justifiably loathed its policy toward the surrounding neighborhoods. These people felt helpless in a struggle against a large, white institution and sought a way to fight back.

To make matters worse, Columbia was not alone in its ambitions for expansion in Morningside Heights and Harlem. Columbia was part of two organizations, the Morningside Renewal Council and Morningside Heights, Inc. (MHI). The former consisted of university representatives, local community members, and politicians. As one council member explained in a letter to Mayor John Lindsay, "The Council is an advisory body to the Housing and Redevelopment Board for the General Neighborhood Renewal Plan for Morningside Heights and West Harlem."[59] Members included politician Basil Paterson and concerned citizen Dwight Smith. The overarching goal of the council was to facilitate the renewal of the Morningside and West Harlem areas. Although this was typically the group with which Columbia consulted in regard to expansion, the organization was not always favorable to the university's plans. In conjunction with Morningside Heights, Inc., the Morningside Renewal Council worked to move a renewal plan through city channels.

Established in 1947, Morningside Heights, Inc., was composed of many of the larger institutions in the area, including Columbia, Barnard College, Union Theological Seminary, Jewish Theological Seminary, Teacher's College, St. Luke's Hospital, St. John the Divine Church, Corpus Christi Church, International House, Julliard School of Music, Riverside Church, and the Interchurch Center. These institutions believed they had a vested interest in the welfare of the neighborhoods that surrounded them. Many of the institutions' investments came in the form of tenant buildings in the Morningside Heights and Harlem areas.[60]

The members of MHI sought to protect those interests and investments with guards. In 1962 the organization established the Morningside Community Patrol. The members of MHI felt that "we cannot fully perform our work of educational, cultural, religious, and health services if people are fearful for their own safety and the security of their personal property."[61] MHI hired security guards from Industrial Security Service for $150,000 a year. Columbia University covered 38 percent of the cost.

A few years earlier, MHI had paid $75,000 to a firm to conduct a study of the Morningside area for the potential of development. The completed study indicated that the area needed rehabilitation, and that much of the area could be available for institutional use. When released in 1959, the study revealed some of the plans that Columbia and other institutions had for the neighborhoods. The timing of the study worked well with the city's desire to improve the Morningside area. MHI chair David Rockefeller had sought aid from the federal urban renewal administration to advance the MHI study with New York City and, according to a report of Columbia's Citizenship Council, the study provided the basis for the Morningside General Renewal Plan that the city presented in 1965.[62]

The Morningside General Renewal Plan worked in favor of Columbia and the other institutions. The goals of the plan were to decrease overcrowding, rehabilitate run-down edifices, remove dangerous and uninhabitable buildings, and create housing options for people of different economic backgrounds.[63] The plan also included the improvement of Riverside and Morningside parks. That was a tall order, if not utopian. As it was, the plan benefited the institutions that had already laid plans for the neighborhood. It allowed Columbia and the other institutions to include all of the buildings that they could potentially enhance or renew. With the release of the plan, institutions, especially Columbia, could freely remove tenants as part of a city-sanctioned plan. Indeed, the plan provided even more power and official credence to Columbia as it stretched outward.

By the end of 1965, various members of the community began to organize against the plan and Columbia. Although most of the Morningside and West Harlem community members may not have been aware of Columbia's involvement in MHI and the renewal plan, the residents felt the impact of institutional expansion. Some resisted Columbia's ambition by way of protest, speaking up against Columbia's actions as a landlord and also its ideas for the green space. They also demanded that Columbia include the community in its planning for expansion. This demand was lost on the university. In one article in the *West Side News and Morningsider,* civic activist George Weiser noted that when Columbia submitted its plans to the Board of Estimate (a municipal ruling board), which oversaw the approval process of the Morningside General Renewal Plan, the university did not indicate which tenant buildings it planned to renew. Thus the community did not have a say as to what would happen to the undisclosed buildings. Weiser protested the fact that "Columbia in effect used the Board to circumvent the democratic decision-making process."[64]

The *Morningsiders United Newsletter,* a community organ sponsored by Morningsiders United, exclaimed that Columbia and MHI were not being forthright. Trying to make the residents aware, the newsletter suggested that "the institutions' overall plan for Morningside Heights is being kept secret, presumably to escape public notice until it is too late for the residents to protest the EVICTION of perhaps 20,000 people—including YOU!"[65] The publication listed the buildings that several of the members of MHI owned.

Morningsiders United took pride in its advocacy of the community and tenants. In one letter to its members, the organization claimed that "we helped gain a guarantee from the New York City Board of Estimate that (a) the 14 block area immediately surrounding Columbia be included in the General Neighborhood Renewal Plan; (b) that the reuses in these blocks should be predominantly for conservation and rehabilitation; (c) that, to the extent feasible, at least 25% of the housing should serve low income families, and another 25% of the housing should serve families of moderate income; (d) that the institutions on Morningside Heights shall limit their expansion in the next ten years to 21 specific projects; (e) that the University will relocate in its own buildings as many as possible who are displaced by its expansion."

Another local organ opposed Columbia's plans for expansion. In the spring of 1966, the *Morningside Citizen* exclaimed: "We submit that in this community it is not possible to place a higher value on academic expansion than on the need to house local tenants in their present buildings."[66] The periodical sharply criticized the university and other Morningside Heights institutions for not using the vast resources of the school to help the surrounding neighborhoods. "We decry the failure of the institutions [to] adequately acknowledge their very substantial obligation to . . . our community and adequately to explore with the community the very pressing problems of institutional expansion vs. housing needs."

The city played an interesting role in the controversy over housing. Although it was the city's design to renew the Morningside area, community members asserted considerable pressure against elected officials in regard to tenant removal. With that in mind, those city officials could allow Columbia to go only so far before they intervened on behalf of their constituents. That appeared to be the case in 1965 when famed litigator and Manhattan Borough President Constance Baker Motley declared that "blanket University expan-

sion without consideration of the neighborhood's needs is entirely unaccept-
able; it must not be allowed."[67] Furthermore, she added, "the government . . .
has a definite responsibility to curb the power of private governments—like
Columbia—to remake a whole area of the city."

Along the same lines, in 1966 Mayor John Lindsay issued a statement that
called for the Board of Estimate to reconsider the amount and manner of
expansion that was slated to occur. The statement sought to ensure the cooperation of Columbia with community residents.[68] In the *Morningside Sentinel*,
George Weiser rallied the residents: "Morningsiders! For the first time in the
long history of Columbia's aggression against the Morningside community
we have a commitment from the Mayor to compel Columbia to abandon its
plans to ram its expansion over a prostrate community . . . and to work out
an expansion plan that will be compatible with . . . the principles of humanity,
justice and democracy."[69]

In spite of the encouragement that the mayor's statement may have provided to some citizens, Columbia continued with its expansion operation and
tactics. The *Morningside Sentinel* relayed news that "on August 1, Columbia
obtained control of this SRO [609 W. 115th Street], which is almost entirely
tenanted by Negroes, the majority of whom are working people. Between
August 1 and 25 the number of tenants decreased from about 90 to around
50. This latest Columbia push-out of SRO tenants is also in contempt of the
Mayor's statement of May 20, 1966."[70]

Harlem residents would not have been so skeptical about the proposed
gym except that large, white institutions had a reputation for taking control
of community businesses and institutions. In a previous incident, residents
wondered what would happen to Harlem Hospital when Columbia took over.
At the Columbia Presbyterian Harkness Pavilion Hospital, which Columbia
also controlled, there was one black doctor and few black nurses. At Harlem
Hospital, when Columbia took control, there were few black doctors to serve
their community. The hospital was at one point governed by the city, but
when Columbia succeeded the city the hospital became a training facility
for Columbia medical students and attending physicians (nearly all white).
In one controversy, Columbia replaced a black doctor at Harlem Hospital
with a white physician. To some in the community, it seemed as though
Columbia was making it so only white physicians could work at the hospital.[71] Similarly, in 1966 Governor Nelson Rockefeller announced plans for a
twenty-seven-story state office building on the thoroughfare of 125th Street
in Harlem. Between the buildings that Columbia and the state intended to
erect, many Harlem residents felt closed in by powerful white America.[72]

The Architects Renewal Committee of Harlem (ARCH) was well aware of such plans for expansion and development. ARCH consisted of black architects, attorneys, and city planners who sought to lead the way in design for Harlem. Created in 1964, ARCH received financial backing from the federal Office of Economic Opportunity, private grants, and various commissions. ARCH assisted the community in acquiring federal assistance for low-income housing and deciphering the many housing and rent regulations. One of the problems that ARCH noted was the fact that, when any buildings were designed or even demolished in Harlem, most of the people in charge and most of the people working were white. Then, mostly white laborers constructed the buildings. During a time when black people had troubles finding jobs, seeing people from outside the community coming in to work caused resentment.[73] In some ways it added insult to injury because it further illustrated the lack of black ownership of land, property, and power in a black neighborhood.

Keeping in mind the renewal plans of the city and Columbia, ARCH intended to garner more power for black people and Harlem. As one article indicated, ARCH sought to provide "soul architecture."[74] In the late 1960s the architects of ARCH considered themselves to be revolutionary and part of the Black Power movement. The members suggested that "there should be more important functions for precious city land than making money."[75] Furthermore, ARCH believed that "the ghetto architect should be a representative of the poor people, responding to their wishes, rather than an advocate of the white middle class imposing its compartmentalizing values . . . upon Black and Spanish-speaking people who have quite other social ideals."

Those beliefs motivated ARCH to win a $97,000 antipoverty grant that would assist the group in submitting its own plan for renewing Harlem. As the executive director of ARCH, C. Richard Hatch, stated, the group wanted to put forth the "people's plan."[76] The assistant director, John M. Bailey Jr., concurred and explained that ARCH was attempting to "give people the professional planning help they need if they are going to effectively confront the public agencies that make decisions affecting their neighborhoods." So, with the grant, ARCH provided literature to residents on zoning and housing laws, secured a lawyer to assist in conflicts that arose concerning housing, and hired staff for a relocation office.[77] In the end, the members of ARCH worried that "if development is not controlled by Harlemites, it will lead to an increase in land costs and rents and thus not serve the people of Harlem."[78] For that reason, ARCH opposed Columbia's plans for West Harlem.

As Columbia's ties to Harlem stretched thin, the university went on the offensive. James Booker of the *New York Amsterdam News* reported: "Columbia

University officials meet this week with Harlem leaders in an off-the-record session to try to develop ways they will spend the $10,000,000 they received from the Ford Foundation." In exasperation, he wrote: "Let's hope there is more than talk, and it is backed up with action, not more studies."[79] Booker was referring to the fact that the university allocated part of the money it received from the Ford Foundation to conduct a study on "urban minority problems" and housing.[80] Incidentally, the paper noted that there was only one African American on the twenty-four-member advisory team.[81]

Columbia also made an overture by opening an account at a Harlem bank and offering assistance to Harlem students. In November 1966 the university established a savings account at Carver Federal Savings into which it deposited $10,000. Columbia's community relations director, Wesley Furst, hoped that the deposit would be viewed as "another vote of confidence in the people and the community of Harlem."[82] The university also provided assistance to Benjamin Franklin High School students by sponsoring mathematic instructors to help tutor. To the bank and to the students who benefited from the deposit and tutoring, Columbia's overtures were welcome and long overdue. Many other residents, however, continued to observe the university with suspicion.

2

Gym Crow

Recreational Segregation in Morningside Park

Part of Columbia's and the city's plans for redevelopment (and expansion in Columbia's case) included Morningside Park. To some people in the 1960s, the park meant "the only place you could go to get mugged," but to others, who lived near and used the park, it represented a piece of land that not even a rich and powerful, predominantly white institution like Columbia University could take from them.[1] Indeed, to the people of the adjacent Morningside Heights neighborhood and the mostly black Harlem community that sat below the prestigious Ivy League school, the small, green park between Harlem and the university belonged to them. In 1958 most community members were unaware that Columbia's President Grayson Kirk had approached New York City Parks Commissioner Robert Moses about the purchase of an area in Morningside Park on which to build a university gymnasium. When the university declared two years later that it planned to lease the land in the park, the proposal was not really an issue.

In the early 1960s very few people were aware of the university's plan for the park. The trouble started in late 1965 and early 1966, when the newly appointed New York City Parks Commissioner Thomas Hoving, who took over in 1960, first criticized the school's intentions, claiming that a private gymnasium should not be built in precious public park space. In addition, various community organizations initiated protests against Columbia. Shortly after the commissioner had voiced his complaint, the New York City chapter of the Congress of Racial Equality (CORE) protested, as did groups like Morningsiders United and the West Harlem Community Organization. In July 1967 the tension increased with a Harlem neighborhood rally at the proposed gym site. There, Black Power advocate H. Rap Brown threatened that if the university continued with its plans, the black community would not hesitate to burn down the structure.[2]

While the Harlem and Morningside Heights citizens had other grievances against the university, such as its tactics as a landlord and landowner, in the late 1960s residents focused specifically on the issue of the gymnasium. If constructed, the gym, like the rest of Columbia University, would stand as a constant reminder of the affluence of white society and, in the opinion of many community residents and students, its oppressive nature.[3] In the late 1960s the gym in the park became more than just a symbol; it also provided a rallying point for black people in the community and at the school to gain a say and some power in predominantly white America.

While various news sources took into account the opinion of the residents surrounding the park, university officials apparently did not. After survey-ing a sample of residents, a *Spectator* poll indicated that 45 percent of the sample "favored the gym," while 29 percent were against the gym project, and 25 percent "had no opinion."[4] Surveys conducted by Public Opinion Surveys of Princeton found that out of 508 residents surveyed in New York City, 41 percent favored construction of the gym, 33 percent opposed it, and 25 percent had not formed an opinion on the project in the park. Subse-quently, Columbia University's Bureau of Applied Social Research conducted a study on a sample of 228 Harlem residents in regard to the gym issue. The study revealed that 58 percent of those who advocated the construction of the gym did so on condition that the gym be shared equally between the community and the university. Although a majority of those polled favored gym construction, the percentage who did not or could not form opinions about the project was a clear sign that the project was not very popular with the neighboring community.

The gym and park issue presented an interesting controversy because it did not involve living space but rather recreational space. Almost as coveted as residential space in the city were green areas like parks. When Columbia released plans for and began construction on its much-needed gymnasium, a storm ensued. This chapter provides a short history of Morningside Park and Columbia's desires for a new recreational facility. It then highlights the conflict that occurred among the community, the university, and the city over rights to the park.

Morningside Park was one of the most unique parks of those situated on the Upper West Side of Manhattan. In the late 1890s, when Frederick Law Olmsted and Calvert Vaux designed the park, they observed that with the steep inclines and narrow allotment of land, there was very little area that was flat. Making use of the flat areas became a major objective for the designers. Samuel Parsons Jr., who was superintendent of parks at the time, noted that "it would be hard to conceive of a more rugged or precipitous park or one that would cost more to construct."[5] In spite of the ruggedness of the landscape, Parsons admitted that "it was a park that peculiarly lent itself to views outside of the park, as well as pictures within the boundaries. . . . Probably no park of so small an area presents as diversified a series of views." Considering its inclines and views, the city set about building the park. Parsons revealed later, though, that the city did so trying to save money. "Unfortunately, Morningside Park was built economically. New York is willing to spend untold sums for . . . public buildings but not for parks," he exclaimed. Parsons remarked: "There is, doubtless, no city in the country which has parks designed with the high degree of art and skill and there is probably no park in the country, at least in the East, where the work of construction has been as badly done."

That comment could have been made about the maintenance of the park as well. One of the problems of Morningside Park in the 1960s was the city's maintenance of the grounds. Parsons, decades earlier, explained that in spite of a great design, the park did not receive the type of maintenance it should have. He wrote: "Civil Service has tended of late years to lower the standard of park work. . . . Probably we can blame politics to a certain extent." He admonished future municipal administrations: "I should not, however, minimize the value of good maintenance."[6] In the case of Morningside Park, that warning apparently fell on deaf ears.

By the 1960s, one report called Morningside Park "the most feared park in the country."[7] As it was, in the early part of the decade, concerned citizens invited the borough president to see just how bad the park had deteriorated because of the neglect of the city. "We saw shattered steps, broken walks, eroded slopes, and playground equipment wrenched from its supports. Broken glass sparkled in the spring sunlight," one citizen relayed.[8] Even the then borough president, Edward Dudley, had to note the disrepair of the park. The *Morningside Citizen,* a newsletter sponsored by the Morningside Citizens Committee, made its request emphatically: "The neighborhood wants a crash program of rehabilitation in the park, better maintenance and better policing." The community had good right to be concerned, as muggings frequently occurred in the park. Even Columbia faculty members fell victim to muggers.[9] It was in the interest of everyone who lived near the park to push for better maintenance of the park.

Columbia had that in mind when it made an arrangement with the city to use the park for recreational purposes. While many Harlem residents complained about Columbia's tenant-removal program by the late 1960s, a

decade earlier there were some positive aspects of the university's relationship with the community. For example, the school constructed two softball
fields in the southeast corner of Morningside Park, one of the only flat areas
in the park.[10] Because the university built the fields on public land, the city
parks department made arrangements with the school to allow nonstudents
to use the fields on weekends and during school breaks. Early on, the university and the community of Harlem cooperatively hosted youth baseball
and football teams. Proud of the joint venture, the university boasted of its
relationship with the Harlem community in publications like *Partners in the
Park*, which told of "Bobby Smith."[11]

Until Bobby started participating in Columbia's Community Sports programs, Jim Young, the director of the Columbia–Community Athletic Field
Program, described him as "shy and introspective . . . [with] little self-confi-
dence." Contributing to the boy's reticence was the harsh "underprivileged"
environment of West Harlem where he lived, the document implied. Mi-
raculously, after three years of participating in the university–community
program in the park, Young reported that Bobby had transformed into a
confident leader, able to withstand criticism as well as to improve his athletic
skills. Both Jim Young and the Columbia University publication contended
that "Bobby's case [was] not an isolated one."

That might have been the situation with Bobby, but one of the early criticisms of the university was the fact that the fields and the athletic program did
not serve those who could have benefited most from their existence. Roger
Starr, who was head of the Citizens Housing and Planning Council of New
York in the late 1960s, noted that the fields were open to the community's
youth only when a member of one of the university-authorized athletic teams
was present. Then, he continued, the program recruited children from poor
backgrounds, but not necessarily the youth who could most use such a program. He suggested that delinquent or predelinquent youth in Harlem were
not chosen to be in the program, but rather those poor and minority youth
who would go on to become Harlem's middle class. If this were indeed the
case, then the program could have been viewed as only a superficial gesture
to improve relations with Harlem and Morningside Heights youths rather
than as a sincere effort to improve the opportunities of truly at-risk youths
in the city.

The Columbia–Community Athletic Field Program, in spite of such criticism, received adulation from sources outside the university as well. Hulan
Jack, the borough of Manhattan's first black president, had given his approval
of the Columbia–Community field. Many of the local establishments and

people, such as the settlement houses, community centers, and merchants, sponsored the youth league baseball teams that used the fields. Even organizations such as the Urban League praised Columbia University early on for the community athletic program.[12]

University officials believed that the school's purchase of buildings, leasing of land, and construction of fields satisfied their community service duty as leaders of an institution so close in proximity to Harlem and Morningside Heights.[13] University Trustee Harold McGuire recalled a conversation he had with Young, who was proud to brag that the program "can field a team with a Chinese boy on first base and a Puerto Rican boy on second base, and a Negro lad at shortstop, and a white boy at third base, but they can all make the double play."[14] McGuire assessed the university's community service youth program, testifying that "[a] terribly important aspect of this program, we feel, is the fact that it has really been an experiment, and a successful experiment in harmonious living."[15] He claimed that this "harmonious living" strategy took place in a very diverse urban area yet still succeeded.

A critic might have asked what the university meant by success. If it meant that many young people involved themselves in the program, then the university was correct in stating that its program was successful. If, however, the university meant that it was living harmoniously with its neighbors, and that its neighbors enjoyed the university's looming presence, then that success was less substantiated.

Until the mid-1960s, when Columbia incrementally cut off community access to the fields, many residents enjoyed and supported this arrangement. By the late 1960s the university was spending $25,000 a year to fund the program, and all was relatively well. Soon, however, the residents of Harlem noticed that the gate that surrounded the fields stayed locked more than it stayed open. Dwight C. Smith, chair of the Morningside Renewal Council, which was interested in improving the appearance of Morningside Heights, wrote to the editor of the *New York Times*: "[A]s the neighbors look at the locked fence around the ball field on what was one of the most available play areas in Morningside Park, they seldom see it occupied by other than Columbia students."[16] The residents feared that university acquisition of more parkland would end with similar results.

Nearly a decade before the 1968 crisis, President Grayson Kirk, realizing that Columbia University was in desperate need of a new gymnasium, asked Parks Commissioner Robert Moses if Columbia could buy 2.1 more acres of land in Morningside Park as the site.[17] Moses rejected Kirk's request to buy the area, suggesting instead that the university should lease the land from the city. Another option was to construct the gym in the middle of the campus or to improve on the university's existing gym. That solution, however, was unpopular for several reasons. First, the university wanted the gymnasium located near the previously constructed softball fields.[18] Second, according to Professor Wm. Theodore de Bary, provost emeritus and chair of the department of East Asian languages and cultures in the 1960s, the university was also making a gesture toward the community. "From the university's point of view," he said, "it was much more convenient [for the gymnasium] to be on campus rather than in the park"; but by building it in the park the community could take better advantage of the various athletic programs.[19]

Roger Starr noted as well that Columbia, being an Ivy League university, needed to keep up with the rest of the schools in its class. These other schools provided their undergraduate males with ample and attractive recreational facilities. Universities like Yale, Harvard, and Dartmouth had beautiful field houses and fields for their students to use, but Columbia, mostly because of its location in the city, did not have that luxury.[20] This was a sore spot among alumni who believed that their alma mater should be as good as any. Columbia University, if it wished to uphold its classification as "Ivy League," really needed to have recreational facilities that matched the standards of the other schools in its class, explained Starr.

In the early 1960s one university publication posed the question: "What should Columbia and the other leading colleges do" to keep abreast of the competition?[21] The article stated: "One indication of a possible direction for the future may be discovered by a look at what Columbia and the other Ivy group colleges have done about the problem thus far. What they have done, almost incredibly, is to expand in both directions. Not only are the curriculums much tougher, but the physical education and intramural programs are slightly more rigorous and widespread." To university officials, the need for a gymnasium was obvious: "Throughout the course of Columbia's athletic history, one note has been dominant: the inadequacy of facilities for exercise. . . . That Columbia College, a relatively small, urban institution with exceptionally high academic standards and the most inadequate athletic facilities of any major college in the East, has been able to turn out respectable teams in many sports, occasionally of championship caliber, is a too-often overlooked miracle."[22]

The article further explained that "colleges such as Columbia which are helping to educate many of society's future leaders have a special obligation to analyze carefully *all* the ingredients of their educational program, including athletics, and to recognize their national consequences." With the fierce competition for recreational space in New York, Columbia should have first considered the local consequences of expansion. That need for recreational space eventually brought Columbia in direct conflict with its Harlem neighbors.[23]

Whatever the location, the school needed a new facility badly, according to Kirk and several trustees. Built in the early 1900s, University Hall, the school's on-campus gym, was sorely outdated. It caught fire in 1914 and the university repaired it, but the school's efforts could not help the overall physical effect of the gym. One critic of the on-campus gym exclaimed: "And as for the smells in the gym! One can assemble hundreds of former students who will attest, if necessary before a notary, that the gym smells are thick enough to cut with a knife."[24] An article claimed that the on-campus gym "created an inferiority complex among Columbia men."[25]

Kirk and the trustees believed that the new gymnasium would allow the university not only to update its facilities, but also to enhance its relations with the adjacent community. In a document entitled "The New Columbia Gymnasium," Kirk said: "Nothing can mean more to Columbia College, . . . and nothing can give us more satisfaction, than the construction of the new gymnasium. . . . [T]his is a project of vital and urgent importance." In a similar fashion, Frank D. Fackenthal, trustee and 1906 graduate of Columbia College, stated: "It is hard to believe so many years have gone by since we first stated a need for a new gymnasium. . . . [W]e must now complete the gymnasium."[26]

In February 1960, after Kirk accepted Moses's offer, State Senator James L. Watson, a black man who represented Morningside Heights and West Harlem in the upper house of the state legislature, proposed a bill that allowed the school to lease a "specified" amount of land from the city.[27] Assemblyman Percy Sutton, also black, voted for the bill.[28] On April 14, 1961, Governor Nelson Rockefeller signed a measure allocating the university its 2.1 acres in the park. The next year, when the university started making its payments of $3,000 per month to the city, the matter stirred little controversy.

The initial outlines of the gymnasium stipulated that the city had "exclusive rights" to the gym. That meant that the university could not require that only its students could use the gym. Columbia also recognized that the gym could be used even when its staff were not present. The agreement also stipulated that the university had to submit a second set of "intermediate" plans within nine months of the initial submission. After the city received and accepted those designs, the university would have no more than five and a half years to complete final design plans. The city further stipulated that construction must begin no later than August 29, 1967, and once started, it must be completed within five years of the day of commencement. As of 1961, the estimated cost of the gymnasium was $6 million.[29]

At this point, the school's relationship with the adjacent neighborhood remained relatively stable. By 1961 the Columbia–Community Athletic Field Program was doing well, and most Harlem and Morningside Heights residents appreciated the opportunity for their children to participate. Community members found that as long as the fields stayed open, there was no problem. So when Columbia initially put forth plans for a gym in the park, they seemed acceptable to the community, considering the success of the previous university ventures there. The planners of the gym believed that they had avoided a sore spot with the community by using parkland instead of buying up more buildings and evicting tenants. In this way, "no Morningside residents would be displaced," claimed the planners.[30] Columbia, again, attempted to promote goodwill in the community by announcing plans to allot two of the ten floors of the gymnasium to public use.[31] The university publication *Columbia College Today* noted that the gym would positively affect the park by making it into "an interracial meeting place full of activity" and "a safe place in which to play again."[32]

That particular statement spoke to the mentality about race that the publishers of the university publication might have had at the time. Some critics wondered if the park "would become a safe place to play again" because it would be an *interracial* meeting place. The publication inferred that as long as there were only black and Puerto Rican people using the park, then the park was unsafe. Only when the university added the idea of "interracial meeting place" to the functions of the park did the concept of safety play a role. If black and Puerto Rican people had been utilizing the park, then it had always been an interracial meeting place. When asked his opinion of the gym proposal, one elderly white man replied: "It's a great idea! . . . Nobody uses this park anyway."[33]

Bob McKay, a lifetime patron of the park and leader of the West Harlem Community Organization, asserted that the park was little used—by white people. He explained that "for them it is even more dangerous than for the blacks."[34] Furthermore, McKay recalled: "Riverside Park was where whitey went and this [Morningside] park was ours." One might have questioned whether Columbia was concerned about making Riverside Park, which was farther away from Harlem, an "interracial meeting place" as well.

In its efforts to sustain a healthy relationship with its neighbors, the university may have been causing more harm than good. Many questioned the sincerity of the large, white institution on the hill and wanted to know who would benefit most from the proposed structure in the park that separated Harlem from Columbia. Author of *Crisis in Black and White,* Charles E. Silberman, in his research on the "Woodlawn Experiment" in Chicago, had made general observations of the relationship between large institutions such as Columbia and its urban neighbors. He noted that institutions often erred when they did not involve those in the community who would have been most affected by future plans: "Public officials, civic leaders, [in this case university officials], and foundation executives frequently draw up and publicize new programs for the downtrodden Negroes without bother to consult those who are to be 'uplifted.'"[35] Silberman's observation was true of Columbia University's proposed gymnasium in Morningside Park.

Several groups opposed the plans for a gym in the park at a July 27, 1961, hearing concerning the new edifice. Most of those organizations were against the proposed gymnasium on the grounds that it would be a private building on public land and thus take advantage of public domain. Those groups, such as the Citizens Union, the Municipal Art Society, St. Luke's Hospital, and the Cathedral of St. John the Divine, resisted the construction of the gymnasium along those lines. Most of the people and local groups who were present at the hearing, however, advocated its construction. The advocates of Columbia's gym were members of the Adult–Youth Association, the Grant–Morningside Neighborhood Group, and the Morningside Citizens Committee.[36]

Outside of the administration and alumni, one of the key advocates of the gymnasium was an undergraduate gymnasium committee, which acted on behalf of the Undergraduate Athletic Council. In October 1963 the proposed cost of the gymnasium had reached $9 million, and the group launched a fund-raising drive to assist the university in building the gym in the park. The committee assigned various representatives to collect money from students who lived in the dormitories and off-campus housing. It also set up desks to accept "donations from commuters."[37] The group recognized that its members would be the direct beneficiaries of a new recreational facility.

Between 1961 and 1965 a great deal happened throughout the world and within the neighborhoods of Morningside Heights and Harlem. The influx of heroin, lack of job opportunities, slum living, and racial injustice infused the residents of these areas with a feeling of resentment against white America that made them prime candidates for civil rights and protest movements. Tired of second-class citizenship, many Harlem blacks decided to change their fate by following the leadership of men like Martin Luther King Jr. and Malcolm X, and by joining organizations like the Student Non-Violent Coordinating Committee.

The followers of King advocated change in the still-segregated and un-just society of the United States. In 1960 in Greensboro, North Carolina, four black student-followers of King from North Carolina A&T entered a Woolworth's store, purchased some clothing items, and proceeded to the lunch counter. Even though the waitress informed them that "we don't serve Negroes here," the students came back each day until the store closed its doors.[38] They demonstrated that they could effect change without violence. In August 1963 that was the message King preached to the thousands who heard, watched, or attended his "I Have a Dream" speech at the March on Washington, D.C.

Members of the Northern Student Movement (NSM) took King's message to heart but attempted to bring further confrontation to the institutional racism of northern industrial cities. The NSM, which visited Columbia's campus in 1963, chose to advance the Civil Rights movement by attacking the circumstances of ghetto life and slum living. According to one article, "the Movement tries to convince Negroes in northern slums that they can confront the non-governmental power structure and make it responsive to their aspirations."[39] This was a slight departure from the movement that King was heading in 1963. King and his followers' intentions were to draw the government's attention to the mistreatment of mostly southern black people. Employing King's nonviolent philosophy in a different sphere, the NSM successfully organized West Harlem residents of a tenement to protest for lower rent. The residents then used the money they saved from lowered rents for building repairs.[40] In doing so, the NSM hoped to equip the "in-digenous leaders" with the organizational and informational tools to stake a claim of power in their living environments.[41]

King's position on nonviolence in the struggle for racial equality did not appeal to every black citizen during the Civil Rights movement. Many of the black residents in Harlem endorsed a different, more aggressive push for rights. Agreeing with King's goal of racial justice but not with his tactics was Malcolm X, a leader of the Nation of Islam, who did not care to integrate, associate, or negotiate with white America about the civil rights of black citi-zens. Many of the black Harlem residents, who lived in slums, welcomed and embraced his words.[42] Unlike King, Malcolm X, who operated from Harlem, advocated self-defense and did not refer to white people as his "brothers and sisters," but rather as "devils."

Malcolm X asserted that black people could fight back against white America by unifying economically through the purchase of businesses in their com-munities and by taking pride in their neighborhoods as well their heritage.[43]

To the residents of Harlem, that advice meant buying into their community and not allowing those foreign to it to purchase large parcels of land within its boundaries, including Morningside Park. In a more real sense, even if Columbia continued with its plans for the gym, it was unlikely that Harlem residents would benefit from the venture economically. It was likely that mostly white, not black, laborers would do the construction work, adding more fuel to the fire that raged against the gym and the white power structure in general. As a side note, the construction company that Columbia contracted to do the work was Crimmins Construction Corporation, a subsidiary of Uris Buildings. Percy Uris, who owned the company, was also a trustee of Columbia University.[44]

At a time when the nation was supposedly celebrating over a hundred years of racial progress, Harlem residents watched southern white authorities unleash vicious dogs on black protesters while police turned water hoses on black women and youth. Then Harlem's own Malcolm X was murdered, causing grief to followers but also igniting his message. After 1965 groups like SNCC abandoned King's nonviolent stance and took up the more aggressive approach to civil rights that Malcolm X had advocated. SNCC became a proponent of "Black Power."

According to the tenets of Black Power, as noted by Stokely Carmichael (Kwame Ture), former president of SNCC, and political scientist Charles V. Hamilton (who would later become a professor at Columbia University), black people must go through several processes to reach a position of power in the United States. One of these was self-definition, which involved the reclamation of the history of black people and black people defining themselves by showing pride in their culture. Another process was that of political modernization, which included three steps: "(1) questioning old values and institutions of society; (2) searching for new and different forms of political structure to solve political and economic problems; and (3) broadening the base of political participation to include more people in the decision-making process."[45] Appealing to the resentment and frustration that festered in black communities like Harlem, SNCC, with its new Black Power motto, urged working-class and lower-class blacks "to get some guns, . . . don't be trying to love that honky to death. Shoot him to death."[46] Institutions like Columbia could easily become the targets of such resentment, especially considering the university's proximity to the Harlem community.

Concurrent with the rise of the Civil Rights and Black Power movements was the increasing U.S. involvement in the Vietnam War. While the war against the North Vietnamese was many thousands of miles away, it had a direct effect on the black residents of Harlem. Many who marched for freedom and shouted "Black Power" were drafted to serve in the war. Until that point, black men had fought courageously in each of the country's wars, including Vietnam. While most black soldiers continued to act gallantly, Black Power forced many of them to question and actively protest their participation in such a politically controversial war.

Wallace Terry, a reporter for *Time* magazine and author of *Bloods: An Oral History of the Vietnam War by Black Veterans*, asserted that "the war was destroying the bright promises for social and economic change in the black community."[47] According to him, black soldiers were dying at a proportionately greater rate than other Americans. While black people made up 12 percent of the American population, they constituted 23 percent of American fatalities in the early part of the war.[48] While people in Harlem witnessed their young men dying in great numbers, there arose a resentment among the residents toward the many white students and faculty at Columbia University who would never see combat because of the ability to avoid the draft as college students or faculty members.

As the Vietnam War and the Civil Rights and Black Power movements occupied the minds of many Morningside Heights and Harlem residents, opposition to the gym stepped up. In late 1965 and early 1966 Mayor John Lindsay and Thomas Hoving, the newly appointed New York City parks commissioner, asserted that Columbia had attempted to fool Harlem and Morningside Heights community members in its offer to share two floors of the ten in the proposed gym. The two city officials examined the actual floor space of the proposed structure and found that the two floors that the community would use made up only 12.5 percent of the total floor space area rather than the assumed 20 percent.

Lindsay and Hoving raised this concern at meetings, at conferences, and in the press. Lindsay, who used opposition to the gym as part of his mayoral campaign in 1965, asserted that "park property should not fall to private builders," particularly Columbia University.[49] Hoving held that "if we are going to have to live with this big ugly structure, built on community land," then the community and not Columbia should get most [of the] benefit."[50] He vowed: "I am dead set against this gymnasium and I will fight as hard as I can to stop it."[51]

Hoving presented a special obstacle to the university's plans for the gym. He, like many New Yorkers, was a staunch supporter of recreational park space. Hoving once stated that "Utopia would mean a park or playground— some large, some small—every four or five blocks."[52] When George Collins, a university professor and opponent of the gym project, asked about Hoving's position on the gym, Hoving responded in a letter. On November 16, 1966, he wrote: "There are many reasons for opposing the [gym] project. First, it is completely out of scale for a park of this size. Second, the design lacks distinction of any kind."[53] As an aside, Hoving contended that "Columbia's capacity to plan and design monstrosities is truly astounding, as Columbia's Professors of Architecture and Fine Arts will admit, privately."

Hoving made an excellent point with his third reason for opposing the gym project. He said that "the 12% figure for community use is totally inadequate. . . . If as Dean Truman says, 12% is *more* than the City asked Columbia to provide for the community, my only response is that this proves the proposal was a mere 'land grab,' with connivance of politicians and bureaucrats who did not serve the Harlem community."[54] There were many thousands more residents than there were students, yet the gym designs allowed the community members much less space.

In Hoving's opinion, one of the most detestable acts possible was placing a large cement building in a green park, and that was exactly what Columbia University, the private owner, intended to do. He wrote in an article in the *New York Times Magazine* that "17 per cent of the city's area—some 37,000 acres—is set aside for parks and recreation space. But 9,000 of these acres are under water. . . . Only 14,500—roughly 7 per cent of the city—is park land located in immediate environment."[55] He observed that that amount was less than that allotted in cities like San Francisco, Los Angeles, Chicago, and Philadelphia.

Hoving was such a protector of park space that he forced the withdrawal of a donated cafeteria restaurant because the donator planned to build it in Central Park. In the same manner, he went so far as to demand that only "moveable," not permanent, refreshment kiosks be allowed in Central Park. More than most, he did not appreciate the university's attempt to place the gym in the park regardless of the goodwill that it was supposed to promote in the community.[56]

The parks commissioner and mayor were only part of a growing group of concerned citizens. On February 1, 1966, Richard Hatch, the executive director of the Architects Renewal Committee of Harlem, also protested to the editor of the *New York Times* about the plan to build the gymnasium at the Morningside Park site.[57] He pledged ARCH's support to Hoving and claimed that the gym would turn out like the school's previous projects, in which the community received little attention. Another opponent, M. M. Graff, sent a letter (which was never published) to the editor as well. He dramatically announced that "the rape of Morningside Park has been carried out with arrogant disregard of the public will."[58] Criticizing the school for its attempt to use public land for private purposes, Graff continued: "Parks are publicly owned land, held in trust for the people, and not to be parceled out for restricted use by any institution, commercial firm, or private egoist."[59]

To be sure, Graff was correct: it was illegal to use public land for private use per se. But the university justified the use of the parkland to the city and the state by allotting the community use of two floors in the proposed structure. Whether the proposed gym was satisfactory to the local residents had little to do with the fact that both the city and the state had authorized Columbia University to build in the park. To complicate matters more, the university had already engaged in a contract with building planners and construction agents and was moving forward with the project with or without the approval of the community.

Agreeing with Graff's complaints against the school, some Harlem residents opposed the raising of the gym for other reasons. Daniel Douglas pointed out that Columbia's gym would have represented yet another attempt of a white institution to own Harlem. Years after the controversy, he explained what institutions like Columbia did: "They own you. They build a gymnasium for you, and then they take it away from you anytime they want. Then they have control of that area. . . . If they build a gym on public land, then they have control over the public and private." Besides, Douglas added, "If that school wanted to help Harlem, then there were more vital things the community needed."[60] Another resident of Harlem, who referred to himself as the Reverend Sam, recalled that, at the time, his feeling was: "If you don't give our people a fair share of the responsibility in running this facility, then you can't come in our community. They [institutions like Columbia University] are trying to whiten Harlem."[61]

Whether the university was really trying to "whiten" Harlem is debatable, but what was interesting about the two Harlem residents' statements was the idea of ownership. They both insisted that the mostly black and Puerto Rican dwellers of Harlem should own the land and buildings in that particular enclave, but instead Columbia was trying to own not only the buildings and land in Harlem but also the people. This point was one that psychologists, sociologists, and economists had been toiling with for some time. Stokely Carmichael and Charles V. Hamilton believed that the black communities in America were colonies that institutional white America controls, and to some extent Carmichael and Hamilton were correct. As had been the case since before the 1935 and 1943 riots, most of the businesses and buildings in Harlem belonged to white people. What was more, the urban renewal that the city made during the early 1960s further "whitened" (to use the Reverend Sam's term) Harlem by making it possible for companies and institutions (nearly all white) to purchase land for fairly inexpensive prices. In that sense, the larger institutions of America would literally own places like Harlem, without ever having to live there. This, understandably, made some residents of the area feel as though they lived in colonies.

Representing the black community in politics, State Senator Basil A. Paterson and Assemblyman Percy E. Sutton, both black Democrats, put forth a bill in each house to invalidate the city's 1960 grant giving Columbia the right to lease the land at Morningside Park.[62] "Columbia shall not build a gym in this park," proclaimed Paterson on April 28, 1966, at an outdoor rally at Morningside Park. In clarifying his statement, he warned, "Let the first bulldozers come here and you'll know what we mean."[63] In a published statement, Paterson and Sutton asked: "Why must the university's obligation to educate its students be fulfilled at the expense of communities hungry for park space?"[64] Incidentally, Senator James L. Watson later explained publicly that he had erred in introducing the bill. He claimed that Columbia had misled him about the community's access to the gym.[65]

Harlem and Morningside Heights residents did not just rely on their elected officials to make their case against the gymnasium; the residents led a grass-roots protest movement to keep their control of the park. A leader in this movement was the Harlem-based *New York Amsterdam News*. An editorial in the January 29, 1966, edition of the paper called Columbia's gym project an insult: "If Mayor Lindsay permits Columbia University to grab two acres of land out of Morningside Park for a gymnasium it will be a slap in the face to every black man, woman and child in Harlem."[66] Pointing up Columbia's relationship to black people and Harlem specifically, the paper noted that "Columbia University, one of the richest institutions in the nation, only admits a handful of Negro scholars each year and its policies in dealing with Negroes in Harlem have been described as downright bigoted." The paper asked: "Why then should the parents of Harlem give up of their parkland to Columbia? What has Columbia done to merit such favoritism?"

Some observers might have claimed that the Columbia–Community program should have counted in the university's favor, but the paper stated plainly that Columbia had done "nothing" that should justify the school's control of more park land. At the end of the article, the paper stated its position: "This newspaper will fight this bigoted act by Columbia with its every resource and we call on the people of Harlem to band together and do the same. This is too much for even Harlem to take. Let's stop this move right now."[67]

Three months later, the *New York Amsterdam News* continued its struggle against the university. In an article entitled "Does Anyone Care?" the paper asked: "Why is the Lindsay administration afraid to tackle Columbia? . . . Does the Lindsay administration really care about Harlem?"[68] The editorial suggested an answer with another question: "Could it be that this is Harlem—and because the issue involves Harlemites—and because it is Harlem . . . Mr. Lindsay simply [does not] care?" Getting directly to the point, the article stated that "it's a matter of whites (Columbia) taking something from blacks (the children of Harlem)." If ever the mayor wanted to do something for Harlem, the editorial claimed, "here is a good opportunity to prove it."

The paper featured a drawing depicting its view of the situation. Entitled "Being Robbed," the illustration showed a white man in a suit with "Columbia U." across the chest pulling up a square of park land that had a slide and the words "Morningside Park Acreage" written on it.[69] While the man was pulling up the land, black children were tumbling off of it. Then the picture showed a black boy in a shirt reading "Harlem" on the front petitioning another white man in a suit. On the side of the man's suit read the words "Lindsay Administration." The man in the suit had his back turned to the situation and blinders on his eyes. Undoubtedly, the picture further entrenched the *New York Amsterdam News* in the movement against Columbia.

On April 24, 1966, members of the Morningside and Harlem communities came together at a rally in the park. The *Morningside Citizen* noted that "there seemed to be [no] one in favor of Columbia University's proposed construction of a gymnasium in Morningside Park." Sponsored by the Ad Hoc Committee for Morningside Park, the rally included protesters decorating makeshift gravestones with wreaths as if they were attending a funeral. The headstone read: "*Requiscat* in Gymnasium, Morningside Park, 1877–1966, Erected in Loving Memory—G. Kirk."[70] There were seven speakers to eulogize the park, including the president of Columbia's student council and the counselor of Protestant students. The student speaker explained that the student council was against the gymnasium and had passed a resolution calling for the suspension of plans for the facility "until a joint agreement between the community and the university had been reached."[71]

In addition to the speakers from Columbia were State Senator Basil Paterson and Parks Commissioner Hoving. Paterson, also the president of the city branch of the NAACP, contrasted the number of students at Columbia with the number of people living in the West Harlem blocks closest to Morningside Park, pointing out that the numbers were heavily in favor of Harlem residents. He called out with confidence that "Columbia shall not build a gym in this park!" Hoving added to the senator's words by simply stating that "I think you know how I feel about encroachment on park land. . . . I will fight to see that it's stopped."[72]

When Columbia's President Kirk became aware of the opposition, he proclaimed that, if the bills passed, the university would sue the state. Kirk noted that "Columbia has two legally binding contracts: one with the city of New York, which if we withdrew would expose us [Columbia] to suit, and the other . . . with the builders."[73] So with legal contracts binding Columbia to the gym, he announced firmly: "Groundbreaking will occur in October."[74]

On November 1, 1966, a *New York Times* headline read: "Columbia Starts 3-Year Campaign for $200 Million." A major contributor to the fund, the Ford Foundation, approved its donation of $35 million to the school on the condition that it "work with the Negro population on Morningside Heights."[75] Implying that the university could improve on its relationship with that community, the president of the Ford Foundation and former national security adviser McGeorge Bundy added explicitly that he and his corporation were "not talking about doing things to the city or *to* the minorities," but that Columbia and the foundation "will concern [themselves] *with* 'the city and the Negro' . . . by cooperation rather than imposed action."[76]

With the university enjoying the funding and advocacy of contributors like the Ford Foundation, the people of Harlem realized that the university had more than enough power to build its gym. In spite of Columbia's access to resources, the climate in Harlem and black America was quickly changing. The long, hot summer of 1966 was long and hot in more ways than one. Black Power fostered a strong resentment of powerful white institutions. H. Rap Brown, categorized at one point as "Amerika's baddest, meanest, most violent nigger," summed up the attitude behind Black Power.[77] When an interviewer asked him if he would ever bring a gun to the Pentagon, he responded: "I'd be unwise to say I'm going with a gun because you all took my gun last time. I *may* bring a bomb[,] sucker."[78]

In many larger cities across the United States, black Americans were fighting back against racial and economic oppression in ways that would force white America to hear their grievances. Columbia University, which was directly adjacent to one of the main black communities in the country, began to reconsider its community relations. The thought of Columbia actually burning scared university trustees so badly that they urged Harold McGuire to authorize the local community's use of a larger share of the gym, "by invitation," of course.[79] The university also offered to add a swimming pool and locker room to the plans for the community portion of the gym. Percy

Sutton, who had since become Manhattan Borough president, accepted the offer, but not wholeheartedly.[80]

Incidentally, it took some negotiation to achieve such a concession from the university. On October 7, 1966, Senator Paterson met with university representative Stanley Salmen to discuss Paterson's opposition to the gym. Salmen explained that "during lunch, [Paterson] informed us that he was going to reintroduce his bill in the Senate to revoke the lease in Morningside Park."[81] The first time that Paterson attempted to do so (on May 17, 1966), the bill did not pass the Committee of Affairs of the City of New York because it was not accompanied by a home-rule message (the complete endorsement of the City Council or mayor). Paterson told Salmen that the only reason the bill did not pass was that the Senate session ended too soon. But it may not have been a matter of timing alone. Salmen had contacted other senators to make sure the bill would not pass. "It is true that Senator Marchi had promised me that it would not be passed through the Senate without the home rule message and Travia had told Mr. Cahill that such a message would be a prerequisite to passage in the House," said Salmen. The university representative further observed that "these delaying tactics worked because Senator Paterson's bill was introduced only a month before the session adjourned."[82]

When Salmen questioned Paterson as to why he would set in motion legislation against the gym, Salmen said that Paterson's response was "to establish a negotiating base with Columbia University." Salmen remarked that if it would cause that much trouble to build the gym in the park, then maybe the university would erect the recreational facility on campus. Salmen claimed that Paterson indicated that "we [presumably Columbia affiliates] needed the gym in the Park, it was the right place for the gym, that the Harlem community needed the gymnasium in the Park, that the rock on which it was built was 'an enticement to the boys' which was dangerous."[83]

According to Salmen, Paterson requested that the community be allotted 50 percent of the gym rather than the 12 percent that the university was offering. Paterson explained that there were nearly one hundred community organizations ready to protest if construction began in the park. Moreover, Amy Betanzos, who was the chairperson of the Ad Hoc Committee for Morningside Park, vowed her support of a new bill against the school's lease of land in the park. With such support, it would be very difficult for the City Council and mayor to not send a home rule message. Indeed, Salmen recognized that "Paterson intends to be the best kind of new leader for Negroes. . . . He is clearly in a negotiating situation." Further, Salmen admitted, "It looks, therefore, as though he [Paterson] were in a position to stop the gymnasium in the Park unless we negotiate with him before January 1st and arrive at some solution which will satisfy him but which would not be a contractual obligation on the part of the University."[84]

In spite of the rising tide of community members, representatives, and politicians against the gym project, one local resident worried that, in the end, the community children would suffer most if Columbia did not construct the gym. M. A. Harris wrote a letter to the editor of the *New York Free Press* explaining that Columbia had made it possible for the neighborhood youth to play in the park with the construction of the school's softball fields and that the gym would provide the same type of services.[85] As a former coach in the Columbia–Community Athletic Field Program, he considered the criticisms of the opponents of the gym as shortsighted. "That is the pity of these sincere but misguided opponents of the gym. Not only do they have NOTHING to lose, but in addition they have NOTHING to give the youngsters who would benefit from the gym," Harris stated. Somehow, he believed, critics had muddled the main issue: "It distresses me to see adults so confuse issues." Harris asserted that the adults he referred to "do not appear able to weigh advantages against disadvantages." The advantage, he maintained, would be a state-of-the-art recreational facility available to neighborhood young people.

Although the addition of a swimming pool to the community section of the gym might have been useful to some Harlem residents, a pool could not possibly satisfy the resentments of many inhabitants.[86] While moderate leaders like Sutton thought that the addition of the pool and locker room facilities might help the situation, more militant leaders like H. Rap Brown, who represented SNCC, and Victor Solomon of the Harlem chapter of the Congress of Racial Equality opposed the "racist gym" in its entirety. Solomon, agreeing with earlier ideas of Carmichael and Hamilton, contended that "Harlem is a colony and is being treated like one," and that the community should impede the progress of the imperialist (Columbia).[87] In a February 1967 meeting, Brown, nearly at the pinnacle of the influence of the Black Power movement, encouraged his audience to protest: "If they build the first story[,] blow it up. If they sneak back at night and build three stories[,] burn it down. And if they get nine stories built, it's yours. Take it over, and maybe we'll let them in on the weekends."[88]

Members of the community continued to mount protests against the gym. Under the sponsorship of the 114th Street Block Association, the Senator Basil Paterson Service Center, the Ad Hoc Committee for Morningside Park, and the West Harlem Community Organization, one rally took place in the park on April 24, 1967. The flyer for the rally read: "Protest Against the Gym That Columbia University Will Build on Space Needed for the Recreation of Our Children."[89] In July of that year, community leaders passed out another hand-bill to people from the neighborhood. It aptly described the way that some residents perceived the controversy over the park. The bill read: "Harlem v/s Columbia Univ. At City Hall; When—July 27th; Where—Board of Estimate; Time—9:30 A.M.; Why—To Keep Segregation Out of Morningside Park.[90]

Community groups planned another rally to protest the gym. It took place on July 29 at 114th Street and Morningside Avenue in the park. Organizations like the Morningsiders United, the Morningside Tenants Committee, and the Grant Parent Community Organization sponsored the event. The planners scheduled politicians Basil Paterson and Percy Sutton as well as community organizers like Bill Stanley to speak against the gym.

For the July 29 event, community members passed out leaflets to moti-vate those who would attend. One of the bills read: "West Harlem Against Columbia University's Segregated Gymnasium," and another asked: "Did You Give Permission for Columbia University to Build a Segregated Gym in Morningside Park?"[91] One clever flyer featured an image of a crow upside down with an "X" for an eye, a bandaged wing, and a crumpled beak. The crow wore a high-top sneaker with an "M" (presumably for Morningside) on the side of the shoe. Directly above the bird read the words "Gym Crow." The remainder of the flyer read: "Stop Columbia University in Morningside Park, July 29, 1967."[92] The community was ready for a battle with Columbia.

Even young protesters joined the effort against the gym. The *Columbia Owl* reported on November 15, 1967, that "a dozen small schoolchildren . . . paraded through the Columbia campus Saturday afternoon."[93] The young people chanted: "We Want the Park, Keep Columbia Out!" Horace Foster, a leader in the West Harlem Morningside Park Committee, led the children through and around campus. The paper reported that "at the same time, ap-proximately fifty adults picketed at the campus gate on 116th and Broadway." At one point all of the picketers gathered to burn in effigy university trustee Frank Hogan, who happened also to be a Manhattan district attorney. Spon-sorship for the event came from the West Harlem Community Organiza-tion. Bob McKay, who was an officer in the organization, commented that they were there "to serve notice on the administration of the university that its encroachment upon the public's property has bred a lot of resistance in the community." Unless the university backed down from the gym project, peaceful demonstrations may not be feasible in the future, McKay suggested. He said: "If the trustees don't reconsider the situation with a view toward the general welfare of the city, this resistance will have the potential of exploding into anger." That sort of rhetoric typified that which was so popular during the Black Power movement.

Ironically the gym issue brought together militant and moderate black leaders. For instance, State Senator Basil Paterson, usually a moderate in the struggle for civil rights, disagreed with the destructive rhetoric of leaders like H. Rap Brown but shared Brown's sentiments about the gym. In December 1967 Paterson contended that he "would stand with anyone [including Brown] against the racist gym."[94] Such an alliance could truly render power. Reminding black Harlem residents of the discrimination of previous times, Brown, Paterson, and other black leaders consistently referred to the building as "Gym Crow," which grew from the notion that the university was forcing the community to submit to acts like those that had taken place in the Jim Crow South.

When the bulldozers began excavating land for the gymnasium, opponents of the facility acted to prevent the workers from doing so. On February 20, 1968, twenty community members and Columbia students went to Morningside Park at 8 A.M. to protest. After arriving at the site for the gym, the demonstrators stood between the construction workers and their machines. In an effort to begin the day, the workers called the police to remove the protesters. Subsequently, the officers arrested twelve demonstrators. Two of those arrested, Robert McKay and Joseph Monroe, were members of the West Harlem Community Organization.[95] With determination, John Love of the Morningside Park Association explained: "After fighting this thing for so many years, we can't give up now."[96] Providing some rationale for the demonstrators' actions, Love expressed his point of view: "We tried to stop the gym by using legal means. Now the only way to protest is by direct confrontation. . . . We can't lose anything." Members of the West Harlem Community Organization voted to hold another demonstration at the gym site later in the week.

The next demonstration involved a larger number of protesters. Indeed, with each event the tension increased. Beginning on the university's campus and ending at the gym site, about 150 gym opponents showed up in the park to prevent construction workers from moving ahead with the project. Both students from Columbia and community members participated in the protest. By this time, Columbia had hired more private guards to protect the gym, and the university urged the city police to step up their patrols. In this instance, the police arrested thirteen demonstrators who were mostly trying to keep a truck from coming to the site. Unlike the demonstrations before, violence broke out at this event, and one student was arrested for felonious assault. The Reverend Kendall Smith from Harlem also faced charges. After he attempted to make his way through a fence that surrounded the gym site, police arrested him for criminal trespass as well as resisting arrest. Many of the protesters loudly criticized the police for arresting him.[97]

Although community protest intensified, so too did Columbia's resolve to complete the gym project. In spite of demonstrations and other episodes, the bulldozers continued to dig out park land. One article in a student news organ appraised the situation: "Each pound of earth removed from the Park means that much more community revulsion against a badly mismanaged building program."[98] Furthermore, the article observed, "the Administration made a grievous miscalculation if they thought they were taking the easy way out with the Morningside Park site." The periodical went on to provide more seething commentary: "Meanwhile, the grey hole that will one day be the gymnasium grows larger and we, for one, are in favor of it. Much more than an ugly edifice squatting on some of the city's preciously needed park space, the new gymnasium serves as a valuable symbol of indifference, shortsightedness, the Administration's consistent failure to recognize the debt it owes the great urban community it lives in. With concrete and brick, the university will convincingly demonstrate, once again the unmitigated power that this particular segment of the establishment has over the people of Harlem." Sadly, the article predicted, the gym would be constructed and expansion would continue to occur.

One local periodical covered the gym protests as well. The *Westside News* featured several articles decrying the university's plans. One issue of the paper showed a snapshot of a child holding a sign that read: "Stop Columbia University from Taking Morningside Park—I Mean It."[99] In regard to the protests, an article noted: "Recent outbursts have been more violent than the earlier ones, but for many, the violence is primarily an involuntary response to a situation that has angered many members of the community."[100] That statement was very similar to those of black rioters who burned cities across the country when they felt ignored, neglected, and disregarded. Moreover, that sentiment provided the vehicle for the transition of the Civil Rights movement to the Black Power movement.

Since Columbia chose to interrupt some of the neighborhood residents' lives, some community members attempted to do the same to Columbia. Each year the Columbia campus hosted the West Side Community Conference, at which people and institutions discussed issues related to the area. That year, demonstrators disrupted the discussion. As State Representative

William Ryan, Sargent Shriver, and Department of Justice appointee Roger Wilkins conducted a panel on "The Urban Struggle for Power," nearly two hundred demonstrators invaded the auditorium where the conference was taking place. At the time of the protesters' entry, Wilkins was making the point that "the benign rubric of citizen participation was causing change."[101] The members of the community hoped that Wilkins was correct.

In addition to the *Westside News* and other newspapers, the *New York Free Press* covered the gym controversy. One photo in the paper showed a community picketer with a placard that read "The Invasion." Below those words was an image of the proposed gym.[102] On the night of March 20, 1968, community organizations led another rally in the park. In the place where so many people had been mugged, nearly two hundred demonstrators from the community paraded. Holding candles to light the night, the protesters chanted and spoke against the gym. One newspaper showed a picture of two West Harlem children holding candles and with smiles on their faces as they marched.[103]

The influence of Black Power was evident in the approach that the community was taking in the campaign against the school. While both black and white community members protested the gym, by 1968 black community representatives like Robert McKay wanted to make it clear that this issue was one on which black people had to take the lead. His efforts led to the entrance of Harlem's Congress of Racial Equality and many other organizations.[104] These community rumblings led to advocacy by local politicians like Sutton, Paterson, Charles Rangel, and Constance Baker. White community members like George Hendricks of Morningsiders United concurred with the idea of black protesters heading the effort to end the school's plans. Of all the community members, the gym issue seemed to have the potential to affect black residents the most. Likewise, perhaps no other group of community members had as much to gain from a moral victory against an institution of the white power structure.

During this time, a pamphlet that was most likely created by students from Columbia made its way to neighborhood groups, residents, and university students. The title of the document was "Gym Crow" and it had different sections.[105] One section called "Separate But Unequal" claimed that "the community will have access to a meager 15% of the gym's facilities and its activities will be supervised by Columbia rather than community-selected personnel." The section also asserted that "the gym will be a conspicuous irritant to race relations in the community, particularly during the summer when Columbia's 85% of the gym will go unused." In another section, called "Community

Gym," the pamphlet pointed out that "money to construct the community section of the gym has been provided by grants specifically designated for that purpose." The document referred to the Ford Foundation grant that the university had received: "The benefits the community will derive from the gym are being provided by the city and the grants, not by the University."

The final section, "Unplanned Obsolescence," outlined the overall inadequacy of the project. If Columbia planned to compete with other Ivy League universities' facilities, then the school on the Heights would still lose with the new gym. The document claimed that Princeton's gym had twice as many seats as were planned for the Columbia gym, and that Yale had two more swimming pools than the proposed facility. A good deal of the space in the gym would also go to the Naval Reserve Officers Training Corps, which the document found to be very controversial in light of the war in Southeast Asia.

Following the lead of William H. Booth, head of the Human Rights Commission, black leaders pointed out that the community section of the proposed building was separate from the portion the university members would use. Some journalists noted that, according to the plans, the allotted section for the university's NROTC branch was even larger than that of the community.[106] Moreover, Booth showed that community residents had to enter through the basement of the structure, just as blacks had to enter through basements and back doors during the Jim Crow era.[107] In defense of the university, the gymnasium was to be built on a ledge, and geographically the entrance that might have been most convenient for Harlem residents would have been at the bottom of the ledge. That does not, however, dismiss the fact that they could not explore the other floors of the structure. Moreover, after realizing that they would receive access to only 15 percent of the proposed structure that Columbia University would control, and be forced to use a different entrance, many black residents in the community saw that things were once more separate, but hardly equal. As they did in the past, black people stood up against what they believed was unjust. Instead of fighting against Jim Crow, the community now fought against Gym Crow.

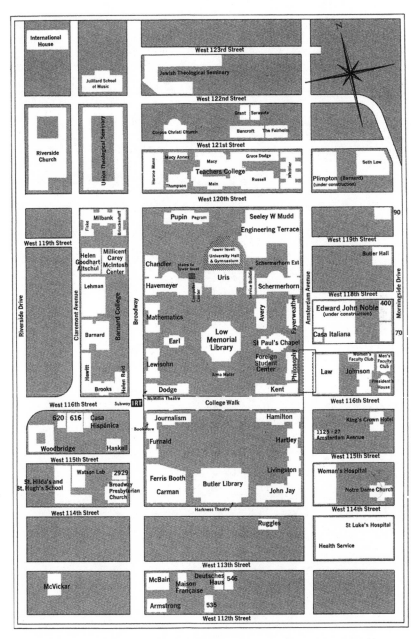

Columbia University Campus, 1968 (with permission of the University Archives, Columbia University in the City of New York).

Project: Columbia University Gymnasium
Architects: Eggers & Higgins
Builder: George A. Fuller Company
Date 4-1-68 No. 9 View EAST

A view of the excavation of Morningside Park and West Harlem from Columbia University's Morningside Heights campus, April 1, 1968 (with permission of the University Archives, Columbia University in the City of New York).

State Senator Basil Paterson addresses crowd in Harlem, 1968 (courtesy of David Finck).

Bill Sales (Mark Rudd to his right) of SAS addresses occupants of Hamilton Hall, April 23, 1968 (courtesy of Gerald Adler).

Steering Committee at work (Mark Rudd of SDS in plaid shirt, Cicero Wilson of SAS against wall in glasses sitting next to Ray Brown of SAS), April 23, 1968 (courtesy of David Finck).

SAS leader Ray Brown, flanked by Bill Sales (*left*) and Ralph
Metcalfe Jr. (*right*), reads new set of demands, April 24, 1968
(courtesy of Nicholas Mirra).

SAS leader Ralph Metcalfe Jr., flanked by Ray Brown (*left*) and Bill Sales (*right*), presents their demands to the media, April 24, 1968 (courtesy of David Finck).

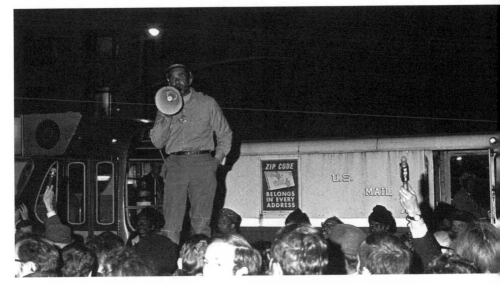

Charles 37X Kenyatta of the Harlem Mau Maus addresses crowd outside of campus, circa April 26, 1968 (courtesy of David Finck).

Black Power activist H. Rap Brown attempting to reach Hamilton Hall, April 26, 1968 (with permission of the University Archives, Columbia University in the City of New York).

With SAS leadership looking on from Hamilton Hall, Black Power advocate H. Rap Brown delivers SAS messages to the press. Standing to Rap Brown's left is Black Power advocate Stokely Carmichael, April 26, 1968 (courtesy of Lee Pearcy).

Harlem supporters march down Amsterdam Avenue, circa April 27, 1968 (courtesy of Richard Howard).

The sentinel of Malcolm X University (Hamilton Hall), April 27, 1968 (courtesy of Nicholas Mirra).

Harlem residents support black student demonstration, April 1968 (courtesy of Lee Pearcy).

SAS members communicate with supporters from inside Hamilton Hall, circa April 28, 1968 (courtesy of Lee Pearcy).

SAS marches victoriously through Hamilton Hall, April 30, 1968 (courtesy of Richard Howard).

A view of Morningside Park from West Harlem, April 1968 (courtesy of Gerald Adler).

3

Up against the Wall
Columbia's Integrated Protest Effort

"Up against the wall, motherfucker, this is a stick-up," white SDS organizer Mark Rudd wrote on April 22, 1968, in a circulated letter to Columbia University President Kirk in hopes of inciting student protest.[1] Rudd's sentence comes from Leroi Jones's (Amiri Baraka's) poem "Black People!" that appeared in the *New York Times* in 1968. The word "motherfucker" allegedly originated in the ghetto. Rudd claimed to have "co-opted the word . . . from the ghetto much as we [the members of SDS] adopted the struggle of blacks and the other oppressed as our own."[2] This chapter details the efforts of student protesters who sought to take on the struggle of the community and to gain power for themselves as students.

The statement that Rudd made in his letter accurately indicated the position in which American universities found themselves as a result of student protests in the 1960s. Beginning in 1964 with the "Free Speech movement" at the University of California–Berkeley, where an integrated group of students demonstrated against the administration's ban on political rallies in a small area on campus known as the Bancroft Strip, universities were under siege.[3] Students from Berkeley were previously involved in protests to encourage the hiring of minority, particularly black, workers in area stores. As a result of their efforts, local storeowners hired black employees; however, those same storeowners pressured Berkeley's president, Clark Kerr, to enforce an existing ban on political activities on campus.

Protesting students, of course, disregarded the ban and held a demonstration anyway in October 1964. When a student was arrested for manning a Congress of Racial Equality table on Bancroft Strip, thousands of student protesters surrounded the police car and sat down, preventing the arresting officer from leaving with his prisoner. After thirty-two hours, and a great deal of negotiation with President Kerr, the student demonstrators allowed the police car to leave, but not without Kerr's promise that the university would not take any disciplinary actions against the student arrested or the protesting students. The negotiations also ensured that Bancroft Strip would be sold to the city, which would mean that it was no longer under the jurisdiction of the university. It also outlined that a tripartite committee of administrators, faculty, and students would be formed to deal with the creation of rules concerning political activity on Berkeley's campus.[4]

The protest at Berkeley demonstrated the power that students could have at their universities, if they only chose to confront those who retained most of the power: university officials. As authors Daniel Bell and Irving Kristol have noted: "When Berkeley became the eruptive focus of student discontent in 1964, it would become a model for students elsewhere."[5] Indeed, students at universities like Columbia used the protest at Berkeley as a model for their own protests. In the 1960s there were several reasons for students' increased courage to confront these powers. The first was that there were so many young students. Because of the baby boom and the upturn of the American economy during the cold war, there were nearly three times as many students attending universities in 1965 as there were in 1950.[6] That translated to nearly 40 percent of young people in America between the ages of eighteen and twenty-two who were attending colleges and universities.[7] Combined with the fact that, by 1965, people in the United States under the age of twenty-five outnumbered those over that age, students and young people represented a force that American institutions like universities had to take seriously. Feeling the influence of the rising New Left and Black Power movements, many of these students saw the benefits of protest. Universities, which until that point had taken the role of *in loco parentis* seriously, were dealing with the results of young people's growing pains.

The second reason was that many of these young people had been exposed to the Civil Rights movement in the South. Students, white and black, had traveled throughout the South, participating in freedom rides, registering voters, and even teaching in inadequate schools.[8] After witnessing firsthand the ugliness of racial discrimination and oppression, many of the student protesters believed that it was their obligation to change society, and that they could start with the universities. These black and white students, taking their cue from the Civil Rights movement, formed coalitions to fight racism in the early 1960s. Howard Zinn, in his account of SNCC, noted the group's experiences in the South and how the youth who participated in the organization should have been compared to the abolitionists of the antebellum years because of their stands against blatant racism. Lauding the racially mixed group of young people who approached the problems of the nation nonviolently, Zinn claimed that they were not ashamed of being "troublemakers" like the abolitionists of old; furthermore, they were proud of their ability to confront racism directly but nonviolently.[9] Many of the students in the late 1960s carried that attitude onto campus. However, the spirit of racial unity, maintained earlier by groups like SNCC, would not endure.

The third reason young people on campuses believed they could successfully confront the power of their respective institutions of higher education was that many American universities provided students with a venue to protest societal issues. Before the cold war, Americans viewed universities like Berkeley and Columbia as bastions of liberal arts education that were almost shielded from issues outside the walls of academia. That changed, however, when politicians began looking toward universities to lead the nation in corporate and scientific research, particularly research concerning war strategy and weapon design.

In the buildup of the military-industrial complex, many American universities were transformed into what some university officials referred to as "multiuniversities," where not only did the nation expect the institution to educate young Americans, but also the university, as an institution, could benefit business and the government.[10] This resulted in the direct or indirect participation of such multiuniversities in the Vietnam War and in racial discrimination. Many students did not view the changes that occurred at their universities during the peak of the cold war as positive, yet they had little say in the decisions that university officials made. Until the 1960s universities like Columbia were typically very authoritative and were run strictly from the top down, with the trustees retaining most of the power, then the administration, and so on. The situation of the 1960s was unprecedented. Never before had universities been confronted with such a large number of students of such a diverse background. Combined with such intense societal issues, this made it extremely difficult to maintain the traditional structure. These reasons were enough to provoke the students on the relatively quiet Morningside Heights campus to rumble in 1968.

Students like Mark Rudd, a junior at Columbia University and leader of SDS, took the lead in the unsettling of his school. His family name was originally Rudnitzky, and for most of Rudd's young life, his family leaned slightly to the left regarding political issues.[11] Reared in New Jersey, he spent time in

Newark, a mostly black enclave similar to Harlem, and he noticed the mistreatment that black people frequently received. After Columbia University accepted him, Rudd attended a youth conference in Cuba, which inspired him to move even further to the left on the political spectrum. Recalling his experiences in revolutionary Cuba, Rudd returned to Columbia University and submitted a "Position Paper on Strategy for the Rest of the School Year—Complicity."[12] In that paper, he stated as his and SDS's goal "the radicalization of students, . . . showing them how our lives really are unfree in this society and at Columbia." He called on students to take part in "striking a blow at the Federal Government's war effort," as it affected the university.[13]

Believing that he had an obligation to stop the university's "complicity" with the war, Rudd looked to ignite protest within the student body. In his open letter, "Up against the Wall," the main focus was on ending the university's relationship with the Defense Department and increasing the amount of power available for students who wanted to take part in the decision making of their school. In the entire eight-page letter, there was no specific reference to the gymnasium issue that Rudd and SDS would later find so controversial.

The internal opponents of the gym further campaigned. On March 27, 1968, the faculty of the School of Architecture passed a resolution stating that President Kirk and the trustees must reconsider the decision to build the gym because the school was not acting fairly toward the community.[14] Two weeks later, at a memorial for the recently assassinated Reverend Martin Luther King Jr., SDS's Mark Rudd seized the microphone from Columbia's vice president, David Truman. As Truman walked to the podium to eulogize King, Rudd beat him to the microphone and asked: "How can these administrators praise a man who fought for human dignity when they have stolen land from the people of Harlem?" He continued: "If we really want to honor this man's memory[,] then we ought to stand together against this racist gym."[15] Rudd scored a valid and probably correct point, but high-ranking university officials could appreciate neither his tone nor his timing. President Kirk responded later by placing Rudd and the other participants in this indoor protest on disciplinary probation.

Rudd claimed that SDS was adopting the struggle of oppressed black people. In urging the mostly white audience of students to "stand together" against the gym, Rudd emphasized the duty of concerned members of his race to fight for downtrodden black people. According to Rudd, SDS saw the unfairness of the racist gym project and committed itself to battling the gym, and in so doing changing society for the better, much in the way that the early SNCC activists did. The white student leader also understood that by demonstrating at the memorial to King, SDS could, in some ways, gain the favor of the increasingly militant black Students' Afro-American Society, who mourned the loss of one of the nation's most revered leaders.

Soon after the disturbance at King's memorial ceremony, SDS began preparations for another mass demonstration. In the evening of April 22, Rudd, along with other members of SDS, met with Ray Brown, Leon Denmark, and Cicero Wilson of SAS to discuss what could be done at the school to address the issues that affected both the students and the community.

Some SAS members had been inspired by their experience at Howard University over the spring break. At the prestigious historically black university, student leaders, like those involved with SAS, took over Howard's administration building, demanding that the university become more relevant to the surrounding black community. To some of the members of SAS, the scenario at Howard seemed reminiscent of that at Columbia.[16]

With the Howard demonstrations fresh in their minds, at noon on April 23 SAS members attended a rally that SDS held at the Sundial, which sits in the middle of the campus. Hearing that the conservative "jocks," or athletes, who usually opposed the demands and objectives of groups like SAS and SDS, would be at the Sundial, some members of SAS arrived to finish a confrontation between them.[17] Bill Sales remembered that "the jocks had been spreading rumors about the members of SAS, and some of us [SAS members] had done battle with [them]." He explained that "we went to [the Sundial to] kick ass. But there were thousands of people there, [and] the radical forces were in the majority," so there was no need to engage the jocks.[18]

Part of the black group's willingness to "do battle" with the conservative athletes was undoubtedly due to the frustration that had arisen among black students in response to the murder of King. Also, the athletes supported the idea of a new gymnasium, as they would directly benefit from its construction. Further intensifying the situation, white SDS leaders were present with their own agenda. They had organized the demonstration to express their radical views on the university and the war, as well as the gymnasium.

After berating the university and its policy toward the Vietnam War and the adjacent community, Mark Rudd suggested that students take the demonstration into Low Memorial Library, which was the location of the university administration. Entering Low could have been particularly troublesome, as Rudd had already been sanctioned for his indoor demonstration the previous month. When Vice President David Truman managed to get to the library and lock the doors, Rudd seemed confounded. As Ornest Ranum, a professor in the department of history, recalled well after the demonstration, "Mark Rudd got up on top of a refuse collector, saying, 'I don't know what to do.

Where do we go now? The Low Library is locked. We cannot gain admission to it. What do we do now?'"[19] In spite of the fact that he had consistently been elected president of his class since elementary school, Rudd's leadership seemed to waiver, as the group of demonstrators grew restless.[20]

Cicero Wilson, one of the leaders of SAS, called for the attention of the crowd. "This is Harlem Heights, not Morningside Heights," he said, implying that Columbia University was part of a mostly black residential area and that the residents in that area had just as much right as the university to make decisions that would affect their homes and lives. Wilson questioned the radical commitment of the mostly white crowd by asking what it would do if somebody tried to take its property or land. He and other members of SAS believed that, if radical white SDS was not even willing to take the demonstration indoors, then SDS was certainly not willing to engage whole-heartedly in a struggle against the university gymnasium. Counterdemonstrators from groups such as the Students for a Free Campus (SFC) and the athletes tried to shout Wilson down, but he explained that it was the duty of both the white and black students of Columbia to help their black and Puerto Rican neighbors keep control over their land and neighborhoods.[21] Then Wilson led many of the mostly white demonstrators to the gymnasium construction site.[22]

Once there, the students began to tear down the cyclone fence that surrounded the site. When the police came, violence broke out between the officers and the demonstrators. After a policeman accosted one demonstrator, the integrated crowd jumped on top of the officer and threw him to the side. When another officer came to his assistance, the crowd jumped him too.[23] Ray Brown and Bill Sales were involved in the struggle. According to Sales, as he and other students tussled with one officer, the policeman went for his firearm. At that point, Sales, who along with other members of SAS had been taking karate, twisted back the thumb of the officer to prevent him from engaging his weapon. Sales has since noted the gravity of the situation, observing: "We could have died that day."[24] One white student protester, Fred Wilson, fought with the police and was eventually arrested on the charge of felonious assault.[25]

Rudd, who had given up hopes of holding an indoor demonstration on campus, eventually met with the crowd at the gym site, but not before ruminating about his indecision. Professor Ranum remembered Rudd saying: "Oh, I made a mistake. I made a mistake. I'm not at the head of the protest movement. That's going to waste our energies. We'll be dissipated. There's no point of going to the gym. I've made a mistake. I've made a mistake."[26] Perhaps Rudd realized that the demonstration was moving on without him, so he met up with the protesters in the park.

While there, Rudd attempted to defuse the potentially riotous situation by gaining the attention of the demonstrators and asking for an administrator. When Dean Thomas Colohan spoke up, Rudd explained to him that the protesters were very serious about the issues that SDS pushed, and that this was just one of the first acts in the struggle against the university. After listening to Rudd's discussion with the administrator, another student yelled out that there was a demonstration building back at the Sundial, and Rudd hurried back to campus to meet with those protesters.[27]

While this scene has not received a great deal of attention in other historical accounts, it was definitely a turning point in the student protest. The seriousness of the confrontation between the students and police should not be overlooked. By engaging the police violently, or at least abandoning the nonviolence stance that earlier student protesters across the nation had advocated, the white and black demonstrators did indeed put a great deal on the line. The student who was arrested further galvanized the protest against the gym by sacrificing his own freedom. It was one thing to protest the construction of the gymnasium with rhetorical speeches, but it was quite another to destroy the school's property and then fight with police officers to keep the university from going forward with the gym and to advance a protest.

After talking with Ted Gold, the leader of the group of protesters that remained on campus and the former leader of the Columbia chapter of SDS, Rudd again urged the crowd to move into Low Library. By this time, Cicero Wilson and many of the other black demonstrators were becoming increasingly annoyed by the seeming indecisiveness of SDS leadership and the mostly white crowd. "SDS would make decisions then undo them and go back and forth. . . . [T]hey were just confused," claimed one SAS member.[28] In a speech, Cicero Wilson implied that his group intended to take over the demonstration: "SDS can stand on the side and support us, . . . but the black students and the Harlem community will be the ones in the vanguard."[29]

Rudd, who had just been upstaged, asked Wilson what his proposals were.[30] Wilson responded that his group had not "proposed" to do anything but to keep the university from building the gymnasium. Furthermore, he stated, the idea that proposals were necessary for the protest intimated that, again, white leaders wanted to decide themselves which path black people should take. In 1966 that very same sentiment among the white leadership of SNCC struck a militant cord among many black participants, who until that point had been willing to share the leadership of the organization. The result of that controversy culminated in the group's purging itself of white membership and calling for "Black Power." Wilson's statements about taking the vanguard and allowing the community to decide for itself what was best were very much in line with the tenets of the Black Power movement, which advocated that black people take the leadership in matters that would primarily affect them and their communities. Off campus, black protesters took lead of the movement against the gym, and so the next step was for black students on campus to do the same. At that point, it became clear to all the protesters that SAS's main concern was with the gymnasium and the university's mistreatment of the adjacent neighborhoods.

Wilson's statements took Rudd and many of the white protesters by surprise because they believed that black and white demonstrators would attack Columbia together as an integrated front. In turn, SAS members began to wonder if SDS was using them to enhance its ideological "revolution." That idea had merit. As psychologist Erik Erikson has noted in his studies on adolescent development, young people resolve their rebelliousness through participation in ideological movements concerned with politics.[31] And if that were indeed the case at Columbia, then, according to Wilson, the protest for the white radicals would be one more of idealism than of pragmatism.

In spite of the debate over the idealism of the white protest leaders, the back-and-forth decision making that was typical of the participatory democracy that the SDS leadership practiced gave some members of SAS the impression that the white protesters were not serious about capturing the attention of the university and, in turn, forcing administrators to reconsider construction of the gymnasium as well as the school's relationship with the surrounding community. Despite their growing distrust for the white demonstrators, the black student protesters did recognize the benefit of being affiliated with the larger, white group. With the louder voice that a larger number of white radicals promised, the black members of SAS had a better chance of bringing their issues concerning their community to the forefront. In this way, SAS used SDS's influence to advance its goals. To that end, Bill Sales soothed the anxiety of the crowd by reaffirming, for the time, the usefulness of the black–white coalition. He commented nevertheless on what he saw as the poor organization of the white demonstrators.[32]

As the situation cooled, Rudd took the spotlight again, but this time he had a definite plan. First, he made it clear that his group was not indecisive but rather was practicing what he referred to as participatory democracy, a system that focused on the individuality of each member of the group. Thoroughly discussed in the Port Huron Statement of 1962, participatory democracy allowed each member of a group to influence the organization's decision.[33] Rudd then suggested to the group that it should take a hostage. While the previous plans that Rudd tried to implement failed, this one attracted the support of most of the demonstrators. As the crowd wondered whom it should take as hostage, someone called for the seizure of Hamilton Hall, a classroom building and the location of most of the administrative offices of Columbia College (part of the larger university).[34]

Although Hamilton was not his first choice, Rudd liked the idea and led some of the four hundred to five hundred students into the building, providing SAS with a successful example of the participatory democracy that SDS practiced. While they chanted "Racist Gym Must Go," Acting Dean of Columbia College Henry Coleman appeared. Rudd ordered the onlookers to clear a pathway for Coleman to go into his office in Hamilton. The dean remembered: "I had to make a decision on whether or not to go in, and it seemed to me that it was my office, my secretarial staff was in there, and . . . that I should walk in."[35] By Coleman actually volunteering to enter his office, he freed the students of any charges of kidnapping. This did not, however, immediately occur to the leadership of the protest. Consequently, Rudd informed Coleman that the students (in Hamilton) were staging an illegal indoor protest; that he and the demonstrators would no longer stand for the university's slowness to restructure; and finally, that Coleman had become the group's "guest of honor."[36]

This particular act illustrated another turning point in the protest. The students believed that they had taken a dean hostage, and essentially they did. The symbolism of holding a dean, someone who represented the university that itself held the black communities of Harlem and Morningside Heights hostage, was not only satisfying but also somewhat overwhelming. In this act of disobedience, the students also held the older generation hostage as well. Because most university officials would have never expected students to have the gall to act this way toward an authority figure, the demonstrators gained control of the situation.

That mirrored exactly the approach that activists of the 1960s took to achieve civil rights: confronting the authorities in ways that the authorities would not expect. The Columbia University protesters broke the law, or so they believed, but they did it for the right reasons, and it appeared to be a victory in their struggle to change society for the better. In spite of the students' self-perception of being outlaws, by voluntarily walking into his office, Dean Coleman actually prevented the students from becoming kidnappers. That, however, was not the important issue; the important issue was that the student demonstrators believed that they had acted badly for a good cause, and that was enough for many.

Rudd then left his "guest of honor," Dean Coleman, and held a meeting in the upstairs lobby of the building. At that meeting he helped to form the

Steering Committee, consisting of the most influential student leaders on campus. This small, racially integrated group included Ray Brown, Leon Denmark, and Bill Sales of SAS; Ted Gold and Mark Rudd of SDS; and students from several other organizations. The purpose of the committee was to communicate the protesters' strategies, goals, and instructions. The committee also dealt with matters such as how to feed the protesters and keep them warm throughout the night.[37]

As the students made themselves at home in Hamilton, the integrated committee put forth a list of demands. They wanted amnesty for Mark Rudd and the rest of the SDS members known as the "IDA Six," whom the university had placed on disciplinary probation for their March 27 demonstration in Low Memorial Library; a permanent halt to the construction of the gymnasium in Morningside Park; the termination of affiliations with the Institute for Defense Analyses; the resignation of Kirk from the IDA executive committee; repeal of the ban on indoor protests; a resolution that students and faculty should decide jointly on judicial matters; and university cooperation in dropping police charges against the protesters.[38] The Steering Committee distributed pamphlets with those demands to various locations, including New York University and City College.[39]

Outside Hamilton, students concerned for the safety of Dean Coleman constantly antagonized the protesters. Two groups objected vigorously to the tactics of the Hamilton occupants: the Majority Coalition and the Students for a Free Campus. Members of the coalition considered themselves the "sane" representatives of the student population throughout the controversy. They met with administrators to discuss the actions of the protesters and to achieve some sort of resolution of the uprising. One member of the Majority Coalition commented on the protesters' demands: "My right to attend the classes I have paid for supersedes any strike demand, especially when the strike demands are so uncompromising. Changes of this scope . . . need not be made overnight."[40] "Who the hell do they [the protesters] think they are?" was the reaction of one coalition member. Another student of the Majority Coalition said bitterly, "I am angry that the school I work to pay for has been virtually destroyed for the semester."[41] Members of the SFC were even more conservative than those of the Majority Coalition. They circulated a leaflet questioning the power structure of the university. It read: "Must one group be allowed to dictate this University's future? . . . Can democracy survive at Columbia University? . . . Will Mark Rudd be our next dean?"[42]

These more conservative students illustrated the debate that took place in the United States concerning the place of the universities and the legitimacy of protest. The primary and sole responsibility of their university, in the eyes of many Majority Coalition and SFC members, was to provide the traditional liberal arts education to young people. Others believed that the actions of the protesters could be viewed as economically unsound. By disturbing the campus and making it difficult to reach certain classrooms, the protesters prevented their fellow students from receiving the services for which they or their parents had paid. In a setting other than that of a campus, actions such as that would clearly have been illegal. Another contingent of students expressed the opinion that the issues were important, but the university was the wrong venue for that type of behavior. They reasoned that, if these students were to become the leaders of the nation, then they must be able to handle problems in a much less disruptive manner. Conversely, the protesting students believed that they not only had a right to deal with what they saw as the wrongdoings of the university but also an obligation to do so before the situation got worse. They chose to confront the university by using disruptive tactics so as to draw attention to the issues they presented.

With conservative student groups bothering them from the outside, the protesters' bond also loosened from within. When President Kirk heard that SDS, SAS, and other students had seized Hamilton, he was furious. "The protest took me completely by surprise," he said later.[43] His first reaction was to call the police, but when he found out that the students held an administrator hostage, he changed his mind. "I demurred [on calling the police], being fearful for the safety of Dean Coleman."

After receiving a phone call from Dean Coleman, Vice President Truman became aware of the possible conflict between SDS and the black protesters. When Truman finally contacted Kirk, the president's anger quickly changed to anxiety. He was deeply concerned over the possibility of violence after he listened to Truman's account of the bad relations brewing within the racially intermixed group. History professor Ornest Ranum remembered meeting with Kirk at the time. Ranum said that "in my discussions with the president, I found him primarily, at this point already, concerned about the negotiations with the blacks in Hamilton Hall, with the SAS."[44] Ranum recognized the fragility of the situation: "I mean . . . the administration was functioning at this point very concisely in an effort to reach some terms with the SAS in Hamilton. This was very clear to me, that the object of their principal concern was that group."

4

On Our Own
SAS's Self-Imposed Separation

Upon entering Hamilton Hall, the student protesters changed the dynamics of the demonstration in general. Until that point, the protesters had given no real cause for worry about racial violence among themselves, but the situation soon changed. Once in the building, the students started to recognize differences—some racial and some tactical—in the way that they wanted to conduct the demonstration. This chapter covers some of those differences and the decision of SAS to break from the larger group of student protesters. It also deals with the alliance that SAS made with the community in Harlem.

Sometime after 7 P.M. on April 23, 1968, a tall black man with three bodyguards disrupted a meeting of the integrated Steering Committee. Some students knew that the committee had contacted residents of Harlem earlier to take care of food provisions, but for the most part, even those white students in the Steering Committee seemed shocked to see the Student Non-Violent Coordinating Committee leader, H. Rap Brown. "I'd like to tell you that the Harlem community is now here and we want to thank you for taking the first steps in this struggle," Rap Brown said. "The black community is taking over."[1]

Fearing the turn the protest was taking, many white demonstrators remained silent to hear what the representative of Harlem had to say. Reinforcing those fears, six large black males approached five white counterdemonstrators who stood guard outside of Dean Coleman's office. The black men then offered to let the counterdemonstrators leave without receiving physical injury. When the white students refused to budge, the black militants reneged on their offer and removed them expeditiously. Subsequently, a new group of black guards formed outside of the door of Coleman's office.[2]

By 2 A.M. SAS and the Harlem contingent had separated from SDS over whether to barricade the building. Rap Brown and SAS supported the measure, while SDS wanted a sit-in instead.[3] SAS's plan to barricade the building would have allowed the students to control who could enter and leave the building. The SDS sit-in would have allowed people to come in and out of the building freely. "At that point it was impossible for the white students to remain," SAS leader Ray Brown explained later; "if they had remained[,] it would probably have diluted the effectiveness of the protest."[4] Black graduate student Bill Sales affirmed Ray Brown's position: "Many of the white students were not prepared to dramatize the issue through a confrontation with students and faculty."[5] He recalled: "They were talking about holding the building but allowing classes to continue so that they could politicize the people that came in and out." Not agreeing with that strategy, Sales and his group voiced their opinions: "We said this is crazy. Don't you know we have committed a crime in here [or so they believed]? We are going to seize this building and make some demands and not move until they are met or until they [the police] carry us out of here." Sales recalled: "We decided we couldn't deal with their madness."[6] Frustrated with the situation, Sales and SAS told the followers of SDS that "you [the white students] got to get out of the building."[7]

This ousting was typical of Black Power in the late 1960s, and furthermore, it was indicative of what had happened on a larger scale with the student movement across the nation when it came to integrated protest. Many black protesters, both on the Morningside Heights campus and across the nation, believed that white protesters, particularly those at universities like Columbia, had too much invested in the "system" to really want to damage it. Charles Silberman, in *Crisis in Black and White*, argued similarly that "Negroes are outside the mainstream of middle-class American life, whereas their [white] liberal allies are on the inside. Hence, the latter have a deep interest in preserving the status quo."[8] He further explained that as "the struggle for Negro rights moves into the streets, the majority of [white] liberals are reluctant to move along with it. They are all for the Negroes' *objectives*, they say, but they cannot go along with the *means*."[9]

In this particular situation, those black protesters and Silberman might have been correct, as the white leadership did not want to go so far as to prevent other students from attending class. Then again, that may not have been indicative of the white demonstrators' willingness (or lack thereof) to damage the system; it just could have been that they did not see the benefit of disallowing their fellow students access to classrooms. Strategically, though, the black protesters were correct in their position because there was a great chance that if they had only staged a sit-in, the authorities would have infiltrated the building and ended the protest within a short period of time, thus lessening its effectiveness. Finally, barricading the building was a better decision because it made it possible for complete control over what happened on the inside, which became very important for planning reasons.

Discipline and organization were of utmost importance to the black protesters. To "dramatize the situation" effectively, they had to do so in a manner that showed that they were serious and focused on their goal. Part of the reason for the black student demonstrators' ability to organize was that many of them had been members of organizations before joining SAS.[10] For instance, Bill Sales had been a member of the Black Student Congress and a secret group called the Cadre. The latter group's role was to involve itself in community affairs and to have its members join local organizations. SAS had formed the Cadre out of the desire to strengthen the ties between black student and community activists. Sales and another SAS member were assigned to the Harlem chapter of the Congress of Racial Equality. Some of the black women protesters, who attended Barnard College (Columbia's sister school), had also organized into groups. Many of those who had protested at Columbia later became members of the Barnard Organization of Soul Sisters (BOSS).

Regarding the demonstration, inside and outside Hamilton, the part that black women protesters played was integral. At least twenty black women from Barnard entered Hamilton Hall.[11] One of their functions was to gain as much information as possible about the neighboring community's relationship with the university. In that way some of the black women acted as liaisons between the community and students demonstrating in the building. The Barnard black women also volunteered to contact the parents of the Hamilton demonstrators. In addition to their other duties, many of the women in Hamilton helped to make policy decisions while also assisting with food preparation and staffing the ad hoc infirmary. Indeed, the black women demonstrators inside and outside Hamilton Hall played multiple roles.[12]

Bill Sales credited some of the organization of the group to the fact that many of the protesters were members of historically black Greek-lettered fraternity Omega Psi Phi, which placed a high value on discipline and organization.[13] As a new chapter of the fraternity had been formed at Columbia in the months before the demonstration, the new members volunteered to participate by protesting the gym.

Several white students agreed with SAS's decision to separate. One remarked: "The real thing about the black/white split was that the two groups realized they had different political agendas. . . . The blacks wanted to stop the gym; . . . the whites' goal was to radicalize other white students."[14] By taking Hamilton, "we were moving too fast" without prior planning or preparation, confessed one white student. Understanding the position of the black demonstrators, another white radical said: "When the blacks saw we were split amongst ourselves, that we weren't disciplined, . . . they asked us to leave."[15]

Fundamental to the separation was the idea that SAS and SDS maintained different agendas, and tension arose because of it. Political scientist Charles Hamilton, who wrote on the Black Power movement, explained: "Black-student protest differs considerably from that of the more affluent white radicals in that the politics of the former is much more *instrumental,* directed toward realistic, achievable goals, whereas that of the latter is inclined to be *expressive,* more oriented toward showing up the 'immorality' of the larger society than to securing an attainable goal," such as the end of gym construction in Morningside Park.[16]

Many in SAS believed that the white demonstrators of SDS did not really care about the very real issue of the construction of the gymnasium against the will of the black community a few blocks over in Morningside Park, but rather they cared to be part of a rebellion. To be sure, the leadership of SAS certainly did not ask the large number of white demonstrators to cease their protest efforts. Indeed, as Judge Loren Miller explained it in *Nation* magazine, "rejection of [white] liberal leadership does not mean that Negroes do not want, and expect, continued liberal aid[,] but they want it on their own terms."[17] In the late 1960s that proved true in the situation at Columbia and other Ivy League universities.

Although the black militants at Columbia disliked the white radicals' adherence to the political strategy of participatory democracy, it was not the only reason the SAS leadership asked the SDS followers to leave. "We felt that we had to have a distinctive identity," Bill Sales later admitted.[18] "We were in there—black folks—taking up for the community, and we had to make that clear. . . . There was no real rift between SAS and SDS." Upon evicting the white protesters, the black students suggested that, if the white demonstrators wanted to help the black community and fight the construction of the gym, they should take other buildings. To the black militants, it was important that they alone occupy Hamilton. By doing so, claimed Sales, they could "focus the protest on the community-wide issues, . . . to forge an identification between what the black students were doing in Hamilton Hall and what the community was doing in Harlem in relation to Columbia University's racism."[19]

SAS's decision to separate itself from the white demonstrators marked another turning point in the protest, one that would have lasting effects. The black activists' request that the white agitators leave so that they could have an identity of their own also indicated the influence of Black Power on U.S. campuses. Black Power advocates maintained that if black people were to advance as a race, then they would have to create and maintain an identity separate from that which white America had given them. Part of the psychological problems that black people maintained resulted from the lack of identity.[20] The mentality that Black Power advocates wanted their people to achieve was that of ownership. They were wise enough to have known, however, that until black people owned their identities, they could never really own anything else, including Morningside Park.

The black university protesters not only created an identity distinct from that of the white demonstrators, but they became a group that required special attention. Occupying the building jointly, the intermixed group would have obscured the purpose of the black students' protest, which was to stop the construction of the gym by drawing attention to the university's town–gown relationship with the neighboring black community. A racially divided protest, however, forced the university to address the issue of race in isolation of other protest issues. That fact made the occupation of Hamilton an extremely crucial part of the demonstration.

In taking control of Hamilton, the black demonstrators obtained a victory over the university that, in their opinion, had taken power and land from the neighborhood for so long. The "Reverend Sam," a resident from Harlem, smiled as he reminisced about the incident. He recalled that, to the blacks in Harlem, when the SAS-led protesters took over Hamilton Hall, it was like "the invasion of the ivory tower."[21] The writer Roger Kahn said: "The men from Harlem were people who had been raised in rats' alleys, offered no hope, or, worse, false hope as they grew. Above them Columbia, the elite fortress, towered on the hill," and they would hold on to any small victory against such an elite power.[22] While not all of the local black residents had grown up as Kahn suggested, he offered an understandable reason why many SAS members favored barricading the entrances to the hall. By ousting the white radical protesters and everyone else, SAS risked losing the support of the larger white group. But the black student demonstrators did not care if they alienated the majority of protesters; they did not work to please the masses of white students—a role that SDS claimed. SAS, its members claimed, wanted to serve the interest of the neighboring black community.

The members of SAS in many ways were closer to the community of Harlem with regard to race and class than were the white students of SDS. The white student protesters of SDS of course were of the same race as some members of the Morningside Heights and Harlem communities, but concerning class status, they were typically quite different from the mostly black and Puerto Rican working-class people of the neighboring communities. Most of the black students were also of working-class background, and most were first-generation college students. After surveying many of the students who participated in the protest, psychiatry lecturer Robert Liebert found that 55 percent of the black demonstrators who occupied Hamilton were of working-class backgrounds, while 18 percent were middle class, and 27 percent were in the upper middle class.[23] Much of the leadership that advocated Black Nationalism and Black Power came from the working class and had enrolled after 1966.[24] Being first-generation college students and of working-class backgrounds placed many of the black students structurally closer to their community.

These numbers, however, were quite different from those of the white students who had invaded the hall. Among these white students, only 6 percent came from working-class backgrounds, 15 percent were from the middle class, and a striking 79 percent were from upper-middle-class backgrounds. This, in fact, differentiated them from a majority of the larger white community at the time, not least of all the community that surrounded the university.

From the perspective of many of the young black activists in the building, their education and their future were at stake. One black student made it clear: "If you were suspended[,] you were instantly faced with the [Vietnam War] draft. With the kind of education you had and having no [vocational or industrial] skills, if another college didn't accept you, where would you be?" A possible answer to that question was "without an education," but another student believed differently. He proclaimed: "I feel education goes on anywhere, anytime. You don't need classrooms." Indeed, by choosing to occupy Hamilton, the black students were gaining not only an education, but also pride. Another student commented: "The possible consequences affected our life more than any whites. Most of us have no money for another school. . . . [A]lso there was the possibility we would get killed by the cops or very messed up." Because the black students realized what they risked by protesting against a white institution like Columbia, Robert Liebert correctly noted that their "vulnerability . . . to administrative discipline was a source of considerable resentment amongst blacks against white radicals."

Considering the racial and class differences between the black and white protesters, it was understandable why many black students were antagonistic toward the white students who attempted to occupy Hamilton with them. While many of those white students were radical in their political beliefs, their class, educational background, and race set them apart from the black students from the outset. Most of the black protesters in Hamilton had attended "urban or small-town public schools," while most white occupants had attended "private or public schools."[25] For many of the black demonstrators inside the building, the gymnasium issue was not an abstract struggle, as some black militants had concluded about the efforts of the white radicals, but rather an actual fight against a tangible, oppressive white America that had for years taken advantage of black people. Indeed, the oppression that America imposed on African Americans had also benefited some, if not most, of the radical white students.

From the perspective of the black members of SAS, white protesters could afford (literally and figuratively) to idealize a perfectly democratic society while not suffering too much in the existent one. As one of the black protesters noted, "It's expensive to be a revolutionary. The [white students can afford the] luxury of ideas. . . . I don't have that luxury."[26] Another student agreed, commenting on the position of many of the radical whites in this society. "A white student can say all he wants against the system, [but he can also] shave his beard and join the system. Black students can't" simply because of the difference in race. With regard to the demonstration, one student recalled that "we weren't just proving it [that they could fight institutional racism] to ourselves; we had an obligation to the community to do something about it."[27]

To view the efforts of the white radicals as abstract is somewhat unfair and skewed. Undoubtedly, the followers of SDS believed sincerely in their cause, and in fact they did have something to lose. They risked discontinuing the university education that they had begun. They, like the black students, risked losing their student status and becoming eligible for the draft if the university chose to expel them for their demonstrations. Furthermore, they risked losing the respect of the people in their communities as well.

While the white radicals might have railed against the oppression that allows a university to build a gymnasium in a park when the community that used the park most did not want it to, they grew up with the benefits of race, education, and class status because of that oppression. It was indeed remarkable that they would rebel against the values that their white, class-privileged parents had instilled in them, and that should be taken seriously. The fact that they had these advantages, however, distinguished them from traditional "revolutionaries" (a term many used to refer to themselves).

Many white people who were less class-privileged than those who protested on campus saw the hope that the nation had to offer them socially and economically, and they did not condone the actions of the radical students. As Kenneth Keniston, author of *The Young Radicals*, explained, working-class and lower-class white youth had the opportunity to experience the "success of success"; that was if they made it to a point where they could rise in economic status to own a house and possibly send their children to universities.[28] That, for them, represented the manifestation of the "American Dream." Conversely, the white protesters at Columbia were experiencing the "failure of success," which occurs often with privileged youth, claimed Keniston. By failure of success he meant that, although the class-privileged white protesters had all of the benefits that society could offer, that was still not satisfactory enough for them. To these types of youths, rebellion was the manifestation of that dissatisfaction.

For the black protesters, Morningside Park was just one more piece of Harlem the large Ivy League school was attempting to take from the people in the community, and that was their main issue. Like the white students, they wanted to ban the Institute for Defense Analyses and sever ties with the Defense Department during the war. They also wanted to create a more democratic society, as the followers of SDS had proposed. But at that moment the university's construction of a gymnasium in the park provided them with a tangible symbol of white America's exploitation of black powerlessness in matters of ownership and community control.

As Hamilton Hall was now the housing structure of a group that represented the interests of the community, the black demonstrators created their own list of demands, one more relevant to their own agenda. The black students' list was substantially different from the one that the integrated Steering Committee had drawn up previously.[29] The first difference was that SAS placed top priority on the halt of gym construction rather than amnesty for the "IDA Six." It demanded that the school terminate the proposed gym and "wipe the slate clean." The second difference was that it demanded that Columbia drop charges against all those arrested in previous demonstrations at the gym site, not those that involved issues such as student power or protests against the war in Vietnam. By making that demand they focused the attention of the administrators back to the issue affecting the community the most with regard to the university: the gym. Third, they demanded that the faculty and administration sever their relations with the IDA. The final demand was that the students (including the white students) involved in the present demonstration receive amnesty. Ray Brown claimed that their position on the last demand was "a moral one."[30] For many of the white students who left, amnesty was first on their list of priorities during the protest. In keeping amnesty as a demand on SAS's list, explained Professor Immanuel Wallerstein, the black students avoided "selling out" the white protesters.[31]

As the students indicated, they were preparing themselves for any and all possible consequences of their occupation of Hamilton, including a "violent bust." Bill Sales remembered that it was very important for SAS leadership to anticipate the reaction of the police to their act of civil disobedience. For that reason, the leadership conducted regular sessions that dealt with what to do in case the police used tear gas, or used dogs, or fired rubber bullets.[32] Drawing on previous experiences, the protesters in Hamilton were quite aware of what the police were capable of doing. One told Robert Liebert that "most black students are in terror of the police. They know what they can do. For the whites . . . the policeman . . . is 'your friend.' . . . The blacks had no illusions."[33] Black people, claimed another student, dealt with the police frequently and therefore knew what to expect. "They build a feeling of being more intelligent than the cop," he explained.[34]

Many different reactions to the occupation of Hamilton Hall appeared in the media. Headlines read: "Students Arrested in Park Due to Violent Protest," and "Challenge to Administration Strongest in School's History."[35] Pictures showing SDS leader Mark Rudd speaking to the protesters appeared in the *New York Times,* which also reported that Harlem groups CORE, SNCC, the Harlem Committee for Self-Defense, and the United Black Front had joined the protest and later had taken over Hamilton, dismissing the white protesters in the process.[36] In Harlem, members of SNCC passed out leaflets and called for "everyone in the community who understands the struggle to support the Black students at Columbia."[37]

On campus, some observers feared for the safety of Dean Coleman, who remained a hostage in Hamilton Hall; others, not affiliated with any organization, were upset at the protesters' disruption. When asked later how he felt about the taking of Hamilton Hall, white graduate student Thomas Kennedy responded: "I was pissed off. I thought 'there are people around here trying to get an education, and I am one of them.'"[38] Another white graduate student, Eric Foner, saw the occupation of Hamilton and the arrival of activists H. Rap Brown and Stokely Carmichael in a different way. "I think everybody felt this was pretty cool. . . . Here's some famous people, well-known in the media. . . . [T]hey were notorious, and they were on our campus."[39]

Wm. Theodore de Bary, a professor in East Asian languages and cultures, was upset about the disturbance of classes: "I felt that they [the protesters] were interfering with the educational process; they were denying me my rights as a teacher, and they were denying my students their rights."[40] Indeed, by barricading the building so the public had no access to it, the black students suspended the operation of classes in Hamilton. Kennedy recalled later that, while the taking of Hamilton Hall had caused a problem, it was not the main building on campus, so people could carry on with most of their daily tasks.

While Kennedy, Foner, and de Bary represented some of the different reactions of white observers regarding the occupation of Hamilton Hall, there were several black students outside the building who also had varying reactions. Some resented the extremely regimented style of the leadership in Hamilton Hall. "The first night was like reading the totalitarianism of Hitler," claimed one black student as he referred to the very hierarchical and tight leadership of SAS. Others stayed out to prove their own independence. "I was testing my ability to reason for myself," admitted one student, while another argued that staying out of the building "solidified my feelings about my individuality; . . . I can't go for black tyranny." Expressing a similar view, one said: "Instead of the white man tyrannizing and brainwashing you, the black man will do it." "It took more courage to stay out than to go in," explained another black student who did not enter Hamilton.[41]

Feeling some hostility toward their fellow black students who did not enter the building, the occupiers of Hamilton put great pressure on them to enter. One protesting black student commented on nonactivist black students: "They were more concerned with their own getting ahead than with those who are left behind." Another occupant viewed the nonactivist black students as part of the problem rather than as individuals exercising their right of free will. The student said: "Either you are with us [the occupants] or against us," leaving no room for the in-between. Another source of pressure for the black males who did not choose to occupy Hamilton were the black Barnard students. Expressing the sentiment of many generations of black women, a Barnard protester proclaimed: "It's a man's role to stand with a group and fight for a cause."[42]

Like the larger Black Power movement, the movement of the SAS protesters on campus involved the theme of manhood. For black men, it was important to be able to protect their own community. Many of the male students who remained inside the building believed that they were doing what a racially oppressive United States had prevented African American men from doing since the advent of slavery: protecting the interests of their race.

While some observers disagreed with tactics and others worried about the disruption that the demonstration caused, at least one faculty member worried about the rumor that some of the black protesters were carrying firearms. James Shenton, a history professor, remembered his anxiety: "I was being told that there were guns in the building and militants in the building. And I might add that I have been told at one point by some students from SAS that, if necessary, they were not adverse to burning the building down to get certain of their demands met."[43] The prospect of such violence was indeed unsettling, but coupled with the fact that a dean was still in the building it gave further cause to fret. "I wasn't sure how seriously I should take what was being said. I really wasn't at all certain, for example, if Coleman was in fact in physical danger. In retrospect, I think that I should have had better sense, knowing, as I do, a number of the SAS students, that they wouldn't resort to that kind of violence." Still, considering the times and the situation, Shenton was not so certain.

The presence of firearms in Hamilton has been up for historical debate. While most historical sources maintain that the black students and community members were not in possession of weapons, forty years later several student demonstrators who were in Hamilton before the separation contradicted that notion. One demonstrator, Juan Gonzalez, revealed that, upon entering a bathroom in Hamilton, he saw a row of shotguns against the wall. An SDS supporter also remembered seeing a duffle bag being thrown out of Hamilton that contained "grey metal objects."[44]

Nearby, at Low Memorial Library, the members of SDS and their followers waged their own separate attack on the university. The serious attitudes of the black students and their decision to hold Hamilton by themselves contributed to the radicalization of many of the SDS followers. As one white student remembered the occupation of Low Library, "It took the example of the blacks to move us."[45] Low, unlike Hamilton Hall, was a building that, if taken, could stop traffic entirely on campus, a situation that SDS subsequently demonstrated. At 7 A.M. on April 24, Rudd, other SDS members, and a number of white protesters took the advice of the black students and moved there and to three other buildings on campus. At Low, the white students, following Rudd, broke down a door in the southeastern section of building.[46] Rudd and the other leaders soon realized, however, that Low was too large for them to occupy effectively, so they focused on a most strategic spot: President Kirk's offices.[47] By taking the president's offices, the protesters believed they would receive the attention of all officials at the university; but most of all, SDS believed that such an action would draw Kirk's attention.

While in Kirk's offices, the protesters embarked on an adventure of discovery. SDS members seized some of the president's confidential papers. Although one white radical claimed that he found documentation proving that the administration intended to suppress SDS, and "a lot of letters about cleaning up the area by moving out the blacks and the Puerto Ricans," most of Kirk's papers were personal memos that dealt with general school matters.[48] As recreated in some media sources, the students ransacked the president's offices. According to Kirk, they smoked his cigars, drank his sherry, urinated on the floors, ripped the rugs, and almost destroyed the Rembrandt portrait hanging on the wall.[49]

In spite of the damage they were causing, many of the white protesters in the building believed that the occupation of Low was a positive experience. Writer Roger Kahn noted that the white radicals "enjoyed the camaraderie of taking buildings . . . and implementing Participatory Democracy."[50] While occupying Kirk's offices, a student named Vicki wrote a letter to a Mr. and Mrs. SLS: "[W]e are all acting amazingly well as a group. . . . It is particularly inspiring to realize how maturely a group of such young people can act."[51] Vicki failed to inform the couple about the demonstrators who urinated on the president's carpet, although she may not have known about such conduct. Another SDS follower related that "there was a total collective feeling. . . . No one really cared about their individual feelings. . . . [I]t was sort of an electric awakening."[52] The feeling in Low was certainly a much lighter atmosphere than that at Hamilton.

President Kirk, whom Bill Sales remembered as "the kind of president who was invisible to students," worked tirelessly to resolve the situations in Low and Hamilton. The president had an unexpected reaction to the occupation of his offices.[53] He worried less about his offices in Low than he did about the protesters in Hamilton. Fearing for the elite, white university's image in race relations (especially after King's death and the resulting Harlem riots), solving the Hamilton problem became the main issue for Kirk and the rest of the university officials. When asked how the relocation of the white students to Low and the black demonstrators' occupation of Hamilton affected his opinion of the protest, he replied: "The fact that a group of black students were in sole occupancy of one of our buildings did complicate the matter."[54] By this, it was possible that the president meant that the concept of a race riot like the one that had occurred in Harlem just weeks before was frightening to him and the rest of the school officials. The president, as well as the black militants of SAS, understood that when both the white and the black protesters were occupying the building, it was an issue of student protest. When SAS asked the white students to leave, however, the issue was no longer simply a student protest, but rather one of a *black* student and community protest.

Fear provided the motivation behind the university officials' actions to quell the disturbance in Hamilton without immediately calling the police. As one white student observed, "It certainly was the fear of blacks holding one building, and what would happen if that building were busted, that enabled the strike to go on as long as it did."[55] The president worried seriously about the potential arrival of a massive group of black protesters from outside Columbia's campus. He believed that "it was quite clear that the people of City Hall would not be happy about responding very positively [to a request for the police] . . . until they made an assessment of the attitudes in Harlem. . . . They were still feeling the effects of the very serious riots in Harlem upon the assassination of Martin Luther King Jr."[56] Philosophy professor Arthur Danto put it well: "Everyone believed Harlem would rise to devastate the campus."[57]

Most of the black students in Hamilton recognized their collective position of power. One maintained that university officials "weren't that worried about a handful of black students at Columbia, but when Harlem protesters arrived, the mood certainly changed."[58] Playing on the university's fear, some black protesters noted that "as a house goes up, it must come down," referring to the possible destruction of Hamilton or the gym. According to another black student-militant, gaining the assistance of Harlem residents would not be difficult. In fact, in the first few hours of their sole occupation of the building, emissaries from Hamilton Hall had raised $125 in local bars in Harlem.[59]

Similarly, most of the food they were eating had come from the homes of Harlem residents who presumably supported their efforts. The student went on to assert that people in Harlem would say: "Look at these brothers up here, who got it made, [they] are revolting against the system too." While standing outside Hamilton Hall on the rainy second night of the students' occupation, one mother from Harlem explained that "rain or no rain, I don't care. We must support these young people. They went out on a limb for us. . . . I for one am coming back and bringing them hot, nourishing food."[60] As Harlemites further conveyed their encouragement and support, school officials recognized the threat of outside interference from residents who shared the race and goals of the students. Administrators worried that it would not be long before the entrance of local black militant organizations or, worse, the destruction of school property.

Kirk could wait no longer to take action on the "black issue." On April 25, 1968, the school's newspaper reported that the "administration wanted to seal off the campus . . . after receiving reports that militant black organizations in Central Harlem were planning to stage a mass protest at Columbia."[61] The night before, fifty policemen secured almost all of the gates of the university. The black protesters' main objective was still to halt construction of the gym, and until the university could satisfy that objective, the Harlem protesters vowed to support the black students in Hamilton. The Fact-Finding Commission later concluded that the seriousness of SAS and community members' demands showed in "their own discipline . . . and their personal conduct . . . [which] was almost military [and] strictly regulated."[62]

Unlike those in Low and the other buildings, the students and community members in Hamilton did not break or seize anything for fear that the university and police would blame any damage or negative incidents on the black students, drawing attention away from their goal to stop the gymnasium's construction. This approach had roots in the strategies of the early Civil Rights movement. Leaders such as Roy Wilkins, Walter White, Fred Shuttlesworth, and Martin Luther King Jr. often emphasized the importance of appearing physically disciplined, clean, and focused. Younger leaders of SNCC and CORE emphasized this as well, when they conducted the "Freedom Rides" from the North to the South to integrate the interstate busing system. These lessons were not lost on the leadership of SAS.

Several observers commented favorably on the way the black protesters conducted themselves in Hamilton. Immanuel Wallerstein, who had contact with the black demonstrators in Hamilton throughout the controversy, said that he was "extremely impressed with their seriousness."[63] President Kirk concurred with Wallerstein in that "the blacks handled themselves very well in Hamilton."[64] Vice President Truman later said that "my respect for them is quite high, and . . . the other group [the whites in Low and the other three buildings], I have no respect for." In an interview with Peter Jansen of *Newsweek* magazine, Truman added, "Those black students are a totally different cut. . . . I admire the way they conducted themselves."[65]

In spite of their admiration, Truman and President Kirk must have been quite unsettled when black militants from Harlem arrived on campus in support of the Hamilton protest. Led by the United Black Front and the Harlem Mau Mau society, black community activists protested outside of the 116th Street entrance to Columbia's campus.[66] Despite efforts to seal the campus off, the police officers securing the gates to the school could not prevent the group of anti-gym protesters from marching through campus.

According to the *Amsterdam News*, "The black students, who launched their protest from Hamilton Hall, were models of decorum, courtesy, cleanliness, and purpose."[67] Roy Wilkins, executive director of the NAACP, claimed that "Columbia's black students showed maturity. They did not choose to impair their position by conduct related, no doubt, to their emotions, but unrelated to their main purpose" of ending gym construction.[68] Senator Basil Paterson, whom SAS allowed into Hamilton, agreed. About the environment inside the building, he said: "Well, it's quite orderly. A number of the students are studying. As I passed, there was almost a class going on in one section of the hall. They're serving food—they were serving food—as a matter of fact, I had lunch with them. And everything is quite orderly and some of them are still cleaning up—they have inadequate facilities for cleaning but they're doing it."[69] The members of SAS maintained a sense of discipline in their efforts.

While in Hamilton, students took up a number of duties. For instance, one black student, James "Plunky" Branch, worked the switchboard at Hamilton. Other students, like Columbia football player Alford Dempsey, took pride in leading the effort to clean the building. Some students kept watch at the door, while others provided the entertainment in the band Soul Syndicate. Each demonstrator seemed to have a role to play for the sake of the movement to stop the gym.

With the movement in mind, the black protesters released Dean Coleman from custody. The manner in which Coleman left should be noted. In not wanting to distract the situation further with kidnapping, SAS's leadership had to choose carefully the way that they approached Coleman and his staff. Rather than telling Coleman that they were releasing him, SAS leadership asked the dean if he and his staff were hungry and "wouldn't they like to go eat lunch."[70] In doing so, the black student demonstrators left no verbal indication that they had been forcing Coleman to stay.

Coleman's exit in no way weakened SAS's position. In fact, on the afternoon of April 26, Black Power activists Stokely Carmichael and H. Rap Brown of SNCC, along with the leader of the Harlem Mau Maus, Charles 37X Kenyatta, appeared at the edge of campus.[71] Local high school students—mostly black—toted signs that read "Support the Black Revolution."[72] The police, whom the university had requested to seal off the campus, formed a tight line to prevent the Black Power leaders from entering. When the authorities did this, the one hundred or so black high school students who had gathered at the scene to support the Columbia black activists pressed against the police. As the police prepared for a struggle, Brown stuck his hand out to shake a high school student's hand. When their hands met, the student quickly pulled Brown through the police line. To the shock of the police and reporters who were present, Rap Brown and Carmichael then marched victoriously through campus into Hamilton.[73]

This scene almost seemed to foreshadow the fact that neither the police nor the university nor anyone else could keep the community from making its presence felt on the matter of the gymnasium. After a meeting, Rap Brown predicted: "If the university doesn't deal with our brothers in there, they're going to have to deal with the brothers out on the streets."[74] He further revealed that he and Carmichael were going back to Harlem "to muster support."[75] In fact, he noted: "Black people are preparing in Harlem to come and deal with Columbia at some point." The *Amsterdam News* confirmed Rap Brown's prediction with the headline, "Harlem Backed Columbia Students."[76]

H. Rap Brown's and Stokely Carmichael's role during the protest was interesting, if not ironic. Since 1966 the two activists had received a great deal of notoriety in the media for their stands against racial discrimination. Internationally known, the two headed the Student Non-Violent Coordinating Committee, one of the first national organizations that black students both created and operated. Besides being leaders of this group, they were leaders of the Black Power movement. Although SNCC was once an integrated organization of students, after the entrance of Black Power in 1966 many of the more militant black members ousted the white participants from the group. Those militants believed that cooperation was no longer the key to beating racism. At the forefront of this decision were Rap Brown and Carmichael. Eventually, Carmichael left SNCC and joined the Black Panther party. Hearing about the protest through community sources, Carmichael and Rap Brown went to Hamilton Hall to aid the black students.

Contrary to what one might have expected from observing previous demonstrations across the nation, the two activists did not come to Columbia University to take over the protest, but rather to assist the black students of the university. As Bill Sales recalled, the members of SAS "had to maintain control of what was going on, . . . so we decided to tell Stokely and Rap what we wanted them to do."[77] Carmichael and Rap Brown, wanting to do whatever it took to advance in the struggle for Black Power, did indeed lend their services to the group. Sales said that SAS told the SNCC leaders that the Columbia black protesters were up against a "press blackout" and that their message was not reaching the public. Using their fame for the benefit of SAS's demonstration, Rap Brown and Carmichael read the protesters' demands and delivered their messages.[78]

Later, on the night of April 26, various other groups and representatives from the community marched onto and around campus to support the black student group's issues. One member of the United Black Front of Harlem stated that "Kirk is the biggest slumlord in Harlem," indicating some of the resentment that community members had because of the school's earlier landownership policies.[79] With that in mind, many of the community members did not see too many positive aspects of the university's gymnasium venture. Blyden Jackson, from the Peace and Freedom party, suggested that the crowd that had gathered on campus for a rally against the gym go to the site "with buckets and shovels and fill that damned hole [where builders had begun to dig] up." To some of the people at the rally, the university's policy regarding the proposed gymnasium was not their only concern. One member of the United Black Front alleged that the "Institute for Defense Analyses [to which the university had connections] provides 'the government with the same kind of information about the ghettoes that it does about Asia.'"[80]

The United Black Front member's statement about the university's provision of information on Harlem's ghetto to the IDA could not be substantiated; however, it showed that the people in the neighboring areas had been observing not only Columbia University's role in the city but also its role in national matters. That night, more than any other, presented a time for the black residents of Morningside Heights and Harlem to air their grievances against the university in such a way that the school had to listen. By the black students independently holding a building on campus and black protesters coming from the community onto campus to support them, black people were placing a great amount of pressure on Columbia to back away from the gym project. Furthermore, the situation gave the community a clearer voice in matters of white institutional and black community relations.

Recognizing the threat that the Black Power advocates' collective influence posed to the university, the faculty engaged in intense negotiations with the students at Hamilton. About the current situation, sociology professor Immanuel Wallerstein, who wrote *Africa: Politics of Unity*, eerily predicted: "Either there will be an irrevocable split of this University into two polarized camps from which it will not revive in the next 25 years, or the burning of this University."[81] Richard Fogelson, a professor of history, exclaimed: "It is time now for professors to interpose their bodies between contending forces. . . . Further[,] we have to be willing to strike."[82] Although the idea scared the newly formed Ad Hoc Faculty Group (AHFG), the members of the group knew that they had an obligation to do something. In an effort to protect its students and state its position on the gym, the AHFG petitioned and pulled at the conscience of the president until he acquiesced. The group put forth a four-part resolution that asked for a halt to the gym construction, a tripartite committee to decide the disciplinary actions against the students, the immediate evacuation of all buildings, and a proclamation by the faculty to stand in front of the buildings to prevent the entry of outsiders, including police.[83] The students, especially the members of SDS, quickly rejected the offer, but the faculty's efforts were not fruitless.

"Gym Construction Is Halted," reported the school newspaper on April 26, 1968.[84] The headline should have read: "Construction Suspended" because only the trustees could make such a decision. Still, the faculty had made tremendous progress in negotiations. The faculty's contribution was of particular interest to the protesters in Hamilton. Professor Wallerstein acted as a liaison between the protesters in Hamilton and the administration. He was one of the only faculty members allowed in the building once the students barricaded the entrances. His contributions to the negotiations were invaluable to the evacuation of Hamilton Hall. Since the gym was the black protesters' main concern, negotiations were feasible as long as the trustees assured them that they would halt construction permanently.

The next day, notable black leaders weighed in on the controversy. About the gym, William Booth told a reporter: "This is not Mississippi, where you have separate facilities for white and black. And what we found has been a separate facility being planned." Booth had been in discussion with the occupants of Hamilton. A renowned and controversial black leader also lent his support to the demonstrators. Bayard Rustin, a pacifist, claimed not to condone the tactics of the demonstrators but believed in their cause. He shared his thoughts on the controversy and gym project: "Well, I believe that Columbia University, which has been very negative to the Negro community, did not consult the Negro community about the gym."[85] Rustin explained that consultation and cooperation were at the root of the racial conflict both on and off campus. He said: "Deep under the problem of housing, schools and jobs is the problem of recognition of Negroes as people, wanting to be consulted, and the desire to be part of decision-making is equal to the desire for housing, schools and jobs."[86]

Politicians communicated about the controversy as well. In a letter to Mayor John Lindsay, local politicians such as Manhattan Borough President Percy Sutton and State Assemblyman Charles Rangel wrote: "Don't let the trustees and administration of Columbia force you into pushing the panic button. Ordering the police to eject physically the students can only cause violence on the campus and clearly increase tensions in the surrounding community."[87] The letter asked that Lindsay "not put the New York Police in the position of being forced to provoke violence, . . . that you use your good offices . . . to resolve this matter peaceably and that you urge that construction for the gym be transferred to a site other than Morningside Park."

In addition to the black leaders and politicians, more demonstrators from Harlem arrived at the gate of campus. The Central Harlem Freedom Marchers shouted: "Harlem, support black students!" and conducted a short rally.[88] In regard to the black student demonstrators and the university, one of the leaders of the Freedom Marchers, Mary Todd, loudly exclaimed: "We want to go in. We want to talk to them. Every time we try to do something, they stop us. They stop us here and they stop us there. We got to keep on fighting. We got to keep on moving. We're going to keep on doing the best we can do to overthrow this corrupt system. We want to go in. We just got to let you know that we support you. We'll support you today, we'll support you tomorrow, we'll support you in two weeks, and if Columbia expels you we'll expel them."[89] Harlem, in alliance with the student demonstrators, made the university listen.

5

Supporting the Cause

SDS, Protest, and the "Bust"

For the students in Low and the other three buildings the SDS followers subsequently took, the situation was different from that for the students who remained in Hamilton. After leaving Hamilton Hall and Low Memorial Library, approximately sixty students decided to take over Avery Hall, which housed the School of Architecture, on April 24. The next day, about fifty protesting radicals, under the leadership of an economics instructor, occupied Fayerweather Hall. Then, on April 26, a group from Low and Fayerweather combined to take Mathematics Hall, where Tom Hayden, an early organizer of SDS, became leader. This chapter will explore the role of SDS in the larger demonstration and its support of the protest against the gym.

For the SDS-led student protesters and supporters, the main issue remained amnesty. Those students refused to negotiate with the faculty, administration, trustees, and city officials, and they boasted that they would not leave until the school accepted all six of their original Steering Committee proposals, making their stance that much more militant than that for which the black student protesters had originally given them credit. Since the faculty and administration could not yet fully fulfill the demands of SDS or SAS, they continued trying to effect a peaceful resolution to the crisis.

The mayor of New York tried to lighten the situation with an attempt at humor. In an April 30 interview with WNBC-TV, Mayor Lindsay said: "Relax. Everything is going to be okay at Columbia. Columbia has not yet used its ultimate weapon. It can always deny cafeterial privileges." When asked why there was unrest among the young people of America, he responded: "Because they got itchy pants."[1] But no amount of humor could ease the tension of the scene.

Finally, on April 30, the university moved to end the protest. President Kirk cut off the water and phone lines in each of the occupied buildings. Realizing that their removal was near, the black protesters in Hamilton and the white demonstrators in the other buildings prepared themselves.[2] Throughout the week, SAS had conducted drills on how to survive tear gas and rubber pellets, but it decided against resisting arrest. In contrast, the SDS leaders pledged that they would not leave without a fight.

The student demonstrators found allies in the faculty. According to a campus minister, the Reverend William Starr, when Vice President Truman announced to a faculty meeting that President Kirk had called the police and that authorities would be arriving soon, the crowd of faculty members erupted in cries of "Shame!" and "No!"[3] Faculty members, worried about the safety of their students, steadied their cordons between the buildings and outsiders.

At 2:30 A.M. a thousand New York City police entered the Morningside Heights campus. After separating into different formations, the police, along with university representatives, approached each of the five occupied buildings.[4] The police issued a warning to the faculty that, by obstructing the police, they were breaking the law. In spite of the admonition, the faculty members held their line and refused to move. This was a tremendous stand on behalf of the welfare of their students. It would have seemed that the faculty would have been an unlikely body to support the students, but in this instance, many of the faculty—particularly junior faculty—empathized with the students' grievances against the narrow, authoritative style in which the university was run. Without hesitation, however, the police broke the faculty cordon and entered each of the buildings.[5]

At Hamilton, the black demonstrators would not accede to the officers' order to come outside. Instead, they waited for the police to get them out. At that point, however, consistent with their agreement not to resist arrest, they left peacefully. That was not before, however, demonstrators rebuffed a police attempt to accost the students from the tunnels below Hamilton with water from a fire hose. Police and other city officials had been in contact with the protesters throughout the week. In fact, two of the highest-ranking black police officers, including Assistant Chief Inspector Eldridge Waithe, were present at Hamilton to ensure that a successful and peaceful mass arrest was made.[6]

Before the arrest, the leadership of SAS requested that some of the Hamilton demonstrators leave the building. Because the leadership realized the possibility that community members would not receive the same treatment within the legal system as the students, they asked their supporters to leave.

Then, SAS leadership urged the black Barnard women to leave before the arrest.[7] The women refused to leave.

Various contingents within the university had requested that the black demonstrators be treated with care. In a report, campus minister William Starr recalled that "the black students had enjoyed 'kid-glove' treatment from the administration . . . while the white students were ignored or denounced by the administration and their spokesmen." Starr illustrated his point by presenting a speech that faculty member Lionel Trilling had made before the arrests. "The black students are newcomers into our society. There has never been a time in which there were numbers of black students in this university. Our actions toward them should be characteristic of behavior to a guest for the first time who is going to become a full-fledged member of the community," Trilling stated. According to Starr's report, Trilling commented further on the matter: "I believe that the white students are undertaking to be political in a very different way [from the black students]. . . . They want power, not for legitimate ends, but to confuse, to open up this situation and see what can be done."[8] Not all faculty members agreed with Trilling, but enough did.

In addition to some faculty members' appeals, several lawyers and other mediators like Whitney Young, Theodore Kheel, Kenneth Clark, William Booth, and Sid Davidoff came to discuss SAS's occupation with the leaders of the demonstration.[9] Columbia was very aware that the eyes of the black community were set upon the school on the Heights. As a result, the police who made the arrests were especially careful not to incite further controversy. Kenneth Clark said: "I didn't hear a single harsh word. There was no resistance, no violence. . . . The students were lined up, as I said, and two students were arrested by a single police and each arresting officer escorted the student down the stairs . . . to the police vans."[10]

Such was not the case at the other buildings. Throughout the removal process and even afterward, observers maintained that the police acted with excessive force against the protesters. Some observers noted how several students in Low were dragged out by their hair or kicked into submission because they resisted arrest.[11] While the police at Low never clubbed any protesters, several students argued that the authorities had mishandled them. A policeman defended his actions: "When the kids go limp and refuse to budge or be touched, all you can do is . . . push them." At Low, few students received serious injuries, but those in other buildings were not as fortunate.

"These kids need to be spanked," complained one frustrated officer. That statement in itself illustrates an important aspect of protest. Given the makeup of the New York Police Department, it suggested the age and class divisions between working-class white people who were thankful for the "American Dream" and upper-middle-class youth who were wholly dissatisfied with the way the older generation viewed society. At Avery and Fayerweather halls, police dealt not only with the students occupying the buildings, but also with the growing crowds outside. Inside Fayerweather, a classroom building that housed the history department, a frightened female protester bit an officer who attempted to remove her. The policeman, bleeding (and possibly equally as frightened), pulled the girl by her hair down the stairs of the building. As the officers threw students out of the building, television and movie cameras were present. Back inside were approximately seventy students who had chosen to resist violently. Upon entering the room where the rebels had barricaded themselves, officers, who heaved furniture in the direction of seated students, felt the pain of the Coke bottles and chairs that the students hurled back at them. The police, short on patience, retaliated by striking the resisters with handcuffs and billy-clubs.[12]

After being beaten outside of Fayerweather Hall, Professor James Shenton and a student left campus crying. A reporter asked the history professor: "Do you see anything in your field that kind of illuminates what happened?" Shenton replied: "No. The only thing I can tell you is that whatever they [the administration] thought they were going to do, they have done the reverse. I could never again trust this administration; I could never again trust it."[13]

In another building, Mathematics Hall, the authorities met violent resistance instantly. As the officers marched up the stairs, students from above threw furniture on them. When a police representative warned of the consequences of assaulting a police officer, they stopped. Their cease-fire, however, was only temporary. According to a university publication, when the students got within sight of the TV cameras, they charged the police to provoke them into acting violently.[14] As Eric Foner, then a graduate student in the history department, noted, "Shrieks of 'police brutality' could be heard everywhere."[15] When asked if brutality actually existed at the removal, he replied: "Absolutely! There was a lot of brutality. . . . The police unleashed a lot of violence, mostly against by-standers." He recalled: "It was like a scene from a Hollywood movie."[16]

In front of Low Library, on a statue of the Alma Mater, there appeared a sign reading: "Raped by the cops."[17] That was the opinion of many of the two thousand spectators on campus. The crowd greatly outnumbered the thousand police, four hundred of whom attempted to form a cordon leading to the police vans and wagons. When a group of onlookers impeded this effort, Foner recalled that "somebody gave the order to clear the campus—and what that meant was the police just raised their billy-clubs and ran around beating everybody they could."[18] A reporter from WABC-TV confirmed that random violence occurred. He reported that he himself had been "grabbed, pushed down some flight of curved marble steps, and all along the way policemen were using handcuffs as brass knuckles [to bash] me over the head as I went down.[19] One demonstrator remembered an incident with a police officer: "I was clubbed on the side of the head with a billy-club, and then I stood up." When the policeman asked if he was leaving, the student said, "yes," but that was not good enough; the officer, according to one report, punched him in the face for good measure.[20] By 5 A.M. the police had arrested over seven hundred people.[21]

Foner, looking back, contended that "the police were mostly Irish-Catholic, working-class people" who resented the "rich, upper-class students." For the mostly white police officers, it must have been disturbing to see young white people who had the opportunity to attend an Ivy League university rebel in such a manner. One student asked a policeman: "Don't you understand, we're doing this for you? You and your kids are going to profit from what we're doing a hell of a lot more than we are!"[22]

Most likely the officer could not understand what the students were doing and especially how they were doing it. In the officer's view, and probably that of many others, receiving a college education without disrupting the university, an American institution, could have been very profitable. Doing so would have resulted in the "success of success" that Kenneth Keniston mentioned in *Young Radicals*. Keniston noted that for people who have been socially and economically deprived, the students' opportunities at the university would have been a dream.[23] The fact that during the removal the majority of officers and students were white further bolstered Keniston's theory. After all, what did the students have to complain about; they were not only rich but also white. The "system" against which they rebelled was put in place for not only their economic but also their social success. With that in mind, many of the police took it upon themselves to make the students and onlookers understand the opportunities they had risked losing.

"They got what they deserved," asserted one patrolman assigned to Columbia.[24] Many of the police force defended their actions that morning. Discussing the issue of brutality, one of them boasted that the beatings that some of the students at Columbia received "weren't half as bad as I would have w[h]acked my kids if they had been there." The brutality that everyone referred to, claimed another officer, was what "one or two cops might have done in the heat of the moment." Others contended that they would have been justified if they had deliberately brutalized some of the demonstrators because "some of these young men were aching for it"; the police withstood "a lot of abuse." In the end, though, most officers did not view the violence on the Morningside Heights campus as the result of their personal vendettas. One patrolman summed up the sentiment of the group: "The truth is that a few guys let off some steam, but basically we were doing a job, and there's just no way to do it without someone getting hurt."[25]

The *Columbia Daily Spectator* called the removal "a brutal bloody show of strength."[26] In a TV interview with a CBS correspondent, Kirk said: "With the utmost regret, after nearly a week of efforts at conciliation, I reached the conclusion . . . that I must ask the police to take the steps necessary to permit the university to resume its operations."[27] Vice President Truman asked himself, "Do you think they will know why we had to do this, to call the police? Will they know what we went through before we decided?"[28] Mayor John Lindsay regretted the violence but commended the Columbia administration for its "remarkable display of patience and restraint" before calling in the police.[29]

On and off campus that day, the discussions centered on the question of whether police brutality actually occurred. Most agreed that, in some cases, the authorities used excessive force. Others, recognizing the effects of the violence that took place, did not blame the police but rather the trustees and administration for calling them. One student contended that "the bloody violence which took place . . . is ultimately the responsibility of President Grayson Kirk and Vice President David B. Truman, the men who decided to use force to empty the occupied buildings."[30] Indeed, it was Kirk and the administration who had called the police onto campus, but it was the trustees who instructed them to do so.

Some of the university trustees, who had pressured the administration to end the disturbance, maintained firmly that no brutality had taken place. In fact, according to the school paper, some even "praised the conduct of the New York City police."[31] Trustee Frode Jensen, who claimed that he spoke to students after the bust, announced: "I refuse to accept the fact that there was any brutality. There was not." He made it clear that "there was resistance on the part of the students." "Incidentally, [the police] did a magnificent job," added Jensen. Agreeing with Jensen, William E. Petersen, the chair of the Board of Trustees and director of Irving Trust Company, said: "The police handled the situation very well." Of course, noted Petersen, "We [the trustees] regret any violence that occurred." Samuel R. Walker, who was the director of Equitable Life Assurance Society of the United States, added that "it was a condition the boys [students] brought on themselves."[32] Another trustee admitted that whatever sympathetic feelings he might have had for the students faded upon inspection of the occupied buildings afterward: "I changed my whole attitude when I saw what the students did inside the buildings."

Running out of answers for why the university had called for police action, Kirk expressed his frustration over the matter. "Despite tireless efforts by hundreds of faculty members and the entire administration," he said, "the student protesters declined to accept any reasonable basis for settlement."[33] The president correctly indicated that the student demonstrators' recalcitrance placed the administration in a very difficult position: "They appear to have regarded the university's patience as weakness." There came a point when patience ran thin and the university had to make a decision. Kirk maintained that the protesters had "been assured repeatedly that we could not indefinitely tolerate a reckless indifference to the integrity of the university and to standards of conduct on which its life as an academic community depends."[34]

During the day of April 30, over 720 protesters attended their arraignment at the Manhattan Criminal Court, which had to employ fifteen more clerks than usual to expedite the process. Most of the students and outside protesters faced charges of second-degree criminal trespass and resisting arrest in violation of penal codes 140.10 and 205.30, respectively.[35] Alumni and other supporters of the demonstration provided the students with money for bail, while Columbia University law students and members of the Lawyers' Guild sought to represent the student protesters in court. The fact that hundreds of students had to face criminal charges in court was a testament of the distance students and other members of the younger generation would go to have their voice heard. Furthermore, it showed the militant black student protesters, as well as the white radical students, that the mostly white student body could be moved to action.

On May 1, while the arrested demonstrators lingered in jail, protesters from Harlem and other colleges and universities staged a demonstration near campus. One of the approximately one thousand demonstrators said: "We support the Columbia students' demands. We call for Columbia University to permanently halt construction of the proposed gymnasium in Morningside Park. We deplore the mass police brutality . . . and join the Columbia strikers in demanding the resignation of President Kirk and Vice President Truman."[36] The demonstrator continued: "As a representative of the Black [and] Jewish Community of Harlem, we are supporting the just struggle of the students who have been carrying this struggle for the Harlem community against imperialistic, colonialistic attitudes of Columbia University that is trying to subvert the social progress of Harlem and turn Harlem into a colony."

H. Rap Brown was with the demonstrators. He, along with the marchers, shouted that in Morningside Park, "we want flowers not bricks," referring to the gym project.[37] Furthermore, according to another demonstrator, "We are going to negotiate with respect to anything that affects our community." In regard to the gymnasium controversy, the balance of power was quickly tipping in favor of those who opposed the project. As the protesters carried on their rally near campus, hundreds of students remained in jail.

A majority of the students who found themselves in jail had never before had any negative run-ins with the law. For Columbia University, however, the situation was unlike that of many community tenants in the university-owned housing units. Those tenants typically did not challenge the school's attempts to remove them from their homes because they feared and misunderstood legal procedures. To the contrary, many of the protesting students, because of their class status, had access to personal lawyers and other representation that would ensure that their judicial process was conducted in a fair and expedient manner. That was the case for the members and followers of SAS, who on the day of their arraignment were represented by the father of one of the demonstrators.[38] What was more, the demonstrators had no fear of the university. Subsequently, upon release that afternoon, some of the arrested students filed suits against Columbia University with the federal court that sought an "injunction against the prosecution of Columbia students arrested in the protest," reported the *New York Times*.[39]

The mass removal represented yet another turning point in the struggle. By first destroying school property and physically engaging the police at the gym site, then separating by race and occupying separate buildings, and then forcing the university to call a thousand police on campus, those who protested against the institution of higher education (for whatever reasons) set the stage for change. One thing that members of the Harlem and Morningside Heights communities, as well as protesting students, wanted was for the university to reconsider its relationship with them, and, because they caused such a disturbance, reconsideration was the least Columbia officials were willing to do. In the minds of the community and the members of SAS, that meant an end to the gym and a change in university expansion policies. For the affiliates of SDS, that meant restructuring the university to allow students more of an opportunity to decide on matters such as the school's role in the war and military research. Essentially, each of these groups had been engaged in a struggle for power, and with the "bust" their chances for receiving that power increased because of the advocacy they would receive from those who disagreed with the school's decision to employ the police.

The string of incidents that shook Columbia's campus emblazoned in the minds of all individuals affiliated with the university and the protest the need for change. University officials took notice of the call for change. "Trustees Express Willingness to Consider Change," a *Spectator* headline read after the mass arrest.[40] President Kirk conceded "that the basic structure of Columbia must be re-examined."[41] In the editorial section of the school paper, students offered suggestions for change. Advice included distributing a memorandum on the gym issue and conducting discussions between Columbia officials and community residents on the school's future plans for expansion. Another suggestion in the editorial section of the *Spectator* was to reduce the administration's power and disperse it to the students and faculty. "This University can no longer remain—in fact or in law—the 'Private Property' of its Trustees and administration," asserted one student. "Columbia must be reorganized from its rancid top to its fermenting bottom," meaning that trustees and administration must give some of the university's decision-making power to the faculty and students.[42] Students made the call for change in an American institution, and this time the institution had to respond.

Foner later contended, and correctly so, that the mass arrest turned most of the students against the administration. "The old administration died that night," he said. "There was no way Kirk could come back as president."[43] Many members of SDS, the student body, and the faculty agreed jointly that neither President Kirk nor Vice President Truman could successfully return to their duties after that morning of violence. Forming the Columbia University Strike Committee (CUSC), undergraduate and graduate students, as well as faculty members, charged that the administration "forfeited its legitimate authority within this institution" when it chose to employ the police to brutally remove the students.[44] Furthermore, the CUSC urged all students and faculty members to stage a strike against the university, starting on May 6, 1968, and continuing until President Kirk and Vice President Truman resigned and the university met all six of SDS's earlier demands.

The students and faculty stood solidly on strike for a full six weeks. For most students, the thought of a strike from school would seem like a much-needed break from the humdrum of daily class work. For the students who participated in the strike on the Morningside Heights campus that spring, their problem was not with the education, but with the way the university operated. With that in mind, many students continued to attend classes, which professors made possible by opening their homes and holding class at alternative sites.

Immediately following the police action, the faculty became one of the main groups to advocate change. It began to restructure the university's communication channels. The Executive Committee, formed mostly out of senior faculty members, gained the power to bypass the president and take appeals directly to the trustees. This move boosted tremendously the power of the faculty, who usually reported their grievances to Kirk, who would then take them to the trustees.[45] Many of the faculty believed strongly that more power should rest in their hands. When asked what structural changes he might make in the university, Lionel Trilling, professor of literature and criticism, answered, "It's plain that the faculty will have to be much more involved in the practical life of the university than it has hitherto been."[46] Some faculty members were even bitter about their prior role at Columbia. "The faculty has been subjected to every conceivable indignity by an administration that is unable to maintain order," said one member; "we therefore ask for a change in the administration."[47] Eric Bentley, a professor of drama, stated that "we [the faculty members] cannot hold any truthful discussions before the removal of the president. All depends on one demand: Kirk must go!"[48] Ironically, that was the phrase the protesters had shouted all week long.

Using what power they had after the protest, members of the faculty approved a "pass-fail grade option," according to the *Spectator*.[49] The decision actually meant that students had the choice, upon meeting with their professors, to receive a pass-fail, a letter grade, or an incomplete in the classes they had enrolled in that spring. The professor or instructor would then extend a passing grade to all students who were indeed passing before the April 23 start of the demonstrations. The students who were not passing before that date would have the option to take an incomplete in their course(s). Taking one step further, according to the *Spectator*, the college faculty decided to "extend the semester until May 29 [and to] abolish the formal final examination period."[50] Members of the faculty believed that the change in the grading and scheduling was necessary in order to continue with the students' educational process.

Another change that was necessary, according to Lionel Trilling, was the expansion of the students' role in university policy. "It is obvious that there will have to be a greater participation by the students in the affairs of the university," the professor explained.[51] After listening to the concerns of the students, the Executive Committee made several suggestions. First, it recommended dropping criminal charges against the students so that they would not have to deal with the disciplinary consequences of both the city and the university. Second, it requested the implementation of the tripartite disciplinary committee that the students had demanded earlier. Third, the body asked that the university abandon the idea of the gymnasium permanently.

The more than seven hundred people whom the police arrested on April 30 faced charges ranging from criminal trespass to assault. To deal with these offenses on campus, Trilling and another member of the Executive Committee successfully changed the composition of the disciplinary committee.[52] In line with the protesters' demands, the committee, which had previously excluded students, expanded to include seven of them and thus became the Joint Committee on Disciplinary Affairs. It then released a five-page report reiterating the Executive Committee's request to drop criminal charges against the protesters, with the exception of those who had committed crimes worse than criminal trespass. The report recommended that each student participant in the demonstration receive disciplinary probation for the remaining academic year and all of the next. Maintaining that only collective punishment was appropriate since "many of those who participated in the demonstration acted out of deep commitment, not personal animus," the Joint Committee urged the university administration to accept its suggestion. With the body's suggestion, each student would have to meet with the appropriate dean, who would then start the disciplinary proceeding. If the protester refused to meet with that dean, the university would impose suspension. If the student denied the charge, that student would go before a five-person tripartite tribunal. Finally, the committee suggested that the president should have the final say on all disciplinary matters, but not the power to increase the suggested punishment.

Kirk rejected the report for several reasons. First, he claimed that "the trespass charges cannot be dropped by the university." Second, "the recommendation . . . that the President should not increase any penalty sustained or imposed by the Joint Committee is one that I cannot accept."[53] To Kirk, the first suggestion seemed like absolution for the students; the second was a direct challenge to his power. By absolving the students, Kirk would suggest that the administration had been wrong in the way it ran the university. What was worse, however, was that he might have also been indicating that the student protesters held the moral ground in the situation by demonstrating against the school. Whatever the matter, though, Kirk could not capitulate completely because he believed that "the model university is the cradle of the nation's future," and thus he could not allow the protesters' actions to go unpunished.[54] He feared that if he and the administration granted amnesty (the primary demand of the SDS) to the demonstrators, "we would have dealt a near-fatal blow not only to this institution but to the whole of American higher education."[55]

The president's decision not to accept the majority of the Joint Committee's report was especially unsettling to the faculty, who claimed that Kirk was a "bottleneck" to progress.[56] While the rejection bothered the faculty, it was also unpopular with the trustees, who chose to back Kirk only nominally. The trustees stood behind Kirk's first claim that the university could not drop charges against the student protesters, but that it could "make recommendations for leniency."[57] Furthermore, they declared their faith in the decision-making ability of the Joint Committee and suggested that it handle all future disciplinary cases. Unlike Kirk, however, the trustees did not reject the committee's request that the president not be able to increase any penalty that it suggested. In the brief statement the trustees gave, they diffused some of the president's power to the faculty and students. To many of the protesting students' delight, Kirk had been defeated.

Although Kirk had to delegate some of his disciplinary power, some students still complained that the Joint Committee's suggestions were unsatisfactory. Many of the conservative students saw the document as a "sell-out" to the protesters and believed that the demonstrators deserved heavy punishment from both the city authorities and the university.[58] On the other hand, the more radical students, many of whom had participated in the protest, contended that the students on the Joint Committee acted as puppets of the administration and represented too many of Kirk's views. Claiming that they could not attain justice from a "biased authority," those students disagreed immediately with the committee's suggestion that they meet with a dean to discuss their case.[59] In spite of the students' growing concerns about the viability of the Joint Committee, the university's allowance of students to sit on the board was the first change of this measure the school had ever made. Indeed, the protesters and faculty, by disrupting classes and demonstrating, forced Columbia to respond to their call for change.

Some students refused to allow the board (especially the administration's representatives) to judge their actions. The members of SAS issued a statement denouncing the validity of the administration to punish students. "We do not recognize the right of the administration to impose punitive sanction upon any persons who engaged in the Hamilton Hall occupation. Any attempt to impose such sanctions will exacerbate the already strained relations between Columbia and Black People," the statement read.[60] SAS confidently explained the situation from its vantage point: "The police were prevented from the use of violence in the clearing of Hamilton Hall because of the superior discipline of the Black students, the presence of certain notables and, most importantly, the fear of an overwhelming response from the Harlem

Community." The statement charged that "it is the administration at Columbia University, through its callous racist policies towards the Harlem community, that is totally responsible for the deplorable situation at this time."[61]

On the night of the mass removal, a disgusted Melvin Morgulis, a student who filmed the incident, cried to a police officer: "Can't you see what you're doing to my buddies out there?" He believed that what he had witnessed was an American tragedy.[62]

What Morgulis observed truly was an American tragedy. The confrontation signified the unwillingness of one generation to give in to the other. It also signified the unwillingness of an American institution to give in to American citizens concerned about the welfare of their neighborhoods. Finally, it signified the climax of the American student movement.

The university, as an American institution, could not allow the students, or anybody else, to challenge its authority. As Jerry Avorn, then editor of the school paper, put it, Kirk believed that "if the administration gave in at Columbia[,] students throughout the country would be encouraged to attempt similar takeovers at their universities and expect to win."[63] Avorn correctly explained that this line of thinking resembled that in John Foster Dulles's "Domino Theory," which maintained that if the United States allowed the Soviet Union to win one nation as an ally in communism, then soon many more nations would follow.[64] Just as the United States could not allow the "evil empire" to prevail, neither could President Kirk and the rest of the university officials allow the unruly students, who wore red arm bands and likened themselves to communist leaders like Ernesto Che Guevara and Fidel Castro, and outside agitators to prevail in their protest efforts.

In hindsight, just as the amount of resources the United States put forth to wage the cold war did not necessarily produce a positive outcome for the nation, the university's use of the New York police force did not bring forth the results that Columbia officials desired. For fear of losing control of the campus and the nation in the immediate present, Columbia University as well as U.S. officials did not recognize that they had overlooked the domestic issues that brought the campus and the nation to the point of chaos. Furthermore, the students, in the eyes of the officials, were lawbreakers. In the fashion of politicians such as President Richard Nixon, who won their elections by vowing to reinstitute "law and order" in a seemingly chaotic country, Columbia University officials, on the morning of April 30, pushed for the reign of the law and the calm of order.

Incidentally, Nixon commented on the Columbia controversy. As the student strike continued, Nixon speculated that the Columbia protests were "the first major skirmish in a revolutionary struggle to seize the universities of this country and transform them into sanctuaries for radicals and vehicles for revolutionary political and social goals." Nixon believed that "if that student violence is either rewarded or goes unpunished, then the administration of Columbia University will have guaranteed a new crisis on its own campus and invited student coups on other campuses all over this country."[65]

It became apparent that the students and faculty, as well as the protesting citizens of the country, needed to convey to the university and the government that it was their school and country too, and that they would take part in the decisions it made. For those students, the protest was far from over, and they wanted the trustees and administration to know it. To the university officials, the physical struggle meant more than just a violent scene; it meant that they could no longer wait to address the issues at hand: student power, the Vietnam War, Black Power, the New Left, and community relations. Fortunately for the Harlem and Morningside Heights community, the black city organizations, and the black students at Columbia, one of the first issues addressed by the trustees of the university was the permanent halt of the gymnasium.

Although the students who demonstrated against the university were making progress with the school, people from the community criticized Columbia for not treating community demonstrators equally. Despite the fact that Columbia eventually dropped criminal charges against the protesting students, the university had not done the same for the community protesters. Several community members sent a telegram directly to the president of the university. The telegram read: "From an institution where law and sound judicial principles are taught, it is disappointing to know that in the case of the undersigned, Columbia University departs from a humane and just path. We protest the use of a double standard of justice in the cases of community residents, arrested at gym-site demonstrations in February, 1968. We respectfully request an appointment with you and the Board of Trustees to discuss this matter. It is our position that court prosecution against community residents be suspended, as was in student cases."[66] Marshall Garcia, Tyrone Geogiou, James Latimore, Bob McKay, Maria Miller, Joseph Monroe, Suki Ports, Rev. A. Kendall Smith, and Bill Stanley as members of the West Harlem Community Organization, ARCH, Uptown Tenants Council, and Beulah Baptist Church signed the telegram.

Additionally, community members rebuked the university for allowing the police to come onto campus. In a "Letter from the Community," residents stated: "Mayor John V. Lindsay and Columbia President Grayson Kirk acted with gross insensitivity in sending police onto the Columbia campus to eject with force the non-violent student demonstrators." In reality, not all of the students were nonviolent, but the vast majority of students were. Lindsay and Kirk, the letter explained, "awarded a priority to property over life and to legalisms over compassion."[67] Notables such as New York State Assemblywoman Shirley Chisholm, State Assemblyman Charles Rangel, and district leaders Margaret Cox, Hugh Ferry, and Franz Leichter signed the letter.

One historic civil rights organization made sure to support some of the students who participated in the demonstrations. *Crisis* magazine reported that NAACP lawyers would represent Columbia students. Robert Carter (of *Brown v. Board of Education* fame) stated that the NAACP was organizing a panel of thirty-one lawyers "to assure the meaningful representation of Negroes involved in mass arrests of various kinds in the City of New York," and that included the members of SAS and the community who protested against the gym.

In the "battle for Morningside Heights," the black protesters of SAS used race as an issue to influence the decision of the university to halt construction of the gymnasium.[68] They did so first by separating themselves, in the manner of Black Power advocates, from the white student protesters, and then by using the surrounding black community as a support base whose presence in the protest posed a threat to the university. It was precisely this division along racial lines that allowed white students of SDS to successfully radicalize much of the general student population, and the black students of SAS to halt gym construction. One long-time gym opponent, George Collins, recognized this: "These students accomplished in 48 hours what many of us had labored in vain for many years to bring about—namely, suspension and reconsideration of the building project."[69]

Concerning the gymnasium, Vice President Truman maintained a somber tone. He could not understand what happened. Truman said: "A great many people in the Harlem community . . . have in fact indicated their desire that they want to have the facility in the park, and I don't mean soft-headed people."[70] Perhaps he and Columbia never polled some of the people in Harlem and Morningside Heights who were evicted from the university-owned buildings. When asked about the future of the gymnasium, Truman responded: "Well, I can't make a prediction about the gymnasium now. It's kind of a symbol, unfortunately; I think the discussions and the responses of the gymnasium have gotten so far from the facts, from the real situation that it has to be dealt with in symbolic terms, perhaps. That seems to me a tragedy." While the gymnasium may have become a symbol of sorts, the sentiment of the community and many students was very real.

The protest efforts of black community members, SAS, and SDS, although divided, sparked a six-week student strike that cracked the fault line of the campus and eventually led to change. While on strike, students intensified the campaign against the university while at the same time continuing with their formal education. Students met with their professors at their homes and other off-campus locations. SAS and SDS participated in student-supported on-campus demonstrations throughout the month of May. Providing a crowning touch to the semester, some students even staged a disruptive event at the spring graduation ceremony. Needless to say, the university was literally left reeling after the uprising of 1968.

The student demonstrators received support from all over the United States. From as far away as Seattle, Washington, the SDS chapter of the University of Washington sent a telegram stating "Congratulations for your success in supporting the struggles of black people. The steps you have taken to help build an alliance between black people are a historic event."[71] The Columbia protesters also received words of encouragement from the Communist Party of the United States of America (CPUSA), radical organizations at Berkeley, the Graduate Association of the State University of New York at Buffalo, student councils at Brown University, the Youth Socialist Alliance of Cleveland, the New York branch of the NAACP, and the local AFL-CIO. The members of the National Student Association pledged "to raise the critical issues of racism on campuses . . . whether it involves the admission of black students to the university, or the provision of scholarships for black students in the university, or the relationship of the university to surrounding ghettoes."[72] Indeed, the Columbia demonstrations provided a catalyst to a larger social movement in the United States.

Perhaps it took an explosion for the university to reevaluate its internal and external relationships. Looking back on the events, one article claimed that "Columbia University is 25 years behind most other institutions of its size and importance."[73] The students and faculty at Columbia had been stymied in their attempts to participate in the activities of the university. Furthermore, many university officials viewed the neighborhoods surrounding the school as places to purchase property and to expand instead of places where people lived and held the desire to control their lives.

Fortunately for the school, H. Rap Brown's 1967 encouragement to blow up the gym never came to fruition. Instead, the community, along with student activists, unsettled the university just enough to achieve their goals of stopping the gym's construction and gaining student power. The Harlem community regained sovereignty over Morningside Park and the gym was never built. In 1968 Steven V. Roberts, a reporter for the *New York Times*, correctly wrote in an article for *Commonweal* magazine that "now Columbia knows that almost anybody—students and faculty as well as poor people—will 'cause disturbances' if pushed far enough."[74] More than that, Columbia found that the students, as well as black community members, were willing to shut the university down for their respect and for the power to make decisions that affected them.

6

Black Student Power
The Struggle for Black Studies

As a result of the spring 1968 protest, things changed drastically at Columbia. With the mass arrest that took place on campus, SDS observed the radicalization of many Columbia students. With a large number of students advocating change in the university, President Kirk and the administration had to accede to some of the protesters' demands. That summer, Columbia University students made history at their school with the creation of the Joint Committee on Disciplinary Affairs, which consisted of students as well as faculty and administrators. Subsequently, the group oversaw disciplinary cases. SDS also achieved its goal of having the school terminate ties with the IDA. In the *New York Times* in September 1969, Columbia went "on record for the immediate withdrawal" of American soldiers from Vietnam and its cessation of relations with the IDA.[1]

One last demand that many radical students did not expect President Kirk to meet was his own resignation from the university. On August 23, 1968, exactly five months from the start of the spring demonstration, Grayson Kirk and David Truman stepped down as the president and vice president. This might have been good news to SDS leader Mark Rudd, but he had been expelled and decided to pursue a career as a traveling lecturer.[2] Incidentally, in September 1968 SDS lost its privileges to use on-campus facilities.[3] Andrew Cordier, from the School of International Affairs, took over the reins of the university as acting president; he found that he also would face his share of controversy from SDS and SAS in the upcoming school year.

Like Kirk, Cordier, as president of a white institution, had to deal with the militant black movement known as Black Power. According to the tenets of Black Power, as noted by Kwame Ture (Stokely Carmichael), former president of the Student Non-Violent Coordinating Committee, and political scientist Charles V. Hamilton, black people must go through several processes to reach a position of power in the United States. One of these was redefinition, which involved the reclamation of the history of black people and black people defining themselves by showing pride in their culture. Another process, political modernization, included three steps: "(1) questioning old values and institutions of society; (2) searching for new and different forms of political structure to solve political and economic problems; and (3) broadening the base of political participation to include more people in the decision-making process."[4] Black Power, at its peak during the late 1960s, influenced the protest efforts of Columbia's SAS in its campaign for the academic inclusion of black-focused programs of study, as well as the increased acceptance of fellow black students. This chapter will discuss the rise of black studies and the effort by Columbia's black students to create a black studies institute.

The struggle to include black studies as a subject in the academic curricula of colleges and universities did not begin in the 1960s. Historians such as Carter G. Woodson, William Leo Hansberry, and John Henrik Clarke began the quest for black studies much earlier in the century. In 1915 Woodson brought into existence one of the first organizations dedicated solely to the study of black people. In the executive director's office of Chicago's Wabash Avenue YMCA, Woodson and several of his colleagues created the Association for the Study of Negro Life and History (ASNLH).[5] One of the purposes of the group, according to an association pamphlet, was "to promote the study of black history through schools, colleges, churches, homes, fraternal groups, and clubs." Woodson fortified the ASNLH by establishing "Negro History Week" in 1926 and the *Negro History Bulletin* in 1937. Until his death in 1950, Woodson's work with the ASNLH laid the foundation for black studies as students would know it in the late 1960s.

Starting in the 1920s, William Leo Hansberry did his own part to add to the recognition of black culture and history. After graduating from Harvard University, Hansberry took an appointment at Howard University, where he lectured on the contributions of Africans to world history. The first to teach courses of that sort in any college or university, Hansberry was unpopular among many of his fellow scholars who had not witnessed the careful research that he had conducted. The black scholar then went on to receive his master's degree from Harvard in anthropology, but he was unable to attain a doctorate in his field of choice because no American university, nor even

Oxford, where he was admitted, took enough of an interest in the contributions and history of ancient Africa. His research efforts and dedication would be manifested in the creation of black studies programs and departments in the late 1960s.

John Henrik Clarke also contributed to the rise of black studies. As a member of the African Studies Association (ASA), whose primary purpose in 1957 was the study and dispersion of information regarding Africa, Clarke pushed the group to place mainly black scholars in the decision-making positions of the organization.[6] This effort led to the 1968 founding of the African Heritage Studies Association (AHSA), which was an offshoot of the ASA.[7] The AHSA maintained as one of its goals the attempt to recruit more black scholars and students to the study of Africa. By the 1960s Clarke acted as a main catalyst in the struggle for African and black studies across the nation.

In the late 1960s San Francisco State College was one of the first to witness the effects of a student protest for black studies. On that campus, black students, under the leadership of Nathaniel Hare (once a professor at Howard University), helped to create the nation's first black studies department. During the 1966–67 school year, Hare and members of the San Francisco State Black Student Union led a successful strike involving thousands of students—black and white—for the department. In 1968, as a result of those students' efforts, Hare became the first chair of the black studies department at San Francisco State College and thus provided an example of success to black student protesters across the nation.[8]

The fact that one of the nation's leading educational institutions lacked courses on black culture and history did not go unnoticed. "Columbia U Has No Courses on Negroes," read a 1966 headline in the *New York Amsterdam News*.[9] The article pointed out that "although [Columbia University] has been in existence 212 years it does not offer a single course in Negro history to its undergraduate school." One university official seemed perplexed with the proposition of adding courses in black studies. When asked if the university had any intention to add courses to the curriculum, the director of public relations, Wesley Furst, replied: "We don't know."[10] Furst clarified that although no specific courses existed, the sociology department presented material in some of its classes that "cut across the Negro." For the student proponents of Black Power, that would not do.

During the spring semester of 1969, some members of Columbia University's SAS began their own movement of redefinition, and later, political modernization, with their push for black studies and recruitment. On February 27 fifty black students representing SAS stood up and walked out of the university's first and only African American history course at the time. Eric Foner, a white first-year instructor, watched as Cicero Wilson, a senior and president of SAS, presented an informal plan for a "Black Institute."[11] As Foner's class was the first and only of its nature in Columbia University's curriculum, senior Ralph Metcalfe considered the class a "racist insult" because it attempted to cover all of black history in only one semester. Although Wilson and Metcalfe showed their frustration with the limited scope of the course, they made it clear that their problem was not with the instructor, Foner, but more so with the officials who oversaw the implementation of curriculum. The new program that SAS proposed would be "responsible only to the trustees on budgetary and all other matters." It would also be free to "grant credit and set up degree programs, to hire faculty and staff, to create auxiliary structures necessary for the implementation of relevant curricula on the black experience, and to establish facilities to coordinate all recruiting of black students and faculty."[12]

To Wilson, the benefits of a black institute were obvious. First, a black studies program would provide students with more knowledge about a previously neglected subject. Ideally, American students should fulfill the obligation to learn about the history of fellow Americans, and the American university provides the perfect venue to complete such a task. As Wilson believed, white students should learn about black culture "because no matter what they do . . . there are race problems in all spheres of life," and having some exposure to black culture could help to solve those problems.[13] Another benefit of having a black institute at Columbia would be the school's ability to compete with other Ivy League schools such as Yale and Harvard, which had already established black studies programs. Because Columbia had not yet created such a program, Wilson asserted that his school rated "by far in last place in the Ivy League [regarding the move] toward relevant education."[14]

By the time of the Columbia 1969 protest, black studies was becoming an issue at other Ivy League colleges and universities as well. Observing the example that students set at Yale University in 1968 by forcing their school to create a black studies department, in 1969 black protesters at both Harvard and Cornell fought for black-centered programs. Under the leadership of Afro (a group similar to SAS), student demonstrators at Harvard called for a black studies program that would allow the students to participate in faculty hiring and tenure practices.[15] At Cornell University, a black student group known as the Afro-American Society militantly protested for a black studies program. In addition, the Afro-American Society demonstrated against what it considered to be the racism involved in the suspension of five black students whom the university had disciplined for a previous demonstration.[16] The Cornell protest involved some of the students carrying weapons to protect themselves from racist white backlash. Even closer to Columbia University, in February 1969, the women of the Barnard Organization of Soul Sisters gave the men of Columbia's SAS inspiration for their struggle against Columbia by influencing Barnard to adopt a black studies major.[17]

Of particular interest to SAS was the successful protest of BOSS. As Barnard was the sister school of Columbia University, the male-dominated SAS had a special tie to the black women of Barnard's student group. Mirroring some of the aims of the larger Black Power movement, some of the primary goals of BOSS were "to bring about the changes in the [Barnard] College necessary to make it more relevant to Black students, and to give us a voice in controlling our own environment."[18] According to William Sales, a graduate student and leader of SAS during the 1968 protest against the gymnasium, BOSS's function was to provide SAS with information about the university's relationship with the community.[19] When asked if the fact that black female students at Barnard won a victory for black studies in 1969 affected the will of the male members of SAS, Ray Brown, a senior and leader of SAS, admitted that "black women are always the bulwark of any black activity. Their input and participation was valuable to the struggle for a Black Institute."[20]

After observing the protests of BOSS, on March 4, 1969, the members of SAS brought a list of demands to Columbia University President Andrew Cordier. One of their demands was the creation of a twenty-five-member board consisting of black students, faculty, and community members. SAS also wanted an interim budget of $100,000 for the board to use at its disposal. The students made another stipulation that the board be responsible only to the trustees. With the school funding the institute, SAS wanted black students as well as black faculty and black community members to have autonomous control over the program.

Control became one of the most controversial issues affecting the viability of the program. There were three interested parties in the debate over the institute: the students, faculty, and the administration. For the students, particularly the black students, autonomous control over the program was absolutely necessary, as it became a racial issue. This view held true to the Black Power strategies espoused by Ture and Hamilton. They claimed that if any program should affect black people directly, then black people should have direct control over it.[21]

Many of the militant students argued that white administrators and faculty members did not have enough of a cultural background to regulate matters regarding black studies. Ray Brown explained that the university's administrators and faculty members knew little about the needs of its black student population: "I think their assumption was that we were just white kids with black faces and forgot that we were people that had been the product of a totally different experience."[22] Because of legal segregation and the rise of the ghetto, many of the black students on Columbia's campus had never before attended school with white students, and many others had attended inadequate urban schools. Brown maintained that school officials "didn't know that we were students for whom some additional outreach was going to be necessary." SAS had previously made appeals concerning increased black recruitment and curriculum, but, as Brown noted, "the people we were talking to were the very people who had grown up in and were comfortable with that system [of Jim Crow segregation] and had not challenged it."[23]

SAS leadership asserted that the administration and faculty would choose professors and chairs of the program that met the "traditional" academic standards of the university, which usually did not take into account the view of a black, minority program. Making its point clear, SAS contended that in the department of economics, the university used those trained in that field to decide who should join the faculty. So, for a black studies program, SAS argued that the university should allow those trained in the culture of black people to decide which potential faculty members to hire. Since very few of the nearly all-white faculty members could boast of those qualifications, SAS suggested that a twenty-five-member interim board of black consultants would need to be created.

This argument fit into Ture and Hamilton's model of redefinition and reclamation of black history, which called for blacks to define themselves by their own standards and to portray black history from black perspectives. The students of SAS also believed that if the selection process were left to the present white department chairs and faculty members, then those chairs and faculty members would look over the available black candidates and find the candidates to be lacking traditional qualifications. Instead of hiring more black faculty members, SAS asserted, the hiring committee would hire white faculty that, while meeting their outlined qualifications, failed utterly to meet the criteria of SAS, the black students, and the community. Senior leader of SAS Cicero Wilson stated that "our standards are much higher than theirs [white faculty members']," and so SAS should be able to help choose potential instructors and chairs.[24]

For many of the faculty members, who, just the year before, were in full support of SAS's demand that gym construction in Morningside Park be permanently halted, giving up control of any academic program was not an option. As liberal as many of the faculty members were, they realized that to allow students, for whatever reason, to have the final say in matters of curriculum was to set a dangerous precedent for the future of education. As Charles Frankel, one-time Columbia professor and assistant secretary of state for educational and cultural affairs, stated in his book *Education and the Barricades,* "Academic freedom [particularly the freedom of the faculty to chose potential faculty members] is the product of a long and difficult struggle. It has been achieved by excluding all groups but professors from any formal power over what goes on in the classroom."[25] That exclusion applied to students. On this issue, the alliance between the faculty and black students that had existed during previous protests broke. A new struggle for power arose between the black student protesters of SAS and most members of the faculty.

One of the reasons that many professors (not just at Columbia) believed that students should not have the right to create and control their own black studies programs was the fact that students were transient in nature and did not have enough invested in the university to really care about the direction of higher education. "Students are on a campus only briefly, and cannot be given the power to dismantle arrangements about which future generations of students may have different opinions," argued Frankel.[26] By the time the positive and negative results from those students' protests manifested themselves, most of the students would have graduated and went on to their respective careers. Frankel explained: "Students have no common professional perspective or shared occupational interest in academic freedom." More than thirty years after the 1969 protest, Eric Foner, as a professor, agreed. "The problem is that student opinions are short-term and departmental opinion is long-term."[27] He believed, as did many faculty members, that at the university, it was the students' job to take the classes from professors, not to select the professors and design the classes, a position arrived at after many years of experience with higher education.

Another reason that many faculty members shied away from allowing students to participate in selecting potential instructors was the possibility of students choosing the most popular candidate versus the most qualified. Frankel anticipated that such a process would foster an unhealthy classroom environment and one "inappropriate to teaching." The classroom, and education in general, he asserted, has little room for democracy.[28] As with most American institutions, Columbia's leadership (in this case, the faculty) did not achieve its rank by being popular with those whom it served, but by be-

ing appointed by a body of peers and ranking officials. This mode of operation, as SAS leaders had noted, was counterproductive for the creation of a
black-controlled black studies program.

Several white professors agreed with the idea of a "black studies" program
but disagreed with an autonomous black institute that would have the final
say on matters that concerned the appointment and promotion of faculty.
One of these figures was history professor Graham Irwin from Australia.
Professor Irwin, who was white, studied African civilizations and drafted
a proposal for a program of Afro-American Studies that would have gone
into effect in the fall of 1969. He projected that the program would have
eventually led to the creation of an "Afro-American Institute." He strongly
opposed, though, the immediate implementation of the black institute that
SAS proposed. He explained that he was afraid of "possible separation of the
institute and its curricula from the rest of the academic community."[29] His
program would utilize several of the college's courses that already existed
and would adopt four new courses. Concerning the four new classes, Irwin
admitted that he was having troubles finding people "suitable [to teach] . . .
these courses."[30]

On this last point, SAS leader Cicero Wilson criticized the faculty proposal.
He noted that, "although faculty members are willing to admit that they are
ignorant in the subject, they are still intent on having themselves set up and
control a program on black studies."[31] If the people who were in charge of
hiring the instructors for a program had little knowledge of black culture,
Wilson reasoned, then the program was destined to fail. About Irwin's plan,
Wilson commented that "their own program . . . must inevitably be as bad
as most similar programs already established throughout the country." The
black studies program at Columbia, if left to black planners, could set the
example for those programs to come across the nation, Wilson suggested.

One particular group of faculty members immediately backed the efforts
for a black studies program. The secretary of the Faculty Civil Rights Group
(FCRG), professor of government Peter Juviler, claimed that the group gathered more than a hundred signatures from the faculty in support of a black
institute that differed somewhat from that supported by SAS. The faculty
organization suggested that the divisions of the university create "informal
policies" of admitting black students to different colleges. It also proposed
courses on "The Economics of the Ghetto" and "Black Literature in the United
States." One of the group's final suggestions was for the university to "develop
a 'resource file' to facilitate the recruitment of black professors."[32] Regarding
the hiring of black faculty members, the participants in the FCRG stated that

"we believe their absence has been one of the products of historic injustice, and that their presence in significant numbers would be one step towards redressment. . . . Their presence on campus is necessary to fulfill the social role of the University." Immanuel Wallerstein, who assisted as a liaison between the administration and black student demonstrators in 1968, was one of the signers of the statement.

SAS could count on the support of some of the university's maintenance and food staff as well. In this way, SAS attracted support for its cause across traditional class lines, as it had done with the gymnasium the year before. In a document entitled "Employees for March 25th," members of the staff pledged their "Support for the Student Afro-American Society Demands for an Interim Board to set up a Black Studies Institute. . . . Only black people can decide what education is relevant to their needs."[33] The fact that various students and members of the faculty supported the demands of SAS was not surprising; however, that the members of the staff would take up the protest of SAS and walk out for a day was remarkable. It spoke to the staff's perception of the black student group's demands as legitimate and worthwhile. The act of the staff also illustrated the tension that existed on each level within the university. There existed (as demonstrated in the 1968 protests) several groups struggling for power within the university, and the staff represented one of them.

Student opinion about SAS's proposed black institute varied. Some, particularly several *Columbia Daily Spectator* staff members, appreciated SAS's attempt to create a black institute, but they hedged at the idea of only black people controlling it. Robert Friedman, editor-in-chief of the *Spectator*, posited that SAS's desire to have an autonomous program was "both understandable and reasonable."[34] "It is now necessary to break away from the stagnating departmental standards that have led to this situation," explained Friedman. Berating the present system, Friedman explained that by "clinging to their outdated notions of 'quality control,' they refuse to admit that departmental control and faculty approval over programs and appointments frequently causes inertia, inappropriate criteria, and meaningless education." After claiming to support the black students of SAS, though, one staff member wrote that the "support was predicated upon the belief that white students would be free to involve themselves in the program's activities and that there would be no prohibition on white participation that will create and later control an Afro-American studies institute."[35] That white people could take part in the program's activities SAS never denied, but control of the program was a different matter.

Much to the dismay of many students, the proposal SAS had put forth made it clear that white participation in the decision making of the institute was neither desirable nor necessary. To this, the staff of the *Spectator* replied: "We believe that it would be a grave mistake for SAS to continue to maintain its position that the power must be exclusively in the hands of black people."[36] As students of the university, the members of the nearly all-white staff believed that they had a right to take part in an academic program that would affect them. By printing their opinions in the newspaper, which was the main media source on campus, the members of the *Spectator* staff must have also influenced the mindset of many observing students. The staff asserted that black people "hold neither exclusive knowledge nor the exclusive right to determine for others the course a black studies program should take." Since Columbia University was called King's College in the 1700s, school officials had created every other program in the school's curriculum that way—only white people determined the courses of study.

At that time, and in the 1960s, white people essentially controlled all other academic programs at the university concerning students. Since there were only two tenured black professors at Columbia in 1969, it was presumably mostly white faculty members who were in charge of those programs, but the newspaper staff never contested that point. The issue confronting many white students was the fact that they had never known black people to manage any facet of academia (or much else). Therefore, they believed that white people should inherently have a hand in the planning of most, if not all, programs concerning academia. For them, white control was normal, but black control was rare and somewhat startling.

When black people demanded autonomous control over a program, the members of the white newspaper staff and faculty saw it as discriminatory. When, however, for centuries white officials controlled all other programs, few if any people other than the black students made the charge of discrimination. Even if not by outline, until the suggestion of a black-controlled program, every other academic program had been exclusively white-controlled. By hiring and granting tenure to so few black professors in the various subjects, the university essentially led students to believe that exclusive white control was acceptable and normal.[37]

One student in particular questioned whether fellow students should be allowed or even consulted in the restructuring of educational curriculum or the raising of a new department. In a letter to the *Spectator*'s editor, Walter James Peoples asked the university, "Who are these [black] leaders," that they should play a role in such a monumental change?[38] "The sanction and opinions of SAS should not and cannot be the sole criterion for evaluating the merit and relevance of such a revolutionary change in the format of our education." Voicing his concern, he explained that "this educational change does not affect simply the school's black population or the college's present student enrollment." Toward the end of his letter he posed the question: "Can we students determine what those who follow us must learn?"[39]

The arguments that Peoples made against the black-dominated institute and black studies program represented the views of many students and faculty members. One of the most interesting parts of his argument was his characterization of the change to the current curriculum. He maintained that the addition of a black studies department or program would be "monumental" and "revolutionary." If the changes were to be truly revolutionary, then power to control such a program and institute could not be given solely to those officials who had heretofore been guarding the status quo. If university officials had previously placed a black institute and black studies program higher on their list of priorities, then the black students would not have had to protest for those changes.

One of the amazing facts about the generation of the 1960s was its immeasurable dedication to righting the wrongs of the past and the level of intelligent debate in which members of the generation engaged. Just as some students, like Walter James Peoples, opposed the methods that SAS used to bring to fruition an institute, a number of white students went along totally with SAS's program. The members of SDS responded to the more conservative students' and newspaper staff's articles. "We must see the demands, which you [the *Spectator* staff] call separatist, as simple attempts at [the] self-preservation" of black people, SDS asserted. "Such control is necessary."[40] To SDS, black control over the program would have been a necessary step in the race to overthrow what it referred to as a "racist system."[41]

The unity of black people, the radical white group suggested, was essential for its survival, and white people should not disrupt that unity. Agreeing with the members of SAS, the SDS representatives contended that "Columbia [had] been, through its courses, participating in a systematic cultural genocide upon Black people."[42] By creating and operating a black institute, black students, faculty, and community members would reverse that process of cultural genocide by participating in the academic process that affected so many black minds. SDS would only be satisfied, it claimed, when "Columbia, which has oppressed black people through expansion, denial of unionization on campus, selective admissions policy, and curriculum irrelevant and often offensive to black students," conceded autonomous control to the black interim board that SAS proposed.

In 1969, while the population of black students at Columbia College was less than 120 out of 2,750, there was still a divergence of opinion among them on the issue of an autonomous black institute. One black student, Oliver Henry, a self-proclaimed "Negro," commented on the "folly" of the "black" student. In the black students' attempts at the "liberation of black people by any means necessary," he rejects "academic success and a broad-gauged college experience" and instead wastes his time joining organizations in the name of the revolution, claimed Henry.[43] He suggested that in order for these protesters to validate themselves as "black" students, they wage their campus revolution with "demands for Afro-American Studies Programs wholly controlled by blacks," when it would benefit them more to work for the "inclusion of the Negro in American History where he, as an American, belongs."[44] Furthermore, explained Henry, the demands of the black students influence the weaker-minded white students who were unwilling to confront the black students. "Negro students must fight for the real revolution against white students, who paralyzed by guilt complexes, countenance anything, any idea espoused by the loudest, the most boorish blacks." He urged black students to end their push for their proposed black institute and to deal with the fact that, in the United States, they would have to work and live with white people.[45]

George Schuyler, a conservative black journalist, mirrored some of Henry's opinions in the national debate over the legitimacy of black studies. He suggested that classes in black studies "seem to have the double purpose of flattering frustrated Negro Youth (whose parents failed to do their homework) while at the same time brainwashing white students to facilitate racial equality—whatever that means."[46] Not seeing the need to have a separate department or program created in the name of black culture at universities, Schuyler contended that people, particularly black people, should learn about black culture in the home, at church, or at some other community venue, but not at school. Many of the disturbances that black students had caused across the country for the sake of black studies, he claimed, were efforts to "make the Negro look good" in history. Schuyler, however, doubted whether looking good in history would improve the plight of black people in America.[47]

Schuyler did not stand alone on his opinions about the legitimacy of separate black studies programs. The executive secretary of the NAACP, Roy Wilkins, disagreed with the students' demands for a black-controlled black studies department and threatened to file a suit against the creation of such programs, claiming that they were unconstitutional.[48] He considered those types of departments "another version of segregation and Jim Crow." In some ways, the aging civil rights leader's argument was correct. By calling for an all-black institute, the black students pushed for a certain degree of separation, but they did so because of the neglect they had experienced from previous segregation within American society. In 1968 SAS protested the school's construction of the gym in Morningside Park partly because the actual structure segregated the "community" portion from the university part with different entrances. In 1969 SAS members demanded the ability to segregate themselves from white faculty and administrators with the black group's push for a separate interim board.

Magnifying some of the contrasts between older activists from the Civil Rights movement and younger advocates of the Black Power movement, William Sales and Ray Brown disagreed with Schuyler's and Wilkins's viewpoints. Sales and Brown also criticized Henry for his depiction of the black students' struggle for a black institute. In an article entitled "Response to a 'Negro Negative,'" Sales commented on Henry's claim that black protesters rejected academic success by wasting their time joining groups like SAS. Sales said: "Success within the present educational structure is not indicative of real learning or preparation for relevant action in the Black Community."[49] "The American university," he continued, "and especially Columbia are repositories of racist European values and attitudes." While Henry urged black students to abandon the idea of a separate black studies program and to try to increase black recognition within the existing courses, Sales considered that proposal senseless. "Survival in America is based on ethnic power, not assimilation." Sales continued, "It is not our intention to blacken white history."

Sales intended to put into practice what Ture and Hamilton termed redefinition and reclamation. "Black people must redefine themselves, and only they can do that. . . . Blacks are beginning to recognize the need to assert their own definitions, to reclaim their history," explained Ture and Hamilton.[50] They further contended that "a black student, by studying his people, adds depth to his understanding of the traditional academic disciplines." Applying their ideas to his situation at Columbia, Sales explained that "militant black students do not repudiate the study of mathematics, chemistry, European History, or English but utilize the works of Carmichael [Ture] and Hamilton, Fanon and Malcolm X, in order to put these disciplines in a perspective relevant to the struggle of Black people against racist oppression." Agreeing with Sales, Ray Brown addressed Henry's assertion that SAS attempted to create a black institute in the name of the "revolution." He said that "we [the black protesters of SAS] knew that this was not the revolution, per se, but that it [the fight for the black institute] was part of an ongoing struggle to improve the lives of black students and black people in general."[51] As Sales exclaimed, "A black student must deal with racism wherever he finds it."[52]

On a different front, that April the members of SAS began to implement what Black Power advocates called "political modernization" in order to improve the lives of black Columbia students and local black youth. The group declared that "Columbia has been and still remains systematically racist and oppressive in its relations with black people." With that, on Monday, April 14, about fifteen members of the black student group staged a demonstration in the admissions office of Columbia University. Located in Hamilton Hall, which was in the center of campus, the admissions office became the target of SAS's protest. Incidentally, Hamilton Hall was also the first building that the nearly five hundred protesting students captured in the previous spring's demonstration against the gymnasium in Morningside Park. In the present demonstration, there were two main issues at hand: the autonomous black institute and an all-black admissions board.

Shortly before 9 A.M. on April 14, the SAS members entered the admissions office and sat down to protest the lack of black student enrollment at the university.[53] As they sat in the office, the staff worked around them and campus life continued as usual. At 5 P.M., the time when the office usually closed, the dean of Columbia College, Carl Hovde, came to inform the group that "their sit-in was an illegal demonstration," and that they were subject to "disciplinary actions [taken] by the university."[54] Disregarding the dean's warning, Leon Denmark, a sophomore member of SAS, issued a statement on behalf of the group that included a list of demands. Questioning the existing system, part of the statement read:

> Black students state and affirm that: the current admissions board has proved to be unwilling and incompetent to successfully address and correct existing inecquities [sic] in the admissions and funding of black students. On this basis, black students . . . demand that:
>
> 1. An experienced and capable admissions board, nominated and authorized by the black students[,] be established to evaluate and determine the admission and funding of black students and be employed by 1969.
> 2. An admissions staff, nominated and authorized by black students and employed by Columbia University to determine and enact recruitment, admissions, policies and programs for funding black students. Further, that any and all staff appointments be sanctioned and authorized by black students.[55]

In a general sense, the black students wanted to help solve the political and economic problems of black people by pushing for increased admissions into college, which was the first step of political modernization. Their suggestion for a new black admissions board fell in line with the second step of political modernization: "searching for new and different forms of political structure."[56] Their suggestion also touched on the third step in the process, which indicated the need to broaden the base of political participants. In the opinion of the students, by having a special black admissions board, the university would benefit as a whole from the entry of more black students.

Initially, Dean Hovde rejected SAS's demands outright. To the black students' demand that an admissions board that they would authorize would retain autonomous control on matters of acceptance and rejections, Dean Hovde replied: "I find that this is a demand that I am personally not willing to accede to."[57] The university, by this time, had already appointed several mostly white faculty members to a special board to consider black and Puerto Rican applicants. Hovde believed that the current board was sufficient to oversee the admissions of those groups. "I am strongly of the view that the present admissions committee of faculty must have final powers of admission."

In spite of Hovde's views, the members of SAS vowed to "stay until negotiations prove fruitful or until other action is deemed necessary."[58] With that, President Andrew Cordier, who was out of town at the time of the demonstration, instructed Dean Hovde to engage in negotiations with the students.[59] From 9 P.M. that night until 3 P.M. the next afternoon, Hovde and the demonstrators talked without coming to any decisions. On behalf of the faculty, the dean presented a proposal to the black students that allowed for a separate board, which the black students could choose and which would have the power to admit black students, with the review of an "arbitration panel." The black students quickly rejected the offer on the grounds that they demanded an autonomous board that would have to answer to no other power in matters of black and Puerto Rican admissions.

By 3 P.M. the next day, several hundred people had gathered outside of Hamilton Hall. As the observers waited for news from the university about the board, Kenneth Clark, the City University of New York psychologist, as well as several faculty members, attempted to reach an agreement with the sixteen SAS members remaining inside Hamilton. Clark, a Columbia University alumnus and arbitrator for the spring 1968 protest, was against the idea of a separate black admissions board, as he believed it was "separatism" on behalf of SAS.[60] Again the faculty put forth a proposal, and once again the students rejected it.

Meanwhile, outside the building nearly two hundred white followers of SDS marched and chanted "Racist Admissions Must Go!"[61] SDS showed up in support of SAS's demands and presented a list of its own demands. They included open admissions to Columbia and Barnard for all black and Latino "working-class" students from the neighboring schools, no tuition for the students, automatic bachelor's degrees despite their grades, and a change of course material to better suit black and Puerto Rican students. SDS explained that its demand for "open admissions . . . seeks to break down the elitist, racist nature of the university which excludes people by race and class under the guise of high standards and 'objective' tests. It works towards uniting Columbia students with the struggles of high school students and community people."[62] While SDS's demands must have seemed noble to the radical group's members, there was little to no possibility of the university accepting or even acknowledging such demands. If the radical group made the demands as a means to expose the lack of recruitment for black and Latino students, then it probably achieved its goal. If the group, however, expected the Ivy League school to take seriously its demands, then its struggle was futile. By making such extreme demands, the white group made SAS's demands seem more reasonable and legitimate.

The university, not achieving much progress with SAS through negotiation, was under pressure to vacate the protesters from the admissions office. Very strategic in their planning, the students of SAS staged their protest just as the admissions office prepared to send out 1,200 acceptance and 2,100 denial letters to high school students across the nation.[63] This meant that the longer SAS drew out their demonstration, the longer the university had to wait to notify those students. Meanwhile, high school students who had not heard from Columbia might choose to attend another university. With that in mind, on the night of April 15, the university presented the students with a restraining order issued by the New York Supreme Court. At 2:45 A.M. on April 16, the sixteen black students who had occupied the admissions office for almost two days bolted out of the front doors of Hamilton Hall, scattering in different directions. The choice to leave the office came after Ted Van Dyk, vice president of public affairs, promised the students that the administration would address each of the issues that led to the demonstration as well as the demands SAS had made during its occupation of Hamilton.[64]

Before withdrawing from the office, SAS issued a statement, warning that if the university did not accede to their demands, the controversy would "push this isolated racist bastion over the cliff in Morningside Park down into Harlem for its first confrontation with reality."[65] The statement referred to the support that SAS received and was continuing to receive from the black community of Harlem. Affirming the statement, Victor Solomon, who had protested on behalf of the community against the university's gymnasium the year before, stepped forward again. As director of New York Congress of Racial Equality, he stated: "We are back here again. We were here just about this same time last year. . . . We have come to fulfill a pledge."[66] Solomon proclaimed that "the demands of you black students are as legitimate as apple pie."[67]

The push for increased black and Puerto Rican admissions did not just affect the college students but also some high school students as well. After leaving Hamilton Hall, the leadership of SAS announced plans for a one-day strike that would take place on April 17. Just before midnight on April 16, however, the group canceled its plans to allow SDS to conduct a rally involving local black high school students, which would start at approximately noon the next day on Columbia's campus. Representing a group called "Soul Unlimited," one black high school student explained why the younger students wanted to protest against the university. "One day soon, many of us may want to matriculate here at Columbia University. . . . This racist admissions policy here at Columbia has to go or we'll help close it down and no one will go here."[68] The high school students provided an interesting angle to the story, as the chances of a student from Harlem attending Columbia had been conspicuously slim in the past. Even Columbia officials acknowledged as much throughout the 1960s. In May 1968 then vice president Truman admitted that most of the black students that Columbia recruited came from the South and Washington, D.C.; very few came from the black neighborhood that sat just below the university.[69]

By inviting the high school students onto campus, SDS caused a controversy. Many black university students believed that SDS was using the younger black students to validate its own white protest. Believing this, only a few members of SAS showed up at the rally. To keep the focus on black issues, many of the black students held to a code of strict separation from the protest efforts of the white radicals. The members of SAS had espoused this belief in the spring of 1968, when the group asked white students to leave Hamilton Hall so that it could keep its protest focused on the proposed gymnasium in Morningside Park. One black university student explained that it was necessary for SAS to "[hip] the brothers in high school to a lot of things about their cooperating with whites."[70]

As Black Power was in full thrust, its politics influenced the actions of the SAS members. From the Black Power movement, the students learned that coalitions between black and white groups were generally not, in the end, advantageous for the black group. In *Black Power*, authors Ture and Hamilton explained, "Black people must ultimately come to realize that such coalitions [between white and black groups], such alliances have not been in their interest. They are 'allying' with forces clearly not consistent with the long-term progress of blacks."[71]

Remaining consistent with their actions the spring before, the members of SAS made sure that they distanced themselves from SDS, who wanted to achieve different goals. SDS demanded the release of twenty-one Black Panthers for their purported part in a bomb plot; the eradication of the Reserve Officers' Training Corps; the cessation of military recruiting and research on campus; and the availability of 197 university-owned apartments to community usage. SDS maintained that the goals of the black students concerning the university's admissions policies were primary to any of the demands that it was making. In this way, SDS again played a supportive role for the black students who were protesting. During the protest in 1968 and in 1969, however, the goals of SDS were not absolutely analogous to those of SAS.

SAS made sure that SDS's role in its struggle was clear: "If SDS is to be relevant to this struggle, [it] must be subservient, and the black students must be in the vanguard."[72] Again, the black students fell in line with the philosophies of Ture and Hamilton: "Black Power simply says: enter coalitions only after you are able to 'stand on your own.'"[73] It was important for the black students to not let SDS co-opt their movement by playing too large of a role in their struggle for increased admissions and the black institute. The students of SAS were, at this point, powerful enough to stand independently because of their victory over the university's gymnasium and because of the support that the Harlem community offered it. As a group that had shown its unity and strength, SAS was able to enter into a coalition on stable ground.

Others in the community agreed with the sentiment of Ture and Hamilton and even offered further suggestions. "Do not allow the SDS to use you to disrupt; . . . their interest is not in your education or welfare," wrote one concerned community member to the *New York Amsterdam News*.[74] "It is up to you to see through groups like SDS (Students for Destroying Schools). . . . Put SDS down, stand up!" The community member referred to SDS's national reputation, but also to the way the mostly white group left buildings in disarray after their previous demonstrations on the Morningside Heights campus. For example, on April 17, the night of the rally, SDS had entered Philosophy Hall only to leave it in shambles with furniture broken and papers scattered. Such was the case in the previous year's protest, but in that instance the group vandalized Philosophy as well as three other halls. An article in the *Village Voice*, a liberal periodical centered in New York, claimed that "disruption is the game they [SDS] play best," as the group was, at its core, anarchist.[75] This was in contrast to SAS, whose members, the article contended, "don't want to destroy the University, they want to use it as a lever to pry the black man loose from poverty."[76]

While SDS waged its own separate protest, in part to support SAS, the students of SAS continued to negotiate with the administration. In addition to the original two demands concerning admissions, SAS made the acceptance of the twenty-five-member interim board to oversee its proposed black institute a nonnegotiable demand.[77] The group also called for a campuswide evacuation on April 22, 1969.[78] SAS chose an evacuation instead of a strike because it wanted to give the administration a peaceful environment in which to decide on the protesters' demands. In a press release on April 22, President Andrew Cordier offered his opinion of the proposed interim board. He agreed that there should be an interim board. His agreement, however, was very conditional. He suggested fifteen members instead of twenty-five, denied the board the right to "hire faculty and staff," agreed to let the board coordinate all programs concerning "the study of the Black experience at Columbia University," denied the board the right to be "responsible only to the trustees," and agreed to grant an initial $100,000 budget for the board.[79] Finally, the president indicated that the validation of the interim board would be contingent upon the will of the College Committee on Instruction, composed of various faculty members and department chairs. Despite Cordier's concessions, his conditional response to their demands dissatisfied the members of SAS. "He wants to consult and discuss, we want the Interim Board," stated Marvin Kelley, a junior and member of SAS. Unwilling to negotiate on those terms, SAS denounced Cordier's offer.

SAS's proposed interim board met stiff opposition from the faculty. Many members of the faculty were against releasing the traditional power of the faculty to hire and promote other members. One economics professor, Peter Kenen, considered the demand for an autonomous board "unreasonable."[80] "No division can be given complete autonomy in budgetary matters and complete power in faculty appointments," he emphasized. History professor Steven Bruchey concurred: "The faculty must have the final right to decide on these issues." If the university allowed any group to do so, Bruchey asserted, "the essential structure of the university would be in jeopardy." Ironically, this argument fell in line with the argument that the administration and trustees had made during the spring 1968 protest. Then, university officials asserted that the right to decide on university matters must remain in the hands of the administration and trustees because if they relinquished too much to the faculty and students, the structure of the university would also be jeopardized. In spite of different functions and locations, the faculty and administration were similar in that they refused to share whatever power they maintained.

Many of the faculty members' decisions to oppose the board came after observing another Ivy League university's acquiescence to a black student group's demand to participate in the appointment and granting of tenure to faculty in the newly formed black studies program at Harvard University.[81] After their own week-long demonstration, the members of Afro were able to achieve this most controversial demand. The victory of the students at Harvard was very rare, and the majority of faculty members at Columbia wanted to ensure that the administration did not capitulate under the pressure of student protest.

As the end of the school year quickly approached, SAS was running out of time to reach its goals of creating a black institute and a separate admissions board. Throughout the remainder of the semester and the summer break, SAS was fairly quiet, and the administration was content to let the group's protests fade, making no decisions on either of the two major proposals. With students leaving campus and concentrating their efforts on non-school-related items (such as work), the coming of summer gave the university the advantage in this battle for control.

"Black Admissions Board Denied," read a headline in the *Spectator* on October 6, 1969. Paul Mendelson, assistant director of the College Admissions Office, reported that after serious consideration, more than one admissions board was unnecessary. He explained that "in choosing freshmen, we [already] evaluate blacks on different criteria because often they haven't received a fair break.... [W]e bend over backward to make some adjustment for them."[82] Wondering who the "we" was that Mendelson had referred to, SAS suggested that if there were a black admissions board, there would be no need for the admissions office to do any "bending or adjusting" to review black applicants. Still, though, SAS's efforts did have some positive results. The number of accepted black students in the college rose from 58 in the 1968–69 school year to 115 in 1969–70.[83] This meant there were 120 black and Puerto Rican students in the college for the 1968–69 school year and 179 for the 1969–70 school year. In terms of total enrollment, the total percentage of black and Puerto Rican students jumped from 4.4 to 6.8 percent.[84] SAS's efforts would have further impact on black enrollment in the future.

The university boasted of the efforts it had made to satisfy SAS's demands and to increase black admissions. An Office of Public Information report disclosed that "the college accepted 145 out of 265 black and Hispanic student applications for 1969–1970, a ratio of about one to two. Of the 3,300 overall applicants, the College accepted 1,200, a ratio of about one to three."[85] Columbia also allocated money to black university students who traveled to different cities to recruit fellow black students, and to a weekend program that allowed potential black students to visit the campus. The office also claimed that the school gave "scholarship aid [to] an estimated 95 percent of the black students at the College . . . [with] the average scholarship grant . . . nearly $1,000 a year higher for black students than for all others." These increases and concessions were due largely to the protest efforts of SAS.

As for the black institute, SAS never reached complete satisfaction of that demand either. The Office of Public Information reported on April 29, 1969, that "the Board of Trustees . . . gave final consideration to the program submitted by the Students' Afro American Society."[86] The trustees authorized an interim board, "in accordance with the program outlined by SAS [to] design and effect a black studies program." The Committees on Instruction of the college and the University Council (a body that consisted of forty-two members of the faculty, nineteen deans, and thirteen administrators) would have to certify the program, stated the trustees.[87]

This program was, of course, not the autonomous interim board that the black group had been advocating. In spite of that fact, some months later, one black professor in pan-African history, Hollis Lynch, was confident that Columbia had the potential for a quality program. "The black studies offerings here compare very favorably to the much better patronized black studies departments at say Harvard and NYU," he claimed.[88] In the end, the university would offer courses in black studies. Carl Hovde, dean of Columbia College, compiled a list of twenty-two courses falling under the realm of black studies that would be available for patronage the next school year. It would not be an official program, but it would be a step closer to one.

Professor Lynch was optimistic in the late 1960s, but somewhat less so in the 1980s. "Columbia has not done what it should," he asserted. Regarding black studies as a curriculum, Lynch claimed: "There's no question that Columbia has responded most inadequately" to the demands of a substantive program.[89] By 1984 Columbia did not have a black studies program, but it still offered courses in the area. The debate still raged over whether an official program was viable and most beneficial for the students. One of the obstacles, according to the associate dean of the College of Arts and Sciences, Michael Rosenthal, was that "there has never been, so far as I know, any enormous feeling that a group of concerned faculty members wanted to get together" to create an official program.[90] This may have had to do with the makeup of the faculty, which in 1984 included only three tenured black professors.

That does not mean that all three would be interested in establishing a program, or that any of the remaining white professors would not be interested in constructing a program; it simply means that there was still no program available to students.

Another impediment, claimed deputy to the president for Student Affairs Philip Benson, was that "our faculties never, in my judgment, received a well thought-out proposal for a black studies program."[91] That argument was interesting on three levels. First, the members of SAS did deliver a proposal for an institute and program in the late 1960s, but the faculty and administrators did not accept it. Second, if Columbia had the wherewithal to recruit faculty members and acquire resources to design multimillion-dollar gymnasiums and buildings, why then could the university not make a similar effort to put forth a plan for a solid black studies program that would enrich students' education? Finally, it was most ironic to have an institution of higher learning geographically set in the middle of a black mecca that did not even offer a program that studied black people and culture. As it was, the School of Arts and Sciences would not recognize a black studies program until 1987. In 1993 the black institute came to fruition with the establishment of the Institute for Research in African-American Studies.[92] As director of the institute, Manning Marable was able to assist the university in recruiting more black faculty. Eventually Columbia would have the highest number of black faculty members in the Ivy League.[93]

Whereas in the 1960s the protesting black students of SAS could not say that they won the battle for their proposed autonomous black institute or an all-black admissions board in the way that they could say they had defeated the university's plan for a gymnasium in Morningside Park, they could say that they helped the people of their race and society by drawing attention to the very traditional and conservative ways of Columbia and many other universities. As one university publication noted, "Never before has Columbia made such a strong effort to abolish all traces of neglect of the blacks and to aid the black movement."[94] By the fall of 1969 Columbia had hired several more black professors to teach the courses it offered in black studies, as well as another black admissions counselor. Although some students considered the university's efforts as tokenism that would eventually cause more harm than good, for the time, it was progress nonetheless.[95]

The members of the faculty and admissions office, in their own opinion, had been doing all they could to help black people advance in American society. By protesting what the faculty and admissions office believed was their best, SAS made them aware that they were not, in fact, keeping time with society. Different from ever before, young people wanted control, students wanted control, and most importantly for this protest, young black students wanted to control their university.

Outside of Columbia University, black people were fighting for their right to participate in the institutions that for hundreds of years had not let them do so. The students who were protesting had themselves experienced the negative results of the "separate but equal" experiment and attempted to reverse those effects. They did so by employing Black Power to increase the admissions of black and Puerto Rican people to the university and by trying to broaden the amount of knowledge about black people with their proposal for the black institute. In taking seriously the rhetoric of the Black Power movement and attempting to put its ideology (redefinition and political modernization) to use, the members of SAS were able to help change a traditionally white and exclusive institution for the better.

Additionally, the members of SAS exercised their rights as Americans. As the United States is a democracy, in theory, its citizens have an obligation to protest what they believe is wrong, and that was what the members of SAS did. Putting democracy into practice, the black protesters at Columbia University provided an example of how to effectively deal with the grievances that people have against their university, society, or government. Ray Brown, who graduated in May 1969, looked back on his and SAS's protest efforts and recalled that it did not matter so much whether they won or lost any particular battle, but how the students as black people fared in the larger context of society.[96]

7

Striking Similarities
Columbia, the Ivy League,
and Black People

What happened at Columbia University in the 1960s was very much a local matter; however, it was not entirely a unique situation. As a white institution that existed in a city, Columbia's problems matched those of similar institutions. For instance, Harvard, Yale, and the University of Pennsylvania all faced space conflicts in their urban settings. And although schools like Cornell were located in rural areas, they, like Columbia, had strained relationships with black people as well.

It is not hard to understand why black people resented institutions like Ivy League universities. Many of these universities rested very near to urban communities but rarely admitted black students or hired black professors. As was the case with Columbia, they did occasionally hire black people, but typically to fill staff positions. Eventually, in the late 1960s, many of the Ivy League schools began recruiting and admitting larger numbers of black students.[1] In the process of doing so, however, conflict arose between those students and the universities over issues of curriculum and housing as well as the treatment of the students themselves on campus. As the tentacles of Black Power reached out across the nation, even the most elite institutions felt the impact of the movement. This chapter will place Columbia in the larger context of elite white educational centers that fostered tenuous relations with not only black residents but also black students in the era of Black Power.

The Ivy League universities most similar to Columbia in setting were Harvard, Pennsylvania, and Yale. Like Columbia, these universities dealt with issues of expansion. Harvard, whose main campus is in Cambridge, Massachusetts, moved outward into working-class ethnic and black neighborhoods in the same way that Columbia encroached into West Harlem. Similarly, the University of Pennsylvania increased its landholdings in West Philadelphia, a largely black area. The situation was the same for Yale University, as it expanded into the poor neighborhoods of New Haven, Connecticut.

As did New York City, Cambridge underwent urban renewal. Universities like Harvard and the Massachusetts Institute of Technology called Cambridge home. After the Second World War, many black migrants moved from the South and settled in Roxbury, a neighborhood bordering Cambridge. Like Harlem, the economic life of Roxbury boomed and then declined in the postwar years. Just as Morningside Heights and Harlem residents wanted to improve their community, Cambridge community members desired a more vibrant residential area. Although the local residents wanted to improve, they did not want to destroy homes. The city was in a difficult position because the lower-income neighborhoods did not produce as much in tax revenue, so it was an attractive prospect to allow large institutions to purchase land and buildings. Although Harvard did not pay taxes per se, the university did make yearly contributions to the city.

Harvard, which was established in 1636, observed the changes in the surrounding Cambridge neighborhoods over the years and, like Columbia, went on the offensive. John Harvard built the university in Cambridge, not Boston, to avoid the entrapments of the immoral life that the city wrought.[2] Describing Harvard and two other elite universities' proximity to the urban environment, author Kermit Parsons noted: "By 1920, Harvard and MIT found themselves near the center of a great metropolis; . . . Columbia was again in the heart of New York, and the University of Pennsylvania was still in the middle of Philadelphia."[3] To make space for itself, Harvard expanded.

When, in the 1960s, the nation's oldest university expanded into the neighboring areas, the residents and students from Harvard attempted to keep the university from destroying homes in the community. At Cambridge City Council meetings, various residents raised their concerns about renewal plans. In May 1962 some three hundred citizens attended a council meeting to protest the initiative to develop their part of the city. When one advocate of renewal referred to the homes in the area as "blight," a council member representing the sentiment of the crowd exclaimed that "homes are not blight!"[4]

Still, Harvard, like Columbia, wanted to find a way to encourage its faculty to live closer to the university. One Harvard student attempted to describe the situation: "The University today is in the position of a man about to be eaten by cannibals. . . . At the moment, the cannibals are in the form of the

Boston metropolitan area. . . . The fully matured product is visible in the slum-surrounded university like Columbia or Chicago."[5] The student further suggested that "it is hard enough to find good teachers. Inducing them to live in slums is next to impossible. . . . The only alternative is to attack the existing pattern through urban renewal." In essence, housing was available, but the type of housing that was open did not appeal to the faculty. If Harvard could have replaced the existing low-rent housing with high-rise apartments and row houses, then the university had a better opportunity to steer middle-income families back to the neighboring areas.[6] Thus the Cambridge Advisory Committee, a group sympathetic to Harvard's desire to expand, urged the university to invest as much as possible in real estate.[7]

During and shortly after the Second World War, rent control was available to residents in Cambridge. In the late 1950s, when the state and federal governments repealed rent control, the cost of housing spiked. At the same time, the amount of available housing quickly decreased. Because of the higher rents, many families had to leave buildings that Harvard owned. One critic of Harvard's expansion claimed that the university had driven many of the Irish residents away by raising prices. That was the same tactic that Columbia used in Harlem. As Harvard acquired and razed residential buildings, the university constructed new housing units for middle-income families. After clearing away the Irish in the mid-1960s, the critic maintained, Harvard set its eyes on the black neighborhoods of northern Roxbury. From a seemingly defenseless position, residents argued that by establishing rent control again, housing could remain affordable and the nature of the neighborhood would not have to change.

By 1969 Harvard and MIT owned over 10 percent of Cambridge's land. Moreover, Harvard did not pay taxes but made a contribution of sorts to the city. Of course, few city officials believed that the contributions that Harvard made were satisfactory and appropriate for the amount of property that the university owned. Indeed, private owners paid taxes at a much higher rate than the contributions that Harvard made. Lawrence Eichel, author of *The Harvard Strike*, wrote: "The only tangible result of the universities' presence that most of the city's residents can detect is an intense pressure on the housing market which caused their rents to skyrocket."[8]

Some of the students on Harvard's campus did not believe that the university's expansion was important enough to displace residents. The members of the Harvard chapter of SDS and the Worker-Student Alliance (WSA) coalesced to fight on behalf of the Cambridge community members who faced eviction or high rents because of the university. Noting that Harvard had purchased some 1,100 housing units in the 1950s and 1960s, the WSA accused the university of trying to make working-class Cambridge into a rich and middle-class depot. In fact, WSA referred to Harvard as the "Urban Imperialist," and the student group attempted to call attention to the fact that the university moved black and poor residents further back into Boston. The WSA demanded that the university roll back the rents of the tenants in the buildings Harvard owned to the rental rates of 1968.[9] Similarly, SDS distributed flyers in the campus residence halls urging Harvard to end its expansion.

Aware of the potential for public controversy, Harvard assigned Professor James Wilson to form a committee that would study the impact of Harvard's expansion on the city. Wilson's committee suggested that Harvard construct more low-income housing so that the university could help to ease the housing crisis in Cambridge. The committee, in a preliminary report, also indicated that Harvard had the need to expand, but that it should do so in cooperation with the Cambridge community. Interestingly, these were the same observations made by a committee at Columbia in the mid-1960s.[10]

In the cool spring of 1969, Harvard University witnessed unrest that could only remind one of the Columbia disturbances the year before. On April 9 hundreds of students, under the leadership of the nation's largest SDS chapter, entered University Hall, the administration building. The dissidents called on the university to respond to their demands concerning curtailment of expansion into the neighboring community, the ousting of the ROTC program, and the implementation of a black studies program. During their occupation of University Hall, the students paralyzed the administrative operations of the university.

Recalling the weeklong occupation of buildings at Columbia University that subsequently led to other protests and strikes, the next morning Harvard University's president, Nathaniel Pusey, immediately called the police onto campus to prevent further escalation of the situation. As did many of the observers and participants in the 1968 Columbia police action, students at Harvard claimed that the police used excessive force in removing them from the occupied building. Arguing that the police had responded brutally and that the university ignored their demands, the Harvard SDS organized a campuswide strike just as Columbia's SDS had done the previous spring. SDS again had managed to radicalize the mostly white, conservative-minded student body of a northern Ivy League university with the help of police action. As many followers had predicted, the New Left group's plan to effect change within the American university appeared to be working in the North.

Backing the mostly white SDS of Harvard was the Association of African and Afro-American Students (Afro). In consideration of the black group's potential influence, SDS added a demand to its list that it had created while occupying University Hall for a black studies program. Although Harvard had already appointed a "Standing Committee" on black studies earlier in the year, Afro rejected the committee's proposal because it did not allow for student participation in choosing faculty and curriculum. Also, the committee had recommended that black studies not stand on its own as a major, but rather in conjunction with the other academic fields. Outraged, the black students of Afro joined the SDS protest, bringing along with them an outlined proposal of their version of the black studies program.

Believing that the disunity of the faculty at Columbia was one cause for the university's disintegration during the 1968 protest, the faculty at Harvard pushed for unity. One Harvard faculty member suggested that at places like Columbia the faculty was not completely loyal to the university, but at Harvard the faculty was much more faithful. "Here at Harvard," the professor boasted, "the faculty is more loyal and committed to the university, regardless of their political opinion, than at . . . Columbia."[11]

With that, on April 17, 1969, the faculty of Harvard submitted a resolution to the administration. The faculty urged the university to discontinue its ties with the Department of Defense through the ROTC program and also offered a plan that would slow the university's expansion into nearby Cambridge neighborhoods and help relocate the local residents who fell victim to the school's accrual of land. James Wilson, whom the university had charged with studying the effects of expansion on the neighboring community, greatly influenced the faculty's position on slowing expansion.

After explaining to his colleagues that his committee was university-sanctioned and not part of any demonstration, Wilson urged the faculty to endorse several of the committee's suggestions. First, he requested that the university create a position for a university official in the way of external issues that involved real estate purchases and management. That person could be responsive to the community's concerns as well as those of the university. Wilson also suggested that the university create a standing committee consisting of administrators, faculty members, and students who would confer with the official in charge of external issues. Finally, and most pertinent to the demonstration at hand, Wilson recommended to the faculty that the university create housing for low- and moderate-income residents, do better in relocating those impacted by expansion, and build on vacant sites for student and faculty housing. The faculty agreed to include Wilson's recommendation as part of its resolution.

Lastly, the faculty voted to wait on the subject of black studies until April 22.[12] The fellows (a title similar to trustees) of Harvard quickly accepted the faculty's suggestions on the issues of expansion and the ROTC in order to quell the unsettling disturbance that was quickly gaining national notoriety. Regarding expansion, the Harvard Corporation (board of trustees) issued a statement. It read in part: "Any future expansion of the university which involves the elimination of housing will include provision for relocating existing tenants."[13] Columbia had also assisted residents with the relocation process. "Moreover, the university will at the earliest feasible time undertake to replace 179 dwelling units for non-Harvard occupants in appropriate locations in the Cambridge area and to build other housing for Cambridge residents as fast as we can, subject to the ability to obtain adequate financing from the Federal Government or elsewhere," the statement read. The corporation's statement must have pleased some of the protesting students as well as some of the community residents: the majority of students voted to suspend the strike for a week.[14] Had Columbia taken similar steps in regard to expansion and community relations, perhaps the gym issue would not have erupted as it did.

Upset that their demands had ranked so low on the faculty's list of priorities, Afro members took their grievances back to the larger group of SDS members to discuss further action. In doing so, the black members of Afro may have stepped out of line with the protocol that Black Power advocates like Stokely Carmichael and Charles Hamilton had set for black organizations in their book *Black Power*. In that volume, the two warned black groups to beware of making alliances with larger white liberal groups, which is what Afro intended to do with the mostly white SDS. The authors of *Black Power* made it clear, however, that effective alliances could be made between a black and a white group only when the power was equally shared. In this instance, the leadership of Afro might have forgone Carmichael and Hamilton's admonishment or it might have believed that its group was cohesive enough to enter an alliance with a larger white group. In any event, the students at Harvard had learned from their observation of the Columbia protest that, while a small minority of black or white students could make noise separately that would attract the attention of the administrators, together they could make enough noise to force the administration to capitulate to any reasonable demand. As a unified group, Afro and SDS threatened to extend the strike if their university did not meet all of their demands, including that concerning black studies. One member of Afro, Myles Lynk, admonished the university: "If the strike is discontinued by the majority, it forces many minority groups into actions which are less moderate and less effective," suggesting the possible use of more destructive tactics.[15]

Recognizing the warning, the faculty, true to its word, met and approved the black studies program. On April 22, 1969, the students at Harvard made history. The faculty of arts and sciences gave "Negro students a voting voice in the appointment of professors in Negro Studies."[16] Passing Afro's resolution 251 to 158, the faculty not only allowed students to take part in the employment of faculty for black studies but also created a "full-fledged department."[17] Outside the faculty meeting, the students of Afro celebrated another victory for student power.

Although some of the scenarios were different, the overall disturbance that took place in Cambridge smacked of the events at Columbia University. The issues of expansion that Harvard faced were much the same that Columbia faced. It seemed as though Harvard responded better to the student disturbance than did Columbia. Although Harvard's expansion problems did not end, the mixed group of students worked quite well together. At both Harvard and Columbia, a fairly small (70–80 members) black student group and SDS realized that each had something to offer that they may not have been able to attain operating solely.[18] The members of Afro provided SDS with an issue that would add legitimacy to SDS's purported goals of making the nation and the university a more democratic place by eliminating racism. In return, SDS provided Afro with an introduction to a larger white audience, which, upon mobilization, would shut the university down. Columbia University's Students' Afro-American Society (SAS) and its chapter of SDS maintained a similar kind of alliance during the protest that would, years later, help to define the 1960s rise of the New Left.[19]

In New Haven the black community drew attention to Yale's encroachment into predominantly black areas. Although New Haven is much smaller than Manhattan, there were still some similarities between the tone of the protests that community members made against the Ivy League university in New Haven and those made against Columbia. Also, Yale met with the ire of black students who wanted the university not only to treat black people outside the university with respect, but to also establish a black studies major.

During the 1960s black people in New Haven, as in many other cities across the United States, struggled to survive. One of the main problems they dealt with was police brutality. They also faced a housing shortage in the same way that black people in Harlem and Cambridge did.

Yale students protested on behalf of the black community as well. At an antiwar campus rally in October 1969, a member of the Black Student Alliance at Yale (BSAY) called for the attention of the crowd of fifty thousand demonstrators. The BSAY decried the fact that black residents had to deal with the horrors of police brutality and that the city of New Haven and the university had been conspicuously quiet on the subject. The moderator of BSAY was quick to note that both the New Haven and Yale campus police victimized black people nearby and on campus. He demanded that Yale use its resources to investigate cases of brutality and to end the practice immediately. Like the Columbia protesters who found the gym to be a local issue that students could easily identify with, students at Yale used police brutality as an identifiable local issue. The scenario was very similar considering the fact that black students forced a local issue to the forefront of the demonstration on campus a year earlier. In support of that effort, the predominantly white Yale Law Student Association issued a statement to Yale University president Kingman Brewster that insisted that he do something about the reckless behavior of the police forces on and off campus.[20]

Part of the brutality to which the students referred concerned the Black Panther party in New Haven. Under the tutelage of national party chairman Bobby Seale, the Panthers started breakfast programs and health clinics. Seale, who had been charged with the murder of another Panther, was scheduled to face trial in New Haven.[21] Seale's notoriety allowed the students to bring national attention to a local problem. The situation was the same when Stokely Carmichael, H. Rap Brown, and Tom Hayden arrived on Columbia's campus in 1968.

Black students at Yale dealt with the same problems that black students at Columbia confronted. One of the issues involved the campus police insistently requiring black students to show their identification cards out of suspicion that they were not students. When the students brought their grievances to university authorities, one official suggested that the black students wear badges identifying themselves. Members of the Black Law Student Union rejected the idea, explaining that white students did not have to don badges to identify themselves.[22] Of course the problem went deeper than the badges: the union was concerned that there seemed to be an imbalance in the number of black people directly outside the university and the number in the university. That was the same concern that members of SAS had at Columbia. Like SAS, members of the union demonstrated in classrooms to dramatize the issue of police harassment. Eventually, the Black Law Student Union in coalition with radical supporters decided to strike at Yale Law School.

At the main campus, the Black Student Alliance at Yale had won a victory for a black studies program. The students on Yale's campus appealed to the faculty and administration to provide a more diverse education for Yale's learners. As at Columbia and Harvard, the students viewed black studies not just as part of a university curriculum, but also as a program that belonged to and was supposed to benefit the larger black community. In 1969 Yale accommodated BSAY's demands for black studies and undertook to create a leading program.

On a different front, the black New Haven community battled Yale as well. Like other urban Ivy League schools, Yale expanded. In doing so, of course, the university sparked controversy. Several neighborhood groups charged Yale with acting callously and greedily by purchasing a great deal of land and property that housed black and Puerto Rican residents. In a letter addressed to Yale's president, these neighborhood groups claimed that Yale valued property over people. The letter read: "Given the history of 350 years of so called democracy in America, black and Puerto Rican people know that it has never worked for their benefit. . . . Also given the recent experience . . . the city of New Haven, Yale, and the private business and industrial community essentially reflected their greatest concern for protecting and saving property rather than the lives of black and Puerto Rican citizens of New Haven."[23]

The letter demanded that "land bought or taken for the benefit of business, industry, and Yale at the expense of the communities of New Haven be returned immediately, free of charge, in conjunction with the city of New Haven." It further demanded that Yale establish "an on-going, revolving defense fund of $1,000,000 for all black and Puerto Rican citizens arrested and/ or charged with a crime." The next demand was that "Yale and the Redevelopment Agency of the City of New Haven immediately meet the costs of a minimum of 10,000 housing units to provide decent housing for inner-city residents . . . at reasonable rents that low-income families can afford." The letter also stated that it wanted Yale to establish educational, health, and day-care facilities that would be available to the residents of New Haven free of charge. Other demands included Yale donating $10 million to a New Haven planning group similar to the Architects Renewal Committee of Harlem; that Yale admit and provide scholarships for all black and Puerto Rican graduates of New Haven high schools; and that Yale Law School provide free legal services to community residents. The letter was signed by members from the Hill Neighborhood Corporation, United Newhallville Organization, Dixwell Neighborhood Corporation, Del Junta for Progressive Action, Fair Haven Neighborhood Corporation, Dwight Neighborhood Corporation, and the West Rock Neighborhood Corporation.[24]

The demands that the letter made were nearly identical to those that Harlem neighborhoods made of Columbia in the 1960s. The demographics of the neighborhoods were similar, as were the problems of poverty and housing. In essence, the community members of New Haven and Harlem wanted Yale and Columbia, the finest educational centers in the world, to contribute to the local community that surrounded the schools. If these universities claimed to be major contributors to the world, then the neighboring residents believed that the universities should start making contributions in their own neighborhoods.

To respond to the community's demands, Yale worked with an organization called the Black Coalition. In the era of Black Power, the Black Coalition pointed to the need for the black community to achieve self-determination. That meant that black residents of New Haven had to maintain some semblance of control in their neighborhoods. With that in mind, the executive director of the Black Coalition, Hugh Price (who went on to work with the Urban League and United Negro College Fund), urged Yale to make donations to the organization and allow various representatives of the community to decide on issues of housing and planning.[25] Yale, through its Council on Community Affairs, promised several large monetary contributions to the Black Coalition to be used for neighborhood development. With some of the money coming from grants and some from private donations, Yale made funds available for housing.[26] This act worked toward lessening the tension between the black community and the Ivy League university in its midst.

In a setting very much like that of Columbia in New York City, the University of Pennsylvania in Philadelphia provided the venue for another struggle for Black Power. There, students and community members alike charged the university with racism. Expansion, employment, and university admissions sparked a rebellion at Penn.

Around the same time as the spring 1968 protest at Columbia, black students at Penn led their own demonstration on behalf of the local black community. At a bank near the university, members of the Society of Afro-American Students (SAAS) protested the fact that there were no black people working for the bank. This particular issue had little to do with the students themselves, but like the members of Columbia's SAS, the student protesters from Penn believed they were acting on behalf of the community. When the bank opened on the morning of April 29, thirty members of the SAAS demonstrated in front of the bank doors. As they picketed, they did not allow the bank employees out of the building and would not let customers enter. This was the same technique that SAS was using on Columbia's campus. When the police arrived, the student demonstrators explained that the bank would not be open for business until the bank hired black employees. The demonstration ended later that morning when members of the SAAS met with university officials. Promising to help resolve the situation, the officials agreed to encourage the bank owners (whom the university officials knew) to hire two black people.[27]

By 1969 the members of SAAS moved on to another issue that directly affected the black community. Penn, like any other university in an urban environment, saw the need to expand to house more students and departments. Black student demonstrators stood with community members against Penn's plans to move into the mostly black Mantua neighborhoods of West Philadelphia. If, for the people of Harlem, Morningside Park marked a symbolic battleground where black people fought institutional expansion, then in 1969 the Walnut Center, for the residents of the Mantua neighborhood, became the same symbol for black people in West Philadelphia. As was the case with Columbia park and the gym, the University of Pennsylvania attempted to point out the fact that no residents would lose their homes if the university demolished and rebuilt over the area where the center sat. Although not a tenant building, the Walnut Center acted as an early educational center for community children. To stop the university, the Volunteer Community Resources Council (VCRC) organized members of the Mantua neighborhoods.[28]

Noting that, for the time being, Penn only planned to demolish the Walnut Center, but in order to complete its expansion program the university would have to demolish homes and displace up to five thousand residents. Indeed, like Columbia, Penn participated in a renewal plan for the neighborhoods that surrounded the university. With the sanction of the federal and local governments, Penn purchased land and buildings and began spreading outward into the nearby neighborhoods. In Morningside Park, Columbia wanted to build a gym; in the Mantua neighborhood, Penn wanted to build a University City Science Center.

The fact that Penn was expanding into poorer neighborhoods and that faculty and staff members would be conducting scientific research during the height of the Vietnam War drew the attention of radical students on campus. In February 1969 members of the Penn chapter of SDS held a rally to protest the Science Center and university expansion. In the same fashion that community members from Morningside Heights and West Harlem met at the gym construction site to protest the proposed structure, members of the Mantua neighborhood attended the event and spoke on behalf of the community. Just as members of the West Harlem Community Organization held a funeral for Morningside Park and burned in effigy Columbia officials, members of various West Philadelphia community groups and students from campus demolished likenesses of the proposed Science Center. Then, like the gym protesters, the group of several hundred Science Center demonstrators confronted Penn's president with the demand that Penn not destroy the Walnut Center in order to build the Science Center. Afterward, the group of protesters held a sit-in on campus. The members of the Society of Afro-American Students arrived to bolster the position of the demonstrators.

As Wayne Glasker, author of *Blacks in the Ivory Tower*, observed, the similarities between what happened at Columbia and Penn seemed to run deeply. The protesting group demanded to speak with Penn's trustees and refused to leave the building until the university responded to the neighborhood's issues regarding university expansion. Unlike the situation in Hamilton Hall, the protesters on Penn's campus allowed people to enter and leave the building that they occupied. Just as the community members of West Harlem supported the efforts of the students on Columbia's campus, contingents from the Mantua neighborhood showed up to demonstrate against Penn as well. Representatives from the community issued a set of demands regarding Penn's and Drexel University's (another university in the area) expansion plans. The demands indicated that Penn should return all of the land that surrounded the proposed Science Center and that Penn should provide money for housing and relocation funds for those residents that had to be displaced. After a week of sitting in, the demonstrators claimed a victory. The trustees agreed to meet with representatives from the group and even agreed to sanction an expansion oversight committee that would consult with the community about future plans. The trustees also agreed to provide relocation housing or funds to displaced residents. Furthermore, the Penn trustees pledged ten million dollars to improve the local neighborhoods by cooperating with the community members on a plan and to provide housing. The actions of the trustees prompted the protesters to end their demonstration.[29]

In 1969, at nearly the same time that the Columbia, Harvard, Yale, and the University of Pennsylvania campuses exploded, students at Cornell University in Ithaca, New York, also protested against the administration. Located on a hill in Ithaca, Cornell's setting is entirely different from that of Columbia, Harvard, Yale, or Penn. Therefore Cornell did not have to deal with the very controversial issues of urban renewal and expansion. Like the other Ivy League universities, though, Cornell had to confront Black Power as the movement swept onto campus. The tactics that Cornell black student demonstrators used to achieve their goals in some ways mirrored those that Columbia's SAS employed. In other ways, Cornell's protesters were much more extreme in the measures they took to exact concessions from their university.

Although the issues that affected students at Cornell differed in some ways from those at Columbia, some were indeed similar. Just as Columbia's SDS had protested the placement of the "IDA Six" on disciplinary probation in March 1968, the members of the Afro-American Society (AAS) at Cornell objected to the threatened suspension of six black students who, at a demonstration for a black studies program, kicked over a candy machine. They also protested Cornell's slow reaction to the burning of a cross on the lawn of a residence hall that housed mostly black women. Like the black students at Columbia who occupied Hamilton Hall in 1968 and the admissions office in 1969 to draw the world's attention to the university's insensitivity to Harlem and black America, those at Cornell seized Willard Straight Hall, the student union building, to show their frustration with racism on campus. While inside, the black demonstrators, like Columbia's white SDS members had done the previous year, demanded amnesty for their actions. In an attempt to avoid a violent situation like that at Columbia's campus the spring before, Cornell's president, James A. Perkins, eventually granted the demonstrators amnesty for their protest.

Between 1968 and 1969 there were fewer than 250 minority (including black) students on campus.[30] The troubles at Cornell concerning black students, however, dated as far back as December 1968. During that month, black students, led by the Afro-American Society, demanded a separate "black college." Some of the students had brought the idea for a separate department back to Cornell after attending a conference at Howard University concerning the move "Toward the Black University."[31] The particular "college" that the Cornell students outlined would have entailed a black studies program that the black students could partially control, which was similar to the demands of SAS at Columbia and of black student groups at other Ivy League schools.

Upset with a curriculum "geared for whites," the protesting students at Cornell claimed that the black studies program would deal with "the whole question of racism in education."[32] When a professor questioned the reasons that underlay the request for a black literature course, the president of AAS, Edward Whitfield, answered: "Why not [study black literature], people study white authors."[33] Responding to the black student's rationale, the white professor reportedly remarked: "Yes, but I think they have more important things to say." While there was the possibility that the *New York Times* had quoted the white professor out of context, his statement, Whitfield believed, pointed up the need for a black studies program.

Many of the students who formed the Afro-American Society had come to Cornell by way of a rigorous recruitment program that President James A.

Perkins had authorized in the mid-1960s. The liberal President Perkins, who earlier in his life had been exposed to the religious ways of the Quakers and had worked for the Ford Foundation (the same foundation that donated ten million dollars to Columbia University during the mid-1960s to improve its relationship with its Harlem neighbors), believed that more disadvantaged black youth should have the opportunity to attend schools like Cornell.[34] As he stated in a speech, "The integrated school and the integrated campus represent our only hopes for future understanding between black and white."[35] His philosophy differed somewhat from that of those who had preceded him, as the goal before he arrived had been to recruit black students who had similar socioeconomic backgrounds to the mostly upper-middle-class white population of the university.

The arrival of President Perkins and his philosophy, in spite of his good intentions for the races, led to the possibility of racial problems in the future. With the implementation of Perkins's program, the Committee on Special Education Projects (COSEP), Cornell began recruiting black students from impoverished ghetto areas.[36] Consequently, many of these students had been exposed to the rising Black Power philosophy that had reached black ghettoes all over America. Although these young people came from mostly impoverished areas, they were no less able as students or more prone to crime than their white counterparts, as some portrayals of black students from ghetto neighborhoods suggested. Like the members of Columbia University's SAS, the recruited black students at Cornell felt the need to band together and form their own identity in the Afro-American Society.[37]

As scholars such as William Van DeBurg and Peniel Joseph explained in their works on Black Power, many of these students prided themselves in the cultural aspects of the Black Power movement by donning the "afro" hairstyle, by wearing dashikis, and by believing in phrases such as "black is beautiful" and "I'm black and I'm proud."[38] These young learners did not represent the types of black people who were overly gratified for white institutions, such as Cornell, *giving* them the opportunity to become part of what many of the young black people called the "establishment." In fact, they made it undeniably clear that they *deserved* the chance to achieve success in American society, and that while they attended schools like Cornell, they would carve out a piece of the institution for themselves. With the esteem that many of the black students had gained from the cultural aspects of the Black Power movement, they attempted to prove that blacks were equal to whites by creating separate black quarters, culture centers, and departments. As did other black student groups around the nation, AAS at Cornell University used its members' status as students to focus on issues that dealt with racism both on and off campus.

President Perkins had made some efforts to satisfy the earlier demands of the black student group. For instance, as per AAS's request, Perkins provided black students with a dwelling that was used for "an Afro-American Center," where the students could congregate and socialize.[39] The president also met the students' demand for separate, private living quarters for black women (unlike Columbia College, Cornell was coeducational by the 1960s) when he authorized the creation of the Wari House. He reportedly made another gesture by allowing members of the Afro-American Society to fly to New York City in the university-owned plane to purchase props and decorations for the Malcolm X Day program that the group had planned.[40]

While President Perkins attempted to aid the black students' transition to Cornell, black students at the university still had other grievances. At one point in April 1968, the students occupied the office of the chair of the economics department to demonstrate against the institutionally racist remarks that visiting professor Father Michael McPhelin had purportedly made in a course on "economic development" earlier in the school year.[41] AAS grounded its accusations in the fact that McPhelin based the early part of his course on the "Western" model of economic development, which excluded the early development of economics in Africa. The black protesters also pointed to the fact that while the class dealt with such topics as poverty and the rise of the ghetto, which are in part based on race, McPhelin rarely if ever referred to African Americans unless he was discussing the racially controversial Moynihan Report.[42] More specifically, McPhelin had considered the childhood games of slum dwellers and urban poor as "sickly and perverted," and that "slums produce young people inclined toward crime and violence."

As Donald Downs, author of *Cornell '69*, noted, "The McPhelin incident inaugurate[d] the politics and pedagogy of racial confrontation at Cornell" in the late 1960s.[43] In the same way that the gymnasium issue was a catalyst for the members of Columbia University's SAS, the protest that resulted from the McPhelin incident led to larger ideological grievances against racism from Cornell's AAS. On April 4, 1968, the protest against the remaining presence of Professor McPhelin intensified as Cornell University officials called three hundred policemen to the edge of campus in case riotous behavior erupted.

Problems on campus only worsened when both black and white students found out about the sudden death of Martin Luther King Jr. Afterward, black students received threatening phone calls from "anonymous sources," while some white students in certain dormitories yelled racial obscenities and fired cap guns.[44] As did many officials at Columbia in 1968, Cornell University officials worried incessantly about the possibility of racial violence erupting. One black student warned that "white people—students—should know that threats will not continue without black response." Veering away from the nonviolent message of the slain King, another member of AAS asserted that "when Martin Luther King died, nonviolence died, baby. . . . They're [the callers] talking about they're going to kill us. I'll be goddamned if they going to kill me!" Taking a stance that Black Power activists across the nation endorsed, the student exclaimed: "Now, if you honkies think you bad enough to fuck with us, just try it!" Then, later in the year, some of the more militant black students had a near-violent confrontation with President Perkins in his office, as the members of the Afro-American Society protested the school's ties to Chase Manhattan Bank, which had allegedly invested in Apartheid-ridden South Africa.[45]

Looking back more than thirty years later, it is clear that Cornell, like Columbia University, had a history of racial tension that would culminate in a campus-shattering confrontation. Along with the McPhelin complaints, much of the 1969 protest hinged on the members of AAS's views on the illegitimacy of the administration in dealing with black students. The views and actions of those students, like those of the black students at Columbia in 1968 and 1969, were extremely politicized. They were, furthermore, meant to unsettle the white university as an institution, which had become a symbol for many black students in the late 1960s of white racism in general.

In December 1968 the Afro-American Society organized and facilitated a series of demonstrations, during which the black students broke a candy machine.[46] The university, threatening to suspend the six demonstration leaders, allowed their cases to go before a judiciary board. Like the newly implemented Joint Committee on Disciplinary Affairs at Columbia, Cornell's judiciary board consisted of several students, faculty members, and administrators. Despite the fact that Cornell students held seats on the judiciary board, the six blacks of the Afro-American Society refused to recognize the committee because no black students sat on it. Moreover, like the IDA Six of Columbia, they saw the university as a "biased authority," incapable of judging them fairly. So, while the university continued to deliberate the case, five of the students (the sixth had dropped out of school) purposefully missed their trial dates.

Four months later, on April 18, 1969, at 2:52 A.M., after trying the five students in absentia, the judiciary committee delivered its verdict. The board exonerated two of them and called for "light reprimand" (disciplinary probation for the remainder of the year) of the others.[47] Less than an hour after the board announced its decision, several black female students found a cross burning on the lawn of their residence hall, the Wari House.[48] The people who had planted the burning cross were presumably upset with the school's decision to exonerate some of the black students and to only punish lightly the remainder of them.

This event, as did the McPhelin incident, provided another motivating factor for the male-dominated black student group's protest against Cornell University that spring.[49] The members of the group would justify their actions by claiming that they were protecting black womanhood, which was an explicit part of the Black Power philosophy.[50] Many black militants, as well as mainstream historians, explained that black men had for so long been incapable of protecting their women because of the restraints that white America had placed upon black men, and consequently the black males' status as men was damaged.[51] They cite instances in American history when black men had no rights to their own families, as the families of black men were nothing more than the extended families of workers for the slave owners. The situation had not improved greatly after slavery ended, and so the frustration that black men felt from not being able to take a stand against the threats to their women further increased. By the late 1960s, however, they believed they had cast off those constraints that prevented them from achieving manhood and took up the militancy of Black Power, which made it an obligation to defend black people, especially women, at all costs. For the black men in AAS on Cornell's campus, that meant that they had to take a stand against the implied threat that came along with a cross burning. This was a chance for these men to assert their manhood and keep black women from harm.

On the other side of campus, at 6 A.M., about thirty visiting parents who were slumbering in the student union building, Willard Straight Hall, woke to the shouts of "fire!"[52] By the time the mostly white parents, who had come to the university for parents weekend, discovered that there was no fire, Afro-American Society members had ushered them out of the building with threats of fire-hose blasts if they did not move fast enough. While the black demonstrators in Straight Hall chained the inside doors shut, other members of the group became active in other parts of the campus.[53]

"We interrupt your regular broadcast for a relevant political message," announced Edward Whitfield on April 19, 1969, on the campus radio station, WVBR.[54] He berated the university for its "racist attitudes" and proclaimed that the Afro-American Society and black students would no longer tolerate them.[55] While Whitfield spoke over the radio station, the black group back at Straight Hall formed an alliance with SDS.

At this point, the events at Cornell followed a different path from those at Columbia. During the first part of the 1968 protest at Columbia, the members of SDS and SAS had attempted to engage the university as a "unified front," but they subsequently split over idealistic and strategic differences. The two groups continued to attack their university on separate fronts during the 1969 protest as well. This, however, was not the case with AAS and the Cornell chapter of SDS in 1969. From the outset, the student groups' protests were separated exclusively by race. As the members of the black group barricaded Straight Hall from the inside, the white students of SDS chose to march around the building "to support the black student demands."[56]

In Straight Hall, the members of AAS issued a list of demands. Like the Columbia demonstrators had done in Hamilton Hall in 1968, the Cornell blacks vowed not to emerge from the building until the university met all of their demands. The members of AAS wanted the school to declare the judiciary board's decision to reprimand the three black students, however lightly, "null and void."[57] The group also demanded "university legal assistance against any civil charges arising out of the occupation of the buildings; a promise that the university would press no civil or criminal charges or other forms of punishment against the occupiers and [that the university] would assume responsibility for damages to the building; twenty-four-hour police protection for the Afro-American center and the [Wari House], and an investigation into the cross-burning" that took place on the Wari House lawn.[58]

While the majority of AAS's demands were reasonable, many administrators and faculty members viewed the group's demands that the school "assume responsibility" for damaged rooms and equipment during the current protest, as well as a demand that the demonstrating students not be held accountable for the damaged vending machine of an earlier protest, as outrageous. These types of demands were typical for black and white student groups in the 1960s. The strategy was to make exorbitant demands with the idea in mind that the university would most likely respond to only a few of their demands. If this indeed occurred, then the protesting group would be in a better position in spite of losing some demands. Also, many of the groups that made demands in such a manner believed that they were forced into committing such acts and that the universities should bear the brunt of the responsibility because they had created the controversial situations.

While inside Straight Hall, Cornell's black student group added a new element to the national student protest movement. As the members of SAS did in Hamilton Hall on Columbia's campus during the 1968 protest and in the admissions office during the 1969 demonstrations, the members of the AAS at Cornell barricaded themselves in Straight Hall and refused to allow anyone (particularly white people) to enter the building without authorization from the AAS leadership.[59] Some of the students who were authorized to enter the building brought with them rifles and other weapons. Although there were campus police officers present, they were unarmed and did not confront the students they saw entering Straight Hall. Unfortunately for Cornell University, not just the campus policemen witnessed the transportation of guns to the black group inside, but so too did various reporters and press representatives.

After thirty-six hours of occupying the student union building, one hundred followers of AAS vacated Straight Hall, some carrying rifles and one even wearing bandoliers.[60] At a cottage that the black protesters had used as their headquarters, President Perkins and several other administrators signed an agreement stating that they would acquiesce to the demands of the AAS. As the administrators signed the agreement, SDS members raised their clenched fists to the black group as a sign of victory. One administrator who signed the agreement with Perkins maintained that he had done so "to prevent the growing and imminent threat to life."[61] This was, in effect, the same comment President Kirk had made when he did not order the police on the Morningside campus early on in the 1968 protest for fear that he might incite a reprisal from the black residents in Harlem. Because President Perkins did not release the authorities on Cornell's campus, the black members of AAS at Cornell claimed another victory for student power and for the black race.

In 1969 the introduction of guns at Cornell University shook the nation to its core. It had a similar effect on the nation as the mass arrest had had at Columbia the previous spring. The nation's reaction to such events was fear, bewilderment, and an acute sense of being threatened by minority groups in uprising. By this time, it was not just the politically conservative who were asserting that student protest had gone too far. By then, even some of the most liberal white and black people became fearful for the future of not just the university but society as well. Indeed, it was a fear-inspiring sight, but the most impressive thing about the introduction of firearms to the protest was that it worked. Several black students at Cornell explained that they had tried different tactics to illuminate the racial discord that took place on campus, but that the administration and the rest of campus did not receive their grievances in a manner that satisfied the group's need for answers to the racial problem.

Only when the militant black students took seriously the words of Malcolm X, who inspired much of Black Power philosophy, did Cornell, Harvard, Yale,

Penn, Columbia, and the rest of the nation sit up and take notice of what the protesting black students considered a desperate situation. Uncannily appropriate for the situations at the Ivy League schools in the late 1960s, Malcolm X made the statement in a 1964 speech that "you'll get freedom by letting your enemy know that you'll do anything to get your freedom. When you get that attitude, . . . they'll call you a 'crazy nigger' . . . or they'll call you an extremist. . . . But when you stay radical long enough and get enough people to be like you, you'll get your freedom."[62] In the spring of 1969 this advice certainly rang true for the black students at Cornell, Harvard, Yale, Penn, and Columbia.

In the case of the black student protesters at the various Ivy League universities, using the traditional channels to voice concerns did not work well and fast enough. Those students chose extreme measures like occupying buildings, inviting infamous black militants onto campus, and taking up arms to advance goals that they believed would have a positive effect on not only them, but their respective universities and communities as well. This was threatening to many Americans who could not fathom a situation so desperate on a college campus as to warrant the carrying of guns. These were people who were often neither black, nor students, nor from impoverished areas where one of the only hopes rested in education. The people with those characteristics had only the highest hopes for the benefits of education, and they forced their universities to live up to the standards that the schools themselves espoused.

Black students at Cornell genuinely believed that their lives were in danger after they found a cross burning on the lawn of the black women's residence, and after white students attempted to forcefully oust them from Straight Hall. Those black students understood realistically that they were a minority on campus and in the nation, and, if the situation came to a violent racial confrontation, they would lose their battle against white racism on that campus. That did not, however, keep them from defending themselves and making their demands clear.

The situation could have been much worse had it not been for the wise capitulation of President Perkins, who did not want to witness at Cornell a scene reminiscent of Columbia's a year before. Although he was fully capable (and in many ways justified) of calling in city and state authorities, he avoided the imminent violence that could have potentially occurred if he had done so. While many of the faculty members criticized his decision to accede to the demands of AAS, Perkins saved Cornell from the far worse fate of having a shoot-out on campus between militant black students, white counterprotesters, and New York authorities. If that meant temporarily sacrificing "academic freedom," about which some professors worried, then his decision was well worth it.

Several professors and administrators believed that Cornell had lost its respectability and authority in the 1969 protest, and in truth it might have done so in many ways; however, the university gained a great deal as well. The school gained a black studies department that would rank among the best in the nation. The school also gained a more in-tune relationship with its students and their needs, which is extremely important to the validity of any university. Most of all, however, the school gained the loyalty of a group of black students who were committed to Cornell University and its betterment, and who sought to help the institution cleanse itself of racism. In fact, one of the advocates for AAS's protest later became a member of Cornell's Board of Trustees.[63] That was not the complete loss that some critics of the president's decision had lamented.

The efforts of the protesters at these elite schools helped to bring about change in their respective Ivy League universities. At Columbia in 1968, the black students of SAS demanded that the school permanently abandon the gymnasium in Morningside Park, and the university did so eventually, reconsidering its expansionist policies. "The decision of the university trustees to meet with community representatives before deciding if construction of . . . [the] gymnasium should be abandoned" was announced by President Kirk on May 8, 1969, and now "the time for protest has passed."[64] The next year, the black students did not win their protest demand for an all-black institute, but they did force Columbia to offer more courses in black history and culture. SAS, because of its 1969 protest, also coerced the university admissions office into admitting more black students than ever before. To the black students, the school's decision to halt the construction of the gym, to provide more classes on black history and culture, and to admit more black students was the manifestation of their highly organized protest and determination to dramatize the university's racist ways and slowness to reform. Involving community members and Black Power advocates in their protest, SAS forced Columbia to examine its relationship with the neighboring communities and the nation in general.

Due to the protests at Columbia, Harvard, Yale, Penn, and Cornell universities, the nation's most prestigious institutions of higher learning changed their outlooks on their roles in society. As black citizens fought for and gained civil rights, and as thousands of soldiers died in Vietnam, the students, community members, and administrators struggled in the battle to uproot racism on campus. The result was the rise of black studies and black culture centers as well as further black representation on campus in the form of students, professors, and administrators at universities across the nation. Furthermore, these universities became much more aware of their settings and roles as members of a larger community. During the turbulent years of the 1960s, students at Columbia and on campuses across the country learned valuable lessons. As one student noted, they found out that they could "exert their collective energies, their power, to bring about change in their local community."[65]

8

Is It Over Yet?

The Results of Student and Community Protest

"The Columbia rebellion was one event in this long term growth in people's consciousness," suggested Mark Rudd almost two decades after the start of the 1968 student demonstrations at Columbia University.[1] The same, presumably, could be said about the later demonstrations of 1969. When Rudd referred to consciousness, he understood it to mean the people's (particularly the young people of the 1960s) awakening and reaction to the problems that had been eating away at a functional American society. Most of America had not, until the late 1960s, been aware that it was in a state of unconsciousness. That was when idealistic, fresh-minded young people like those at Columbia disrupted the "American Dream." This chapter will discuss the aftereffects of the demonstrations that took place at Columbia.

That the demonstrations at Columbia were part of a larger social movement is undeniable. And it was not at all surprising that students and young people took the lead in these efforts to deal with an ailing nation. During the latter half of the twentieth century, young people were typically providing the energy and fervor to various social movements in the United States, especially the Civil Rights movement. Students like Linda Brown and the "Little Rock Nine" drove home the point that racism had to be eradicated from education. In Birmingham, the children who endured the utmost human savagery during the "Children's Crusade," as well as the four young girls who died in a church bombing, provided fuel to the fight that civil-minded Americans would make against racial discrimination. Furthermore, students like Lloyd Gaines, the "Greensboro Four," and James Meredith did a great deal to open the doors for integration and activism both in higher education and in society in general. The same is true for the SNCC and CORE members who traveled to the South to desegregate businesses and to register voters, and who eventually tried to find a way for black people to achieve black power.

The line that these early activists drew was precisely that which the participants in the Columbia University demonstrations of 1968 and 1969 followed. They took the knowledge, experience, and morality that they had gained from these events and applied them to their situation at Columbia, a university that found itself in very close proximity to a black ghetto; a university that had ties to war research; and a university that prized power over morality.

Looking back on the events that took place at the school on the Heights, several things went wrong. First, the university had been resting on its laurels and not striving to progress with the times. This was the way of many universities, but Ivy League universities in particular. Next, the Columbia University administration did not listen to its most prized asset: its students. Also, Columbia, with all its powerful trustees, administrators, and dignitaries, could not find a way to deal cordially and effectively with its neighbors who were from different racial and economic backgrounds. And Columbia, as did many other universities at the time, chose to go the route of the military-industrial complex over the way of the concerned community member that happens to be an educational institution. Finally, and most importantly, the university waited too long to deal with these problems.

Until 1968 Columbia University had been resting on its laurels as one of the nation's most prestigious institutions of higher learning. Many in the administration believed that the university had been headed in the right direction; then the turmoil of 1968 and 1969 occurred and unsettled nearly all members of the university. Almost as if it were resting from the drama that had unfolded in the spring, months after the initial 1968 protest, the university became very quiet. President Andrew Cordier, the successor of Grayson Kirk, stated in 1969, "The calm and unity of the University . . . have provided for the healthy expression of divergent views in the dialogue necessary for restructuring the University."[2] The demonstrations brought to the members of the university a temporary calm but also a sense of urgency to do something positive for the university before it lapsed back into a state of complacency.

Radical historian Howard Zinn made similar remarks in the months following the 1968 rebellion in a speech he gave at Columbia University. In a speech entitled "Students and University in Our Age of Social Action," he explained that "if students are fighting for a more democratic university . . .

[then] the chances are that the university will insist on remaining the traditional university in the face of those needs."[3] Zinn was correct. Just after the spring 1968 incident, Alan Temple, chair of the Special Committee of Trustees, stated in an interview: "With respect to the progress of the committee work, I think the correct description is controlled haste. . . . I would warn my listeners against expecting results too early[;] changes in the basic organizational structure and the statutes of this University will require time, varied research, hearings, study on the opinions of people who have both expectations and concerned interest, reconciliation, and drafting. This cannot be done in a short time."[4]

Because institutions like Columbia had a reluctance to move away from what Zinn characterized as "traditional," there arose a need for students to jolt the university into action. In his opinion, the reluctance on behalf of the institution justified the demonstrations of the students. "If you have an encrusted system of parliamentary change—which means no change at all, well, perhaps gradual change over centuries—then I think the acts of civil disobedience, like occupying buildings, are very minor, they're really moderate acts."[5]

Some Columbia authorities would probably have disagreed with his judgment of the students' campus occupations as being moderate, but Zinn went on to place his argument in context. "When you consider the range of social action as it is taking place in a world of revolution and a world of social change, the kind of acts of civil disobedience that we have seen in the United States in the past few years on the campuses or in the ghettoes, are the mildest form of social action."[6] Zinn was correct. In the late 1960s, serious, bloodletting revolution had occurred in places like Latin America, Europe, and Africa. Often young people, the age of those who attended Columbia University, started these revolutions for political reasons, such as the need to overthrow colonial regimes. After introducing bloodshed, these young people achieved those goals. Universities were not spared from the revolutionary spirit of these young people. To be sure, the Sorbonne in Nanterre, France, and Frankfurt University in West Germany provided settings for that generation of young people's revolutionary acts. As one French slogan went, "We won't ask; we won't demand; we will take and occupy."[7] Indeed, the acts of rebellion at Columbia University in New York were in line with acts that were occurring (or would occur) in London, Spain, Rome, Poland, Czechoslovakia, the West Indies, and Mexico.[8]

To avoid more acts of rebellion and revolution, universities learned from the crisis at Columbia. Long Island University quickly invited students and faculty members to participate in a decision-making committee for the university. The chancellor explained that the student body and faculty as a whole chose the representatives. Radical students all over the country were crying "two, three, many Columbia's." One journalist from the *San Francisco Examiner* explained that "for Columbia, you see, is the temple, the mecca, the veritable Vatican of the American intelligentsia. . . . Hundreds of men who never went to Columbia regard it as their spiritual alma mater."[9]

Revolution for the American students was, in reality, improbable, but rebellion fell well within the boundaries of the American students' behavior. As Michael Hunt has explained, the United States is much more prone to reform than it is to revolution because of the fact that most Americans are too deeply entrenched in capitalism to revolt against it. Simply put, most U.S. citizens have too much to lose and not enough to gain should a revolution occur. With the middle class growing as it was during the 1960s, it was improbable that the majority of its members would be willing to sacrifice their material wealth for the sake of those below them in status.[10]

To many young people in the late 1960s and early 1970s, however, it must have seemed as though a revolution were at hand. Many of the young radicals of that generation believed that they would be the ones to start it. At least that was what Mark Rudd and other SDS members had thought. As real as Rudd thought the revolution would be, decades after, he admitted that the idea of revolution was a fallacy. As he remembered it, "I bought into the fantasy of revolution."[11] The realization that the acts of civil disobedience that the radicals had committed would not lead to revolution came with years of hindsight for Rudd.

In spite of Rudd's "fantasy revolution," according to a declassified Central Intelligence Agency document, officials in North Vietnam believed and were encouraged by the fact that an actual revolution could occur in the United States. According to the document, "American bombing raids have not seriously affected the North Vietnamese morale. . . . On the other hand, the North Vietnamese morale has been boosted considerably by the Civil Rights and 'Black Power' movement in the United States." The North Vietnamese officials were hoping "that the riots and the emergence of the 'Black Power' movement signal[ed] the beginning of a popular revolution . . . against the ruling class."[12] If this were to occur, then the communist-backed North Vietnamese would have a better chance of defeating the South Vietnamese and American forces. Revolution as a result of protest was a real possibility for some, like the North Vietnamese, who had witnessed the violence and turmoil associated with revolt.

While some of the North Vietnamese were hoping for another American revolution, some of the protesting students, like William Sales, had indicated early on in the 1968 protest that their moves to occupy buildings, to take a dean as hostage, and to get arrested were not part of an ideological revolution, but rather were part of a rebellion that would lead to the end of construction on the proposed gym, the dissolution of the relationship with the U.S. Defense Department, and better treatment of minority and poor people in the surrounding neighborhoods. Sales and Ray Brown of SAS had made this point clear when they asked the white radicals, whom Rudd led, to leave Hamilton Hall on the grounds that SAS and SDS had ideological differences. At that point, the radicalization of the student body (an SDS goal) and the end of gym construction (an SAS goal) contrasted greatly and served different purposes for the two groups. By Rudd admitting that the "revolution" for which he and the members of SDS pushed really ended up being no more than "mythology," he further validated SAS's decision to detach from SDS in both 1968 and 1969. SAS, which benefited from SDS's larger protest efforts, acted on the very tangible motive of ending construction on the controversial edifice in the adjacent neighborhood park. As Sales explained years afterward, "There was a different dynamic for black students, in a sense, to that demonstration than to the white students."[13]

One of the legacies of the Columbia demonstrations concerned violence. As Zinn explained, revolution rarely occurs without violence, and the members of the mostly white SDS, claimed a one-time chief inspector of the New York City Police Department, used this knowledge to their advantage. Twenty years after the 1968 rebellion, Sanford Garelik, who acted as chief from 1966 to 1969, made the same contentions that police officers had made during the mass removal of students. "The radical Left emphasized psychological and physical harassment against the police. Their disrespect for the law had reached the point where violence almost achieved respectability."[14] When violence occurred at the 1968 Democratic national convention in Chicago, many were not surprised, and some pointed back to the campus rebellions of the previous spring.

What Garelik considered "disrespect for the law," many young people considered lack of faith in the law and the system in general. In spite of that, Garelik correctly observed that the violence that occurred in the late 1960s drew media attention to the protesting groups and their causes.[15] That attention allowed Americans to view authority figures actually beating American young people. For those viewers, who had not been aware of the students' in some cases provocative actions, the events would have appeared to be extremely brutal. The radicals' efforts provided a model of sorts for these discontented youth who followed.

As mentioned before, this tactic was not new, as civil rights activists during the 1950s and early 1960s tried to make public the senselessness of racially motivated violence. This was how groups like SDS and leaders like Martin Luther King Jr. were able to increase societal pressure on racist authorities and policies. The shock that people received from viewing various events on television or in the newspapers deeply affected their opinions of the war in Vietnam as well. Indeed, overpowering images of violence during that era often did validate the causes of antiwar and antiracism proponents. In this way, the advent of technology influenced social change immensely. Regarding Columbia's rebellion, one observer remarked that, "thanks to the presence of the media, the events at Columbia were more widely influential than the Berkeley strike."[16] This was significant because until the 1968–69 protests at Columbia, the Free Speech movement at Berkeley had been hailed as the most renowned student power uprising at an American university.[17]

In this way, violence did benefit SDS, and that fact gave the group's members the idea that their so-called revolution was valid. It was true that if SDS had left the buildings peaceably, then the administration might have still been debating the issues that the students and community had raised. The part about SDS's protest that was most abhorrent, from Garelik's observation, was that SDS did not actually seek solutions to the problems that the group had illuminated but rather attempted to sustain its feigned revolution. If the members of SDS and the New Left bequeathed anything to future generations, lamented Garelik, it has been "a continuing disrespect for the law and an increased tolerance for lawbreakers."[18]

Garelik might have been correct to some degree. The members of SDS, and later the Weathermen, the Yippies, and what remained of the New Left, did indeed display disrespect for the law, and they even encouraged lawbreaking, but their behavior was not worse than the disrespect that white authorities had been showing for the law as it concerned black people in the United States.[19] The Kerner Report explained this phenomenon well: "A climate that tends toward the approval and encouragement of violence as a form of protest has been created by white terrorism directed against nonviolent protest, including . . . the open defiance of law and federal authority by state and local officials."[20] In simply observing the improper and illegal conduct of authorities such as those to which the Kerner Report referred, as well as the national government's response to the acts, it would have been logical to assume that disrespect and intolerance for the law was permissible. In their political platforms, leaders such as Richard Nixon and Ronald Reagan focused specifically on student demonstrators as lawbreakers, but the lawbreaking those students performed pales in comparison to that which city, state, and national figures had perpetrated in both the North and the South for years.[21]

One result of the confrontation between the civil disobedient student demonstrators and the authorities was the movement of many young people's political affiliation further to the left in the years that followed. One student who observed the demonstrations in the late 1960s shared his reflections about the event. "I realize that by giving Columbia a small jolt, a lot of good has come of it," asserted the student.[22] Others who had been part of the demonstrations found that life as a radical leftist was dangerous and potentially deadly. The *New York Times* reported in 1970 that Mark Rudd, the leader of SDS during the spring 1968 protest, had gone into hiding to escape some of the repercussions of the Columbia and other protests. Ted Gold, a former vice-chairman of the Columbia chapter of SDS, while part of a Weathermen (faction of SDS) unit that was constructing bombs for a planned attack on a non-commissioned officers' dance at a U.S. army base in New Jersey, died in 1970 by way of an accidental bomb explosion in a Greenwich Village townhouse in Manhattan.[23]

The students' move toward the left was cause for concern for many in the nation. In the *New York Post Daily,* Barry Gottehrer, who acted as special assistant to Mayor John Lindsay in 1968, later wrote, "You don't understand how the communists are behind all of this. These white kids are dupes. . . . There is money coming from the communist countries. They [the communist countries] want to start something over here."[24] J. Edgar Hoover, director of the Federal Bureau of Investigation (FBI), also believed that communist infiltration was possible. "If anything definite can be said about the Students for a Democratic Society it is that it can be called anarchistic," stated Hoover.[25] With further disdain, but no real evidence, he claimed that "the SDS is infiltrated by Communist Party members who attempt to develop discord among the youth of this country."[26]

To be sure, spreading discord to the youth was not an exclusive stronghold of the Communist party: very patriotic entertainers, civil rights activists, and even veterans hoped to reach the youth on matters that they considered immoral or hurtful to the country.[27] The chances, however, that the Communist Party of the United States of America or any other country had been the organizers of the students' demonstrations were slim. Edward Pintznuk explained this phenomenon further in his book *Reds, Racial Justice, and Civil Liberties,* in which he discussed the fact that the CPUSA misjudged the mood of the American people as well as the fact that Hoover's Counter Intelligence

Program (COINTELPRO) did a great deal to neutralize the potential for a successful communist movement in America.[28]

As the protests at Columbia took place during the cold war, the FBI believed that the perceived "anti-American" sentiment that student demonstrators displayed had to be terminated. Hoover, as director of the FBI, had attempted to discredit black leaders from Marcus Garvey to Malcolm X, and he would not stop there.[29] He used the bureau's COINTELPRO to infiltrate student protest groups such as the SDS.[30] Columbia's student newspaper, the *Spectator,* claimed to have discovered documents that denoted "a relationship between the FBI and Columbia dating back to 1933."[31] These once-classified documents pointed toward seventeen target groups around the nation that COINTELPRO intended to cripple, and the article mentioned specifically Columbia's SDS chapter.

With the attention and notoriety that student activity at Columbia drew in the late 1960s, tension thickened within the ranks of the FBI itself. A special agent for the FBI asserted that "tensions within the bureau, particularly in Washington [D.C.], were very high," especially after the start of the Columbia rebellion.[32] The agent went on to explain that "I can't classify it as a hysteria but there was a considerable interest." One author, Sanford Unger, believed that that tension led the FBI to neutralize SDS and the New Left "with a vengeance almost unknown in FBI annals."[33]

James Kirkpatrick Davis explained in his book *Assault on the New Left* that after finding no hard evidence, even Hoover had "come to the conclusion that the New Left was not under the influence of the Old Left, the CPUSA or the SWP [Socialist Workers party]."[34] Still, the overarching goal of the agency was to discredit the New Left and SDS, just as it had attempted to discredit the Civil Rights movement.[35] Mark Rudd was of particular interest to the FBI.[36] To further discredit SDS, the FBI suggested releasing a "mass-mailing of anonymous letters to university officials in the New York area and to parents of SDS activists [who were] arrested" during the protest.[37] The letters would contain excerpts from an open letter to President Grayson Kirk that Mark Rudd wrote the day before the April 1968 protest began. It was the letter that ended with Leroi Jones's phrase, "up against the wall, motherfucker."

Another recommendation the document made was to send postcards out to the public "advertising fictitious SDS events." The FBI also floated the idea of creating a photo collage that would "emphasize the strange collection of hippies, dropouts and plain nuts that cling to the New Left."[38] This, the document claimed, "would have a caricaturing effect on the SDS on campus," the article reported.[39] By doing so, the bureau, presumably, wanted to evoke enough distaste for SDS to push parents and authorities to disband the radical group. Eventually, Hoover authorized several of the recommendations, but in July 1968 he balked at the postcard proposal, which he feared might backfire and discredit the bureau's efforts. In August the director did, however, authorize the photo collage, which would be sent to "fraternities, sororities, college administrators, faculty and public officials."[40]

The article also stated that the memorandum indicated several young people who acted as informants. It noted that the bureau claimed to have not recruited the young informants but instead accepted volunteers for the task of infiltration. "Since the initial demonstrations at Columbia[,] . . . seven individuals have contacted the New York office [of the FBI] and have indicated a desire to assist the Bureau relative to the New Left activities at Columbia University."

If, indeed, several young people volunteered to be informants, then the bureau made an important observation about the student movement that has often been overlooked: that members of the New Left, antiwar, Civil Rights, Black Power, and student movements were in the minority. Most young people (most Americans for the matter) did not participate directly in social movements. In fact, toward the end of the 1960s, many members of the conservative and moderate ranks called for an end to the disturbances that these movements had caused. This would lead some young people to work with the FBI in order to quell disruptions on campus and in society.

While the bureau might have claimed not to recruit any informants, another government agency did recruit people to infiltrate groups like SDS. The CIA's Office of Security sent a memorandum to headquarters in 1968 explicating how the "penetration" of the movement would occur.[41] The memorandum stated that "agents will be spotted and recruited to penetrate those organizations and movements in the United States."[42] The organizations to which the memorandum referred were Women's Strike for Peace, SDS, SNCC, CORE, and several other groups. Further, the document requested the support of the FBI in achieving the goal of infiltration. For these government agencies, there seemed to be a real threat of implosion in America, and this motivated the government to check any and all groups that might spark large-scale rebellion.

By 1969 not just government agencies but many Americans believed that the nation was crumbling from within, and some based that feeling on the lack of trust that was prevalent in society. As Michael Wallace, who was a graduate student at Columbia at the time of the protests, put it, "The usual rules of the game in capitalist society had been set aside; . . . it was a political struggle. There was a fucking war on in Vietnam and the civil rights movement. These were profound forces that transcend that moment."[43] Indeed, instability reigned as the Vietnam War swelled and assassins murdered faithful leaders like King and the Kennedy brothers.

Many young people, not without reason, believed that they could not trust the older generation, which had fumbled its chances of bringing equality and, what was more, humanity to American society. And conversely, many of the older, more conservative generation believed that there were those in the younger generation who had lost all hope and who sought the destruction of society as a whole. This was especially hurtful to many older Americans who had the opportunity to watch the United States grow into a major world power during the Second World War. In spite of the U.S. status in the world, young people at Columbia like those in SDS and SAS distrusted institutions like their government and their university because the government had placed order and the fight against communism ahead of justice. Similarly, the university placed expansion and the attainment of power ahead of the civil treatment of its black neighbors in Harlem and Morningside Heights. Students distrusted a government that would blur the line of democracy by unleashing government agents to discredit social and political groups that questioned the legitimacy of the government's policy makers. Government agencies like the Office of Security, the CIA, and the FBI, as well as officials such as J. Edgar Hoover, played a large part in this rising distrust and the younger generation's encouragement of Americans to be leery of the government.

If the government, specifically agencies like the FBI, did not trust its student-citizens, then certainly the student-citizens would not trust the government and its relationship with the university. There could be nothing but distrust for the university and the government if students understood that there were secret dealings concerning FBI investigations and contracts with the Defense Department (an issue during the 1968 demonstrations). While government and university authorities believed that they were protecting society and the university, the officials' actions had an adverse effect on those who insisted on questioning the officials' authority in the first place.

Mistrust of authorities was not the only outcome of the Columbia rebellion; there were positive results as well. Aside from the tripartite committee for disciplinary matters that demonstrators in 1968 had demanded from the university, the students also gained access to the university Senate.[44] The Senate was a body that housed representatives from the administration, faculty, and student population. This newly created council provided a way for students to positively and constructively restructure the university. While the formation of the body might have seemed reactionary on the part of the university (especially because it was formed directly after the 1968 protest), it nonetheless spelled progress for the school and the students.

Twenty years after the 1968 student protest at Columbia, two of the school's professors reflected on the demonstrations. Carl Hovde, who acted as dean of Columbia College from 1968 to 1972, asked a most critical question of himself. He wondered: "Is Columbia better because of what happened in '68?"[45] Using the university Senate as an example, he contended that the rebellions were, in the end, for the best. Another professor, Melvin Mencher, who was a nontenured faculty member at the time of the demonstrations, made similar observations of the Senate. After two decades of the Senate's existence, Mencher praised the council with its "twenty-six voting student members and many nontenured faculty members" who participated in it.

Hovde extolled the Senate for two specific reasons. The first was that it made for a positive dialogue between students and authorities: "People get to know one another and in varying measure to trust one another."[46] It is worth noting that Hovde cited trust as an important part of restructuring the university, implying that the lack of trust was an underlying cause of the student revolt. Another reason he cited was the increased amount of tolerance for differing opinions that the protests caused. "In a crisis," he explained, "people have already learned to work together in some ways. Often enough they won't agree, but they will at least be able to talk to one another." His main criticism of the university during the late 1960s was the way each of the major groups (students, faculty members, and administrators) found themselves isolated from one another. Avoiding this isolation, Columbia learned a lesson from the disturbances and uses the university Senate to address issues affecting all members of the institution.

After the protests of 1968–69, a former black graduate student and leader of SAS, William Sales, explained that his main point of pride concerning the demonstrations came from the ability of himself and the other members of SAS to establish and maintain ties with the black community in Harlem. He saw the students' efforts as being part of the "black liberation struggle," and he realized that it would take a coalition between the black students and the local black community to achieve the goal of racial equality.

In doing so, the black activists not only would help to achieve racial equality but would attain Black Power in its most essential form. For the black students and community members, what occurred during the 1968–69 protests was truly amazing. Those two groups managed to overcome class divisions to ally themselves along racial lines. As members of the black intelligentsia and working class, they were able to manifest power by using their race to invoke fear and reconsideration in a powerful white institution, and this was extremely rare for black people in the United States. For white America, power had manifested itself in the same way since the founding of the country. From the seventeenth to the first half of the nineteenth century, white people agreed to put their race (meaning free status) above their class differences. After slavery ended, the white alliance continued, with even populists choosing their race over their economic welfare. The White Citizens' Councils and Ku Klux Klan of the mid-twentieth century worked together to protect the interests of their race. Leaders such as George Wallace and Strom Thurmond received the support of those whose politics were not similar but whose race matched. Black students and working-class black community members did the same in 1968–69 when they achieved a measure of power. In creating this alliance, black people forced Columbia to approach the local commuity with respect and awareness of the fact that the people would not remain quiet forever. That was Black Power.

This fact had crossed the mind of William Sales. For him and other black students, "the Columbia uprising was not essentially about black student issues. It was about Columbia University's relationship with Morningside Heights, to Harlem and to the Harlems of the world."[47] The seriousness of the protests allowed young people the opportunity to gain organizational experience and to meet and debate with civil rights leaders and politicians such as Stokely Carmichael, Basil Paterson, and Percy Sutton.

There were not many things that black students at Columbia University asked for specifically in the late 1960s and did not receive. That, however, occurred only after a great deal of protest, patience, endurance, discipline, and devotion. The same is true for the Civil Rights movement that preceded the black students' actions, and civil rights activists had to endure even harsher treatment to achieve their goals. In 1954, after several trial cases, civil rights activists brought suit for the legal integration of public schools and received it when the Supreme Court overturned the decision of the *Plessy v. Ferguson* case. Unfortunately, southern officials resisted the order until the federal government used army troops to protect desegregating students. In 1955 black activists desegregated the bus system in Montgomery, Alabama, only after walking, carpooling, and boycotting for more than a year. In 1964 Congress passed the Civil Rights Act, and the next year Congress passed the Voting Rights Act only after black citizens died from firebombs or lynchings or some other form of violent racism. Even then, some suggest that Congress did not move on the bill until white activists like Michael Schwerner and Andrew Goodman died attempting to register black voters in Mississippi. Unfortunately, black and white citizens died attempting to do what should have been normal. Then, in 1968, after the assassination of King, came the Fair Housing Act, which resulted from the efforts of black residents frustrated by housing discrimination and the barriers between them and decent housing.

In the same vein, black students demanded entrance into traditionally white universities and achieved that goal, but not without receiving death threats and ill treatment. This, too, took a great deal of protesting and demanding as well as discipline and militancy. Those black students who arrived refused to be the "tokens," however, and demanded further admission of their fellow black students. With the new black students came a new attitude that the students had acquired from their home communities.

The more militant attitude of the students led them to believe that they deserved to be a part of these traditionally white universities and, specifically, Columbia. These were the children of the *Brown v. Board of Education* decision, and they knew what education was supposed to look like, and so they settled for nothing less than equal access to classrooms. This attitude of militancy also gave steam to a movement for black studies programs that would allow black students attending these predominantly white institutions the opportunity to learn about black people's past and the problems that currently affected black communities. In many places, university administrators capitulated to the students' demand for black studies. Taking the movement to a new extreme, the students who had been recently recruited to these universities made the bold demand to take part in the structuring of these programs, namely, the hiring of faculty members and the selection of courses. Considering the fact that most of these black students were on some sort of financial aid, and thus beholden to the university, their acts of defiance were that much more brazen and noteworthy.

Why would these young people who had the privilege of opportunity sacrifice their own personal gains for those of future generations and classes? There is no measurable answer other than the students' sense of community and the need to obtain power in a collective sense. These black students had witnessed what happened to young black people who did not follow the rules set by white society. For examples, they needed to look no further than to men like Lloyd Gaines, who disappeared after attempting to integrate the University of Missouri, or Bob Moses, who was nearly beaten to death as he tried to register voters in Mississippi, or Jimmie Lee Jackson, who died during a march for voting rights.

Fresher in the minds of black students in the late 1960s, however, were the acts of Thomas Smith and John Carlos in the 1968 summer Olympics. The simple act of raising black-gloved fists created a major problem for the Olympic officials and caused embarrassment for white American officials.[48] Smith and Carlos were part of the rising Black Student Power movement that affected colleges and universities all across the country. As students, Smith and Carlos soaked in the philosophy of Black Power and the effectiveness of militancy from people like San Jose State University professor Harry Edwards.[49] By giving the Black Power salute during the playing of the U.S. national anthem, they ironically committed one of the most racially charged acts of the latter half of the twentieth century. In doing so, they lost the medals they had just won in the two-hundred-meter dash and their status as Olympic athletes. In spite of that, these student athletes proceeded with their act of defiance much as the black students on Columbia's campus defied school authorities to get black student demands met.

At this point in American history, the tide was right for such revolutionary change. At least outwardly, the nation was making an attempt to heal its racial wounds. Black people, on the same note, believed that they deserved to be consulted on matters that concerned them and to be in charge of programs that directly affected them. For that reason, black students and community members were able to justify confrontational demonstrations against Columbia University's proposal for a gymnasium in a nearly all-black neighborhood park and against other universities that denied them the opportunity to control black studies programs.

Today, one would be hard-pressed to find an accredited university that did not have a black studies program or at least course offerings in black studies. This is a result of the work black activists did in the 1960s. Equally important as the presence of black studies courses and programs is the presence of African American students on campuses all over the United States. As it is, more black students are attending college than ever before, and this is a positive result of the 1960s Columbia student demonstrations.[50]

Aiding in the manifestation of these black student activists' goal of increased admissions of their fellow black students was the Pell Grant, which was named after Claiborne Pell, who had attained a master's degree from Columbia University. As a senator representing Rhode Island, he pushed through the Basic Education and Opportunity Grants in 1972 that provided federal money to students from low-income backgrounds.[51] By providing the money directly to the students and bypassing the institutions that might unfairly distribute the grant money, Pell, in many ways, assisted the entrance of black people to institutions of higher learning like Columbia University.

Also contributing to the increased enrollment of black students was the advent of the black athlete.[52] Harry Edwards explained that many of these student athletes had come to predominantly white universities under "special adjustments." Due, in part, to these special terms, a great deal of these black student athletes did not ever achieve graduation.[53] These young blacks did (and do), however, allow predominantly white educational institutions the opportunity to boast about the efforts of the universities to integrate and add "diversity" to their campuses. More than that, these black student athletes have provided a great deal of revenue for their schools.[54] While this may not have been what the black activists at universities like Columbia had in mind when they demanded the increased enrollment of black students, many of the recruited black athletes viewed themselves as activists as well.[55] And that in itself created a stark contrast to the contingent of Columbia University's white athletes (or jocks) who acted as counterprotesters during the 1968 rebellion. In spite of counterprotesting athletes, in the late 1960s black student athletes as well as traditional students embraced Black Power and rebelled against institutional racism.

Columbia's admission and enrollment of black students was inconsistent after the protests. By 1973 the university accepted only 100 black students in contrast to 136 in 1972.[56] That marked a 27 percent difference in the two years. A report in the school newspaper indicated that in 1976, "Black Applications Increase at Three Ivy Colleges"; Columbia was not one of them.[57] Furthermore, the number of black applicants to the school on the Heights decreased 20 percent from the previous year. The paper noted increases in black applicants to Brown, Princeton, and Dartmouth.

As Columbia sits very near one of the nation's largest black communities, those numbers mystified some black community workers. The East Harlem Coordinating Program director at Park East High School, Rita Bayron, believed that "Columbia is not working hard enough to recruit black students from New York City."[58] She observed that the program had ties to other New York universities, but that "Columbia is the only school we don't have an ongoing relationship with." Her sentiment mirrored that of Gino Rusch, the director of the College Readiness Program for Harlem public schools. "We don't have a strong relationship with Columbia," he stated. "I think it's not enough to send out some catalogues. Columbia has to go out and actively recruit."[59] The fact that the school newspaper ran these stories showed that the concerns that protesters had in 1968–69 were still very real.

The controversy over the presence of these black students on campus, however, has intensified over the years.[60] A *Journal of Higher Education* article reported that only one of four black students believed that their school provided an excellent or "very good" campus racial climate.[61] Some of this is due, in part, to the increased rise of conservatism, the lack of nonacademic support for black students, and the lack of commitment to affirmative action, claimed the article.[62]

As the economy weakened in the early 2000s, the U.S. government, which had pledged itself to righting the wrongs of racial injustice in the late 1960s, began scaling back affirmative action programs that would allow for minorities to have opportunities for admission to predominantly white government-funded schools. In states like California and Texas, the state supreme courts and voters have cut affirmative action programs.[63] California Governor Pete Wilson campaigned on a platform that appealed to voters who believed that black citizens and other minorities were receiving too many preferences at institutions of higher learning.[64] As the *Regents of the University of California v. Bakke* case of 1978 reached the U.S. Supreme Court, affirmative action began to meet a great deal of legislative resistance.[65] Although the decision upheld affirmative action, it was a serious blow to some blacks because it inhibited the ability of institutions to use a candidate's blackness as a factor when trying to achieve diversity on campus. Unfortunately, for so many years, a candidate's whiteness allowed universities to show preference.

In his book, *And We Are Not Saved,* former Harvard law professor Derrick Bell aptly described the struggle that black students and affirmative action face in higher education.[66] By pointing to the fact that there are often "unspoken" limits on affirmative action, he showed that the nation and particularly those who occupy positions of authority in higher education are not as devoted to erasing racism as they might claim. Administrators, he suggested, place unspoken limits on affirmative action for fear of losing the cultural integrity of their universities.[67] While these universities might have been willing to hire one or two black faculty members or enroll a few more black students, when the percentage of black students and minorities reaches or exceeds the percentage of blacks in the nation, the institutions stop recruiting black students.[68]

Manning Marable, who became the founder and first director of Columbia's Institute for Research in African-American Studies, attributed this limit to affirmative action to the need of white academics to have "ideological hegemony."[69] He explained that that was the natural response of white people when challenged with the prospect of losing control. In this situation, that meant white people losing their status as a majority to those who would have previously been considered minorities. This, he claimed, was not a conspiratorial act on behalf of white people but more one of self-defense.[70]

If racial preferences in favor of black people and minorities have unsettled white officials in such a manner, then the struggle of the black student activists of the 1960s has not been laid to rest. Casting an even darker cloud over the matter is Derrick Bell's prediction that "if a case reaches the Court involving racial classification . . . a majority of the Court will reject it. They have already done precisely that in a number of cases."[71] As there is currently a case against the University of Michigan concerning its affirmative action program, Bell's prediction as to the potential reaction of the Supreme Court becomes that much more interesting and crucial.

What happens in the courts will eventually have an effect on what happens in higher-level schools like Columbia. Theodore Cross, who as editor of the *Journal of Blacks in Higher Education* has written extensively about affirmative action, has attempted to show how rulings against affirmative action at schools such as the University of Texas would affect private universities.[72] Considering data on the role of the SAT, a standardized college admission test, and that of "nonracial personal qualifications," Cross concluded "that if all racial preferences in college admissions were abolished, [then] more than three quarters of the black students currently enrolled at the nation's 25 highest ranked universities would not be accepted for admission."[73]

While black student activists at Columbia were able to win some victories in the way of increased enrollment of black students in the past, the challenges in doing so today are just as great as ever. The members of SAS, if anything, left the younger generations of black students with a model of struggle that could be employed in the face of white recalcitrance in regard to the prospect of increased black enrollment. Touching on some of Bell's fears, Cross noted that recalcitrance is only one part of the problem facing this younger generation of black students. "There is already a strong body of established federal law that private universities that receive federal aid or subsidies may be treated legally as a public institution and therefore made subject to the regulations that govern state institutions," commented Cross.[74] If this scenario came to fruition, it might have a leveling effect on the entrance of black students into universities like Columbia.

At the same time that affirmative action is under attack, the number of black studies programs, in spite of their remarkable rise since the 1960s, is currently dwindling, due in part to the lack of interest on behalf of younger generations as well as higher-education budget cuts.[75] An article in the *Jour-*

nal of Blacks in Higher Education showed that instead of black studies, most African American students today are majoring in the field of business.[76] Part of this phenomenon might be due to the fact that black people have further assimilated into American society and have accepted many white middle-class values, especially those concerning the achievement of success in the business world.

As times change, so too do the attitudes of students concerning their place in education. One of the issues that differentiate students of the current generation from those of the 1960s is politics. Much of the way that students carried themselves in the 1960s depended on the social issues that affected black people within and outside the walls of education. That is why the members of SAS could view themselves as black activists and not just as students. The efforts of those students made it possible for black students today to view themselves simply as students and not necessarily as black activists.

In looking back on the events at Columbia during the late 1960s, if the black student protesters and residents of the local neighborhoods viewed Harlem as a colony belonging to white imperialist institutions like Columbia, then some could construe the protesters' move to block construction of the gymnasium in Morningside Park as an attempt at the "decolonization" about which Frantz Fanon wrote.[77] Author of *Wretched of the Earth,* a book that many of the period's black student protesters had read, Fanon asserted that decolonization, the taking back of land, resources, and sovereignty from foreign imperialists, almost always involves violence. To achieve decolonization, Fanon claimed that "we [the colonized black peoples] must use all means to turn the scale, including, of course, violence."[78]

The prospect of violence for the black residents of Morningside Heights and Harlem was not out of the realm of thought because many members of the community had participated in earlier riots against what they perceived as the white establishment.[79] Columbia officials could look down on Harlem from their offices on the Heights and realize the potential for that violence to reach the school's campus, especially when residents specifically indicted the school for the mistreatment of the community. As the protesters found, violence (or the threat thereof) produced results, even if they could not justify its use.[80] This, however, was not necessarily positive, according to Joel Rhodes. Author of *The Voices of Violence,* Rhodes concluded that "violence did hurt the movement overall, for both blacks and whites, alienating them from traditional and potential supporters while squandering their [the antiwar and Black Power protesters'] brief hold of politics and the media at precisely the moment that meaningful change was within their grasp."[81]

While that might have been true, the threat of violence and violence itself were not uncommon for American social movements. Violence over racial issues could be recounted in the tales of John Brown, the New York draft riots, the Civil War, Klan raids, and countless riots in the nineteenth and twentieth century. Jerry Cohen and William Murphy, authors of *Burn, Baby, Burn!*, discussed the causes of the Watts riot of 1965, which had some bearing on the potential of another Harlem riot in 1968. Cohen and Murphy pointed to the eerie accuracy of an FBI manual entitled *Prevention and Control of Mobs and Riots*. "When a riot occurs . . . some kind of provocation triggers the violence," the manual observed.[82] It could be as simple as beginning construction on an unpopular gym, or the perceived mistreatment and brutality of black students. "The precipitating incident, even though it might have been completely imaginary [or in this case symbolic], becomes exaggerated through rumor and magnified out of proportion to its actual importance."[83] The gym was not the most important issue to the community near Columbia; the main issue was that the school should have treated community members fairly and respectfully, and that the university should have acknowledged the community members' right to control their lives and their neighborhoods. If the members of the community had to use violence or the threat thereof to accomplish this, then they would do so.

SAS leader William Sales, who went on to become the chair of the African American studies department at Seton Hall University, recounted how the seizure of buildings not only incited the thought of violence in white authorities, but it also forced the white radical protesters to examine their role in the struggle for equality. "It was our insistence on the introduction of a new tactic, the seizure of administration and classroom buildings, that forced white activists to confront their own ambiguities, surmount them and thus precipitate a crisis which was to transform American higher education."[84] He accurately claimed that, in this way, his fellow black students' role was "catalytic" in regard to the huge fallout, including the six-week strike and the later protests over black studies that occurred because of the demonstrations. Part of the fallout also concerned the influence that the tactic of seizing buildings had on other schools, such as Harvard and Cornell, where student protesters held similar demonstrations. Another part of the fallout was the fact that the university had to approach the neighboring community with respect, which in itself conceded power to the black residents of the surrounding neighborhoods. The black student activists at Columbia showed those who would follow what was possible with Black Student Power.

Unlike Sales, not everyone extolled the student movement during the

1960s. In fact, many critics of the students' protest efforts claimed that the demonstrations, particularly those at Columbia, led to the ruin and decline of higher education, pushing it too far toward the liberal left. University of Chicago professor Allan Bloom asserted that the students' efforts to politicize the campus should be compared to the "destruction of the universities in Nazi Germany."[85] These schools, he stated, were "ruined by the intrusion of political activity, mass opinion and misguided moral passion." In his and many others' opinions, American universities were no longer places of intellectual and academic debate, but rather a place for "political correctness" and liberalism. The authors of *Shadow University,* Alan Kors and Harvey Silvergate, agreed with Bloom's contention.[86] They cited several examples of how, recently, being "politically incorrect" has led to the dismissal of professors and students.[87]

If Bloom, Kors, and Silvergate were making the contention that universities, as a result of demonstrations such as those that took place at Columbia, were becoming too liberalized, then they were surely mistaken. At most American colleges and universities, the grand majority of trustees and members of boards of regents are still predominantly white. Furthermore, despite the fact that black tenured faculty members are present at nearly all of the nation's leading institutions, the surprisingly minimal percentage (4.8 percent) of these professors of color also suggests that these universities have not become too liberal.[88] Finally, at least in the nation's leading universities, black enrollment has increased but is not overwhelming, and the percentages of black students attending these schools has not changed markedly since the 1970s.[89] So, while critics might be unsettled by the push toward "political correctness" and the presence of politically liberal administrators and faculty members, substantively, there is nothing that indicates that these universities made overarching liberal changes.

In spite of the arguments of critics, if anything, the student demonstrators promoted divergent ideas and views for their times. As the decade of the 1960s closed, it just so happened that the liberal activists maintained the loudest voice in matters concerning racism and the war in Vietnam. When these demonstrators entered their careers (many in the field of academia), they brought with them their political views. This, of course, would have an effect on how officials currently manage universities. It is somewhat naïve, however, to believe that universities had not been politicized before the 1960s.

To be sure, the presence of politics on campuses was not necessarily negative. In 1988, Morris Dickstein, an alumnus of Columbia, wisely observed, "Yesterday's burning political issues are today's problems in theory and methodology. . . . Some of the energy that went into demonstrating in the streets is now directed toward the curriculum."[90] Is there a better place to deal with methodological and theoretical (political or apolitical) problems than at a university or college, where theory and methodology are and have been most cherished? A professor of English at Columbia, James Shapiro, bolstered Dickstein's point: "Now the political action takes place in the classroom, and in scholarly books dedicated to social change."[91]

For students in recent decades, college has often been viewed as a place that should prepare one for a job. Granted, in many ways that is the function of attaining a degree; however, college for many of the activists in the 1960s was a place to learn and to engage what they were learning. This is certainly not to glorify one generation over the next, but the function of universities seems to have changed in the past few decades. Seldom will there be an issue controversial enough to incite present-day students to protest.

In the 1980s, on Columbia University's campus, however, there was one such issue that invoked student action. Apartheid—government-sanctioned segregation and oppression in black South Africa—managed to stir the emotions of the newer generation. Members of the Black Student Organization (BSO), which had been founded in the 1960s along with SAS and the Barnard Organization of Soul Sisters, demanded that the university divest itself of "holdings in companies doing business with South Africa," reported *New York Times Magazine*.[92] After a three-week demonstration that at one point closed Hamilton Hall (the building that SAS had occupied nearly twenty years earlier), Columbia University acceded to the BSO's demand and divested. This rare political activity on behalf of modern students clearly showed roots that dated back to the black activists' actions of the late 1960s. Indeed, when top university officials explained in 1983 that divesting could be detrimental to Columbia economically (Columbia had upward of $23.5 million of holdings in companies that functioned in South Africa), the rhetoric seemed to mirror the argument against halting gym construction.[93] In this instance, the trustees again rejected the proposals of students and faculty alike to divest. The result was a campus movement.[94] Like those activists of old, the 1980s' black student protesters chose one issue to exploit, and because of their efforts and the sensitivity of the university to charges of racism, they won their battle to have Columbia divest itself of ties to apartheid South Africa. Although the issues were somewhat different, the theme of racial discrimination and colonization still existed.

While protesters like William Sales and Mark Rudd and professionals like Morris Dickstein and James Shapiro believed that the 1960s disturbances had at least some positive effects on future generations, one observer of the protest opined that the "uprising had little lasting impact."[95] In 1988 Sylvan Fox, who reported for the *New York Times* in 1968 and 1969, asserted that Columbia's disturbances were only part of many chaotic and violent events that took place during those troublesome years. Fox pointed specifically to the assassinations of Robert Kennedy and King. He also referred to the numerous upheavals in Europe and Latin America.

Explaining that the events that took place on the Morningside Heights campus were only part of a continuum of youth movements that eventually met their unsuccessful demise, he saw no reason to praise the Columbia events more than any other. If the student demonstrators' goals were to radicalize the majority of young people in society and to create an "authentic New Left," as Fox contended, then they "fell markedly short of those objectives."[96] Adding the hindsight of twenty years, he noted that in 1980 and 1984, it was, in part, the baby-boomers (those who would have been college-aged at the time of the Columbia protests) who voted the conservative Republican candidate, Ronald Reagan, into the office of president. Reagan, while governor of California, gained a conservative following with the stands he made against the student and Black Power movements of the late 1960s and early 1970s. Although Fox could not prove that the baby-boomers who attended Columbia University later voted for the conservative candidate, he correctly stated that the New Left's efforts to permanently radicalize these young people did not, on the whole, come to fruition.

It was true that, because of this failure, many of those once "radical" and "militant" activists lost their zeal as the years passed. Often they found out that there would never be a revolution because revolution is antithetical to the underlying nature of the United States. After eighteen years of reflection, Mark Rudd readily admitted that revolution during the time of the 1960s protests was highly improbable: "We [SDS members] didn't understand American society very well at all. Our only experience was that each succeeding freshman class at Columbia was more radical than the one before it. From this we extrapolated that the entire society was becoming more radical."[97] The sad fact of the matter was that because of the skewed worldview that Rudd and other members of SDS had gained during their short time in college, people got physically and emotionally hurt. In this way, it is understandable how some older people, who were not familiar with the campus culture of the 1960s, might have believed that student groups like SDS did not have valid justification for acts of civil disobedience.

Rudd, to some extent concurred: "I think our Columbia education probably worked against us because a lot of us read about the Chinese Revolution and the Russian Revolution. We just thought our revolution was going to happen . . . like that."[98] Finally, he conceded, "it's obvious as can be that the U.S. was not in a revolutionary or even pre-revolutionary stage" at the time of the 1968 demonstrations. Many of the 1960s protesters recognized this and decided to buy into the system rather than continue to fight it. Rudd explained it perfectly: "We could not have maintained that burning passion for so many years and at the same time accepted the wealth and privileges which are our imperial birthrights."[99]

Rudd's statement, in essence, validated the earlier predictions and skepticism that the members of SAS had of SDS and the radical white group's motivation for protesting. The revolution that the white radicals sought was not much more than a fad, and in time, the participants in that revolution would become part of the system that the radicals tried so desperately to change. At the same time, the members of the black community surrounding Columbia would still be, for the most part, poor and disfranchised, and the white student radicals would be part of the middle class and not living in Harlem.

In direct contradiction to Sylvan Fox's argument that the radicals and militants of the 1960s generation turned to conservative politics after the failure of their movement, the *New York Daily News* claimed that most of those who participated in the 1968 protests at Columbia did not, in fact, go so far as to do such. The periodical asserted that, "according to a survey taken by a university official, among the 700 [plus] who were arrested [in 1968], about two-thirds now are still 'involved' in causes of one kind or another."[100] Andrea Egan, a graduate of Barnard College, who in 1968 got married to a student from Columbia in one of the occupied buildings (Fayerweather), made a similar point. "Very few of us have drifted into 'yuppiedum,'" she boasted. By "yuppiedum," one could only assume she was referring to the yuppie culture that historians have described as one of affluence, class-conscientiousness, and class-privilege. Neither the statistics that the survey revealed nor Egan's testimony can substantially refute Fox's claim.[101]

Still, many of those who participated in the protests did claim to maintain the same or similar political views as they did while they attended Columbia University. Most, however, made the disclaimer that their tactics have changed greatly since then. One of those graduates was Mark Elrich, who came back to Columbia to participate in a reunion of the 1968 demonstrations. "It's exciting to see how many people stayed with the commitment we developed in those years," he remarked.[102] Elrich himself had become a union carpenter and labor leader. Mark Naison, who had joined SDS and protested the gym, claimed that his participation in the events on campus provided him with a badge of honor. "Getting arrested to protest Columbia's attempt to build a gym in a Harlem park was something I was proud of at the time—and am still proud of now," he stated in an interview years later. Naison went on to teach in the black studies department at Fordham University and later authored the book *White Boy*, which spoke to some of his experiences at Columbia.[103]

In fairness, Fox's initial claim about the Columbia crisis being only a small part of the turmoil in the 1960s was, in part, correct. The Columbia University protests in 1968 and later in 1969 were only part of a larger student and youth movement that confronted racism and the Vietnam War. The United States had witnessed the demonstrations of Berkeley students in 1964; Columbia, South Carolina State, and Howard University students in 1968; Cornell, Yale, Penn, Princeton, and Harvard students in 1969; and probably most tragic of all, Kent and Jackson State University students in 1970, where National Guard troops and police officers actually shot and killed students. The events at Columbia only added a boost to these and the hundreds of other protests that took place in the 1960s. While the student movement did much to influence young people like those who would join SDS or SAS on Columbia's campus, the movement did as much to draw backlash from the nation's moderate and conservative contingencies. Historian Lisa McGuir called this the rise of the "New American Right," which later installed the likes of Richard Nixon, Ronald Reagan, and George H. W. Bush into the office of the president.[104]

Of course another result of the 1968–69 student protests was an increase in caution on behalf of the university as it approached its Harlem neighbors. Acting to cut off rumors that Columbia had planned to expand further into Harlem even after the protests, the university issued an advertisement in the *New York Amsterdam News*, a periodical that many Harlem residents read. The title of the piece stated: "Somebody's Trying to Hurt Us Both—Columbia and Harlem."[105] The advertisement cited several rumors about Columbia buying the Theresa Hotel as well as taking over the Lenox Terrace apartments and Harlem Hospital. With a sense of urgency and trepidation, the piece denied each of the rumors, offering explanation for why the university would not want to commit such acts at the time. About the Theresa Hotel, the advertisement explained that the rumors were "absolutely false. Columbia does not own and does not intend to own the hotel." Concerning the Lenox Terrace apartments, it made the same statement and maintained that "Columbia has no interest in them."[106]

Most elaborate, however, was the piece's response to the rumor that the university wanted to take over Harlem Hospital. It noted that "Harlem Hospital belongs to the city of New York, as part of the municipal hospital system." For some readers, this probably was not much assurance, as Morningside Park also belonged to the city and Columbia was able to commandeer the park's most useful areas for the school's own purposes. "The city requested Columbia to work with the hospital. Civic groups in Harlem added their support to the request," noted the advertisement. Again, there was a time when some civic groups supported the idea of a gym in the park, while Columbia ignored the protests of the civic groups and people who did not want to have a gym built in Morningside Park. Then, with an uncanny resemblance to the rhetoric of the university's presentation of gym plans, the advertisement asked: "Who benefits most from the program?" and went on to answer: "the people of Harlem. The university actually loses money on its Harlem Hospital activities." In essence, these were many of the same words that Columbia representatives had used to sell the gym to local residents.

Especially after the protest over the gym, Harlem residents should have been suspicious of any white American institution that approached the community to offer its services for free, let alone one that was offering its services at a loss. Whether the university actually committed the acts that the rumors had indicated was a side note to how university officials chose to respond to the rumors. Columbia had learned that it was better to outwardly discuss its plans with the community rather than to wait until the community found out about its plans afterward. This was indeed a positive effect of the 1968–69 demonstrations.

Community organizations saw themselves as victorious over Columbia. In May 1969 the chair of the West Harlem Community Organization, Edith Pennamon, wrote to her fellow members: "Dear Friend, The Establishment's attempt to use the scarcity of recreational facilities in the West Harlem community as a legitimate excuse to extend their control into the larger community, has ended victoriously for Harlem. Columbia University's abandoned gym-site in Morningside Park stands as a monument of Harlem's will to determine and guide its destiny."[107]

The student and community demonstrations helped to increase the confidence and strength of community organizations in relation to powerful institutions. As one West Harlem Community Organization document explained, "A coalition was formed with Black students at Columbia in opposition to the construction. Out of this experience, and others similar to it, grew the realization that WHCO should strengthen its position as an advocator and leading participant in the developmental activities of the community."[108] Because of the organization's stance on the gym, its membership swelled. The organization claimed to represent seventeen thousand people in a fourteen-block area.

After settling with the realization that the gym would not be built in the park, Columbia hired a designer to study what would be the best location for the gym. I. M. Pei offered estimates to the university in regard to a plan to place a new gym underneath Southfield on Columbia's campus. Pei was an outward opponent of moving any farther off campus to build. Noting the obvious, Pei commented that "the competition for housing . . . has been the root cause of most of the conflict between the institutions and the surrounding community during the past decade."[109] He further explained that "the surrounding community . . . was still distrustful of Columbia and was ready to resist any hint of new growth beyond the campus perimeters; . . . attitudes between some (community and university) groups were, in many ways, still polarized." With that in mind, Pei suggested constructing high-rise towers on campus to house other programs and departments.

After the protest of 1968–69, Columbia was in a bad way financially and could not afford to follow through with Pei's plan. Indeed, by 1970 Columbia had $8.5 million in budget for new construction, but Pei estimated his plan to cost between $15 and $18 million. The new president of Columbia, William McGill, revealed that Columbia, after the years of protest, was "in the red," and that the university was "overextended."[110] Indeed, because of the protests, some potential students chose other universities over Columbia, and some of the alumni refused to donate further to the school. Still other donors saw Columbia as too risky an investment.

Columbia had slowed its expansion into West Harlem, but many people were still skeptical of the school. President McGill wanted to make it clear that in the years after the rebellions, "the university does not act unilaterally, as it once did."[111] In fact, one of the university's vice president's main duties was to interact and dialogue with the community. In his role, the vice president fielded community complaints and explained the university's positions on matters regarding housing and expansion. Even the trustees had to change in the wake of the demonstrations. By 1971 the university trustees established a standing committee on community affairs, which marked a departure from the casual consultations that the university made with selective community representatives.

One of several skeptics, Eric Arroyo, staff director of the Morningside Renewal Council (an organization with which Columbia had consulted in the past), was still suspicious of the university and its motives. Arroyo said that "by no stretch of the imagination are we in love. . . . I think one can say that [the university-community relationship] is not as acrimonious as it was at one time, especially at the time of the gym."[112] He admitted, "And of course the very fact that the institutions in general are not expanding on the scale they were before . . . has toned down the thing." With a touch of sarcasm, Arroyo tried to explain the new relationship: "If I was shooting at you one day and I'm only calling you a bastard the next day, would you say the relationship is better?"[113]

As Columbia began and stopped construction in the park, the community had to deal with the physical damage that had been done. After the controversy, there was one community group that attempted to improve the park where Columbia had left a scar. In one document entitled "Statement of Community Redevelopment Objectives and Criteria for Morningside Park," the West Harlem Coalition for Morningside Park called for the city to construct a childcare facility in the part of the park where Columbia had begun digging. Further, it wanted play equipment, the construction of an amphitheater, the construction of an outdoor swimming pool/skating rink of 50–100 feet, and the implementation of a one-year intensive maintenance program designed to restore the entire park and facilities to good condition.[114]

The School of Architecture and Environmental Studies at City College of New York even submitted a plan for the site to the Parks, Recreation, and Cultural Affairs Administration of the City of New York. The City College proposal claimed that "the most important feature of the development plan is a major indoor facility to be built in the existing excavated area."[115] Unlike the Columbia of the 1950s and 1960s, the indoor facility that City College planned reflected community involvement. "A desire has been expressed by members of the communities surrounding the park that this facility be a link between the communities which border the park, particularly to the east and west." Finally, the proposal indicated that "a children's play area was closed and dismantled during excavation in the proposed Columbia gym. This should be restored in the general vicinity of the original playground."

The West Harlem Community Organization attempted to make use of the abandoned gym site in a number of ways. One of those included a "Morningside Park Festival" that would allow the children of the area to play in the park. In a letter to Christiane Collins, Bob McKay explained that he was in contact with a playwright who could put together performances for the festival. McKay also indicated that another interested community member wanted to put on a "Black Arts Show."[116]

While some onlookers questioned whether the confrontation was worth the controversy it caused, some of the students and community members who participated in the rebellion never wavered in their conviction. In 1974 one of the black student militants, Charles Jones, claimed that in regard to the demonstration, "my opinion on that hasn't changed at all. . . . I still think the university was wrong in building a gym on public land." Politician Basil Paterson still believed the same as he did in 1968: "I think things have happened for the best," he reported to the *New York Times*. "It's too bad we had to go through that period of confrontation, but now people feel there's a new relationship between Columbia and the community," he stated.[117]

Columbia eventually completed its plans for a recreational facility. In 1974 the university sent out invitations to celebrate the grand opening of the Marcellus Hartley Dodge Physical Fitness Center. The gymnasium part of the new facility bore the name of an alumnus (Francis Levien) who donated a million dollars to the new gymnasium fund. Incidentally, the university constructed the fitness center at the site of the old gymnasium—on campus. The university president, William McGill, was proud in the fact that "he had succeeded where four of his predecessors had failed," according to the *New York Times*. Further, he boasted of the "'landmark contract' that required the gymnasium's builder to hire a work force with 20 percent minority representation."[118]

In 1988 Columbia University's president, Michael Sovern, claimed that the school's relationship with the community had improved since the time of the controversy over the gymnasium. "We are in far closer touch with community leaders, their interests and their opinions than we were in 1968," he asserted.[119] Sovern pointed out that the university funded several programs that allowed "Columbia's students, faculty and staff" to work with various community organizations. In fact, he proudly touted, "[Columbia's] students provide legal services to the poor[, and] our dental clinics offer service of vital importance to our neighbors."[120] He did not, however, mention the fact that the mostly black neighbors provided the clinic with patients that are necessary for both funding and grants, and that the poor people that the law students helped with legal matters provided the aspiring attorneys with practical experience that would help with the students' future careers. The proud statement about the university's dental clinic and the services it offered to the community was reminiscent of the way Columbia boasted about its "partnership in the park" during the early to mid-1960s.[121]

In the late 1980s a local politician, Lisa Sostre, questioned the school's sincerity in community relations. She said that "Columbia University's relationship to the community is not a good one. . . . Its relationship with the community is almost a contradiction to the kind of humanism that it teaches in the classroom."[122] Unfortunately for the educational institution on the Heights, critics in the 1980s were leveling the same type of disparaging remarks that critics had offered in the 1960s. William Sales, who at one point after the protests chose to live in Harlem, commented that "from the vantage point of the surrounding communities, there's probably been no real substantive advance at all in race relations and community relations."[123] There was, however, a change in the way that Columbia would approach expansion and other ventures that would involve the community of Harlem.

In spite of the new approach that Columbia had been taking with its neighbors in Harlem, the university still received complaints of poor treatment from tenants of university-owned dwellings. In 1985 a former tenant of a Columbia-owned apartment published a book denoting the continued problems that the university had with its Morningside Heights neighbors. In *We Are Talking about Homes: A Great University against Its Neighbors*, Lynne Schwartz discussed the continued callousness the university displayed when dealing with the issues that neighborhood tenants had raised. When a fire damaged many of the units in her apartment building, Columbia was slow to respond to the needs of the tenants, who were fearful of losing their homes, claimed Schwartz.[124] Residents and city officials also complained of the school's continued expansion. Columbia, instead of expanding farther east toward Harlem, concentrated its new expansion efforts west toward Riverside Park.

This, too, was a result of the 1968–69 protests; the university, aware of the potential uproar of the adjacent black community and negative publicity that further expansion in the direction of Harlem might bring, chose to expand in a different direction. Unfortunately for the school, the residents in those areas felt just as much resentment toward the institution's policies. One city official asked why the university needed more housing units. Eventually the representative pointed toward Columbia's "enclave mentality," not to mention the school's "need and desire to control everything."[125]

One area on which Columbia planners have focused most recently is Manhattanville, an industrial area situated on the Upper West Side of Manhattan. Columbia's desires to expand include the area north of 125th Street, south of 133rd, and west of Broadway. Also included are several blocks east of Broadway and north of 131st Street. As part of Harlem, Manhattanville has become the subject of controversy for many New York residents who point to the large amount of land and buildings that Columbia already owns in Manhattan.[126] While the university has expressed its need to expand to keep pace with its Ivy League counterparts (of all the Ivy League universities, Columbia had the least square feet per student ratio—326 feet per student), community leaders have demanded that low-income housing be placed in the area where Columbia plans to build new campus facilities.[127]

Columbia officials have explained that the university chose Manhattanville as an area of expansion because very few residents would be displaced. As an industrial zone, the school purported to have no intention of entering a situation involving housing. Furthermore, the university officials presented the benefits that the community could receive from revitalization of the run-down neighborhoods. One benefit included job opportunities for nearby residents. Officials estimated that 7,200 new jobs would be created upon completion of the expansion project.[128] Another included businesses returning to the area, which could insert billions of dollars into the local economy. The one-time national director of the Urban League claimed that the Manhattanville area would be better suited for both housing and business, and that Columbia already owns too much land in Manhattan.[129]

To avoid the catastrophe of the late 1960s, Columbia has claimed to make every effort to maintain a line of communication with city and community leaders, including the mayor's office, the Department of City Planning, and civic and business leaders who formed the Columbia Advisory Committee.[130] The university has also made a website, http://neighbors.columbia .edu/campusplanning/campusplanningHome.php, available to concerned residents who have questions or who want to know more about the university's intentions. The fact that the university is making these steps to reveal its designs early is a major departure from the route it took in the late 1950s and early 1960s when community members had no real idea of the school's objectives. Nonetheless, many students and community members remain wary of Columbia's plan for Manhattanville.[131] Undoubtedly, not far from the community residents', students', and school officials' minds is the 1968 controversy over "Gym Crow."

In 2006 Columbia hired a consulting firm to advise the university in regard to expansion and marketing. The firm created a group called the Coalition for the Future of Manhattanville. The coalition, which ostensibly includes community members, businesses, and politicians who have an interest in the area, backs Columbia's plan to redevelop Manhattanville. In direct contrast to the coalition and Columbia is Community Board No. 9 (CB9). When Columbia recently submitted a 197–c plan of redevelopment for community review, CB9 rejected the school's plan and instead submitted its own 197–a plan for redevelopment. One of the major concerns of CB9 is the potential for Columbia to use eminent domain laws as a tool to expand. Many in the West Harlem community worry that Columbia's redevelopment will lead to the displacement of residents as the school acquires new buildings and by the increase of rent that would occur with the creation of new structures. Further, opponents charge that Columbia has made no proposal to create affordable moderate- to low-income housing that reflects the economic status of many of Manhattanville's residents.[132]

At a meeting in August 2007, former mayor David Dinkins and current university president Lee Bollinger met at a Harlem community center to discuss the school's plans with CB9 and observing community members. Dinkins and Bollinger were loudly booed. By September 2007 both Columbia's 197–c and CB9's 197–a had been certified by the Department of City Planning. Both plans will undergo a Uniform Land Use Review Procedure.[133]

In the end, Columbia still has the need to expand, and the community still distrusts the university's plans. The names have all changed, but the scenarios and issues seem to be the same. Instead of Grayson Kirk it is Lee Bollinger; instead of Mayor John Lindsay it is Mayor Michael Bloomberg who is in favor Columbia's plan; instead of the West Harlem Community Organization it is CB9 that opposes Columbia's ambition; and, instead of 2.1 acres in Morningside Park it is 17 acres in Manhattanville. The conflict over space and power continues to rage.

The members of the 1960s generation should be applauded in spite of what some called their misguided idealism. If ever there were a time when the United States would move to strike down racism for good and allow all Americans an opportunity to influence the decisions that their government made, it was during the 1960s. As Todd Gitlin, who was at one time the national president of SDS, stated, the 1960s were "years of hope," and hope is what the young people of that generation did.[134] While some critics of the activists claimed that these young people were acting as if they hated America and wanted to destroy the country, most of these student and community activists, in spite of the destructive rhetoric, wanted to make the nation better, even if it meant causing disruptions. Unfortunately, as Barry Gottehrer, who acted as special assistant to Mayor Lindsay at the time of the 1968 events, understood it, the Columbia crisis "marked the beginning of the end of idealism of the '60s."[135]

By the late 1960s, students at Columbia and universities all across the United States were making their school officials believe that it was wrong to carry on with the colleges' entrenched, institutionally racist ways. The community and students challenged the leadership of white institutions and the government. These challengers thus played the role of a catalyst for positive change. What would make a university like Columbia or other white institutions believe that it could take and control even more land from black people? The answer was power.

Economically, politically, and socially, Columbia believed that it had a right to take up more park space; and, what was more, it had the power and support to do so. Trustees and administrators of an Ivy League university did not contemplate too deeply the effects of removing tenants from SRO apartment buildings in New York City; nor did the trustees worry about cutting off access to softball fields in Morningside Park. Indeed, the trustees did not fret about such matters because the trustees and administrators did not have to live in any of the Harlem SROs and did not have to patronize Morningside Park; in fact, many were afraid of both places. The reality of the situation was that many of the people who did actually live in SROs and who did patronize Morningside Park before Columbia released its designs for a gymnasium were black.

Unfortunately, in the opinions of many white institutions, the ideas of black and powerlessness had been synonymous for too long. That fact makes this story unique and important. For once, Columbia University officials, New York City officials, and even federal officials had to recognize the power of black people. This did not, of course, mean the wholesale defeat of racism but rather a symbolic battle that showed that institutional white power could be checked by a cohesive and focused protest effort.

In a similar fashion, black and white students found that by protesting, they could force a university to share the power that had traditionally been unavailable to students. Much of this they learned from the Civil Rights movement, but the students in the late 1960s chose to apply these lessons to their efforts on campus. The white radical students achieved the radicalization of a large number of the generally white student body and eventually won some protest demands, including the cutting of ties with the Institute for Defense Analyses and of course the increase of student power.

Black student activists were also victorious. By separating from white protesters and allying themselves with working-class black community members, black student protesters were able to exercise Black Student Power. As Bill Sales of SAS put it two decades after the 1968 demonstrations, "We were not depending on anybody but ourselves and our community. That was a phenomenal feeling. It was—it was a way of viscerally learning what a real black liberation would be like."[136] In one form or another, Black Student Power would become an issue with which universities would have to deal throughout the 1960s, 1970s, and 1980s. In the instance of the 1968–69 demonstrations, however, Black Student Power meant the manifestation of power for the black community that surrounded Columbia University in the City of New York.

Conclusion

This work began as a simple project on a community rebellion in New York City, but it grew into a piece that deals with the innermost insecurities of the citizens and institutions of the United States in regard to the implications of race and power. It has attempted to answer several questions: How could a white institution make such a bold attempt to take land and property that belonged to the city and that was used mostly by black people? How did the confrontation methods that worked in the Civil Rights movement play out in the Columbia controversies? Why did black and white students split, and how did their agendas differ? Why did American universities give in to student protesters, and what did that mean for the future of education?

Habit and power are the most succinct answers to the first question regarding the desire and ability of a white institution to take what was public and make it private. Columbia had the money and wherewithal to purchase large amounts of land and property in Harlem, and the two acres in Morningside Park for the gym would have just added to its holdings. Part of this phenomenon was due to the economic inability of people in those surrounding neighborhoods to purchase buildings and land, but more had to do with the fact that no one had really challenged Columbia with the tenacity that black community members and students did in 1968–69. Together, they illustrated that, even with the university receiving grants from the Ford Foundation and making contracts with the city and state, it could be stopped, as could most white institutions, if these entities pushed too far into areas that did not belong to them.

The students and community members blocked Columbia's gym plans by using confrontational and disruptive tactics. These were techniques that civil rights activists were using throughout the North and South in the 1960s. One of the reasons these methods worked so well at Columbia was the death of civil rights leader Martin Luther King Jr., which added inspiration to the efforts of the students. The confrontational tactics also worked because the university did not expect that the students would take matters concerning the gym and the school's ties to the Defense Department that seriously. As President Kirk indicated in 1968 when he found out about the students invading Hamilton Hall, he was surprised. He, like many school officials around the nation, did not believe the students who attended these universities had much reason to protest. Those officials found out that in spite of the metal fences and walls that they erected to keep undesirables out, the problems of the larger society would bleed onto campus eventually.

Although black and white students protested the construction of the gym and the university's ties to the military-industrial complex, they did not do so as a racially integrated group. In this case, the black students and community members who advocated the separation tactics that Black Power outlined showed how black people could use their race, the race of their allies, and the race of their opponent to advance goals such as the end to gym construction and the increased enrollment of black students. By separating from white radical protesters, black students made the university recognize the black demonstrators and their demands as a separate issue altogether. In doing so, the black protesters were able to play on the university's fear of being labeled as a racist institution. In addition, the black demonstrators were able to capitalize on Columbia's fears of Harlem black militants invading campus and rioting in the way they rioted after the death of Martin Luther King Jr. In the end, the controversies at Columbia in 1968–69 marked a time in history when the strategies of Black Power succeeded.

Part of the reason American universities capitulated to the demands of student protesters was fear, but another part was the understanding that universities could no longer shield themselves from societal issues. When universities like Columbia made contracts with the Defense Department, the desires of the students did not play a large role in the decision. American universities quickly learned that students wanted to take part in the decisions that their universities made. Because of generational differences, the desires of the students and those of the universities were often quite different.

The students wanted their universities to use their power to fix the problems of society. University officials wanted their institutions to continue to operate efficiently and without disruption, and to contribute to society as they saw fit. Often these universities neglected their roles as neighbors, and the students pointed out this fact. When the students chose to protest, they set into motion a new way of thinking that would help to rearrange the power structure at universities. While students today may not even recognize the ways that the efforts of the early protesters affect their lives at their universities, the lines of communication among students, faculty, and administrators are much more open than before the students of the 1960s chose to act.

It is an attractive prospect to want to claim that the world changed greatly because of the events at Columbia, but that would be unrealistic. Indeed, change did occur because of the protests, but many of the dynamics of power and race privilege remain intact. In Harlem, the black community is still largely poor and disenfranchised.[1] This is not to say that Harlem's black community is totally voiceless or powerless; it is just not as economically and politically powerful as some of the white institutions that have established themselves in Harlem.[2] Along the same lines, Columbia University still owns land and housing complexes in the surrounding neighborhoods, and, unfortunately, it still faces allegations of racism and imperialism.[3] Even if they do receive input from the faculty and students, Columbia's trustees and administrators still make the grand majority of decisions that affect the school. Again, this is not to negate the gains that students made during the 1960s, but it does show that change is a relative term when it comes to history.

In regard to black students at Columbia, SAS's 1960s push for equal rights on campus and in the community was helpful to the larger black freedom struggle, but students of African descent still deal with issues of whiteness and the effects of white privilege. Fortunately, these students benefit from the creation of the Columbia University Institute for Research in African-American Studies that opened in 1993. Its presence is the manifestation of the dreams of those SAS members who participated in the 1968–69 protests. These sorts of changes (or rather enhancements) occurred slowly, but they should be considered victories nonetheless for those protesters.

If one were to measure the importance of the Columbia events by the greatness of the changes that occurred in the world as a result of the demonstrations, then one might be disappointed. If one viewed the events as part of the larger lessons to be learned about American society, the black experience, and university life in the late 1960s, however, then the importance of those events becomes infinitely more essential. Columbia's history in the 1960s testifies to the fact that universities like Columbia could not remain sheltered from the social and economic strife of the "outside" world.

One of the lessons that can be learned from the Columbia controversies is that large, white institutions are not now, nor were they ever, impregnable.

Considering this fact, the social movements of the day—Black Power and the antiwar movement—disrupted the plans of Columbia University. Black Power, in this sense, meant the ability of black students and black working-class community members to overcome class differences to deal with an issue that affected black people. This alliance, along with the protests of other students, forced the university to back down from its proposal to build the gym.

In the end, the gym was really just a symbol. It was a symbol of what Columbia, and any other white institution, was capable of doing in a black community. For an entity that owned so much land in Harlem, taking a couple of acres of land in a park would not have seemed like an irregular acquisition, especially since the university had undergone the same process to build softball fields. A large business, which essentially describes what a university is when it deals in realty, often makes decisions with the welfare of the people that it intends to serve in mind. The gym, in this case, was originally intended to serve only the needs of Columbia students. Therefore, the needs and wants of the people who already patronized the park were overlooked. By the time the university made an attempt to deal with the concerns of the community, it was too late, and society had changed greatly. This business decision obviously became detrimental to the operation of the university when the Harlem residents and students reacted negatively. As serendipity would have it, the timing for the protests of the community and student activists was perfect, as the mood of peaceful negotiation for power shifted to one of militancy. When Martin Luther King Jr. died, so too did much of the accommodating sentiment that black people had fostered. This time, the power and threat of racial violence, which usually worked for white supremacists, worked in favor of the black community. The community, which had shown what it was capable of during the riots that took place in Harlem in the 1960s, incited fear in the minds of university officials who knew that Columbia could potentially become a victim of Harlem's wrath.

In a different time, the university might have gotten away with building the gym because the school officials could log complaints from people outside the university as just that: reactions of outsiders who did not understand the needs of the university. University representatives could reason (as did one Columbia official) that they expected negative reactions from community members, but that progress was necessary. As it was, concerned citizens on and off campus impeded what the university considered progress.

The fact that the community could count on SAS as an inside connection became a main reason why the university could not complete its project in the park. Like most universities in the late 1960s, Columbia was sensitive to issues concerning race. Allegations of racism in a time when the federal government was forcing universities to open doors to black students meant undesirable attention for institutions like Columbia. As an Ivy League university, Columbia had gained the reputation of being one of the elite institutions in America, and an indictment of racism by black and white students only tarnished that image. Whether officials at the university considered the school to be a haven for racism was of really little import. The fact that a significant portion of its student body, in addition to a large contingent from the neighboring community, labeled it as such was enough to draw negative attention. This was a situation that the university could not ignore, especially in light of the tense racial climate that plagued the 1960s.

Columbia, if anything, learned about the potential of people, particularly young people. For as entrenched as the university was in its ways, the student protesters maintained enough resolve to force the school to address their issues. The university could not take some of the protesters' issues seriously, such as when SDS called for open admissions and guaranteed graduations for local black, Puerto Rican, and working-class white students. Many of the issues the students pressed, however, were valid. Issues like the war in Vietnam and the school's role in weapons research prompted students' anxiety and concern. The presence of African Americans on campus as well as the implementation of courses that dealt with history and culture of black people were equally important. Using the momentum they had gained from the 1968 protests, members of SAS attempted (unsuccessfully) to force the university to start a black institute that would give them the right and means to tell the story of black people. These concerns about the war, race, and power did not just affect the students on Columbia's campus, but traces of the protest that took place on the Heights could be found on the campuses of Harvard and Cornell as well. On those campuses, issues regarding black studies programs, institutional racism, and the increase of student power unsettled students as well. In this way, the impact of the Columbia protests became that much more significant, as the efforts of the Columbia University protesters set the groundwork for future rebellions across the nation.

History has done well to record the events that occurred on Morningside Heights. Columbia in 1968–69 is an exciting story that deals with many of the major themes of the 1960s. Issues of local and national politics, economics, and diplomacy all played a role in the unraveling of those events. Local politicians debated heavily over the necessity and purpose of a private gym on public land, and the election of Richard Nixon and his decision to terminate college deferments made the Vietnam War a reality for students. Economically, the class differences between school officials, students, and local community members contributed to the controversies. Furthermore, diplomatic relations, in the sense of university environment to the Harlem environment, tested the lines of the rebellion that occurred in those years. As a result, the students made themselves more than aware of what was happening in their world. This was what motivated them to shout "Gym Crow Must Go!"

If anything, the Columbia episodes illustrate how history is inevitably connected, and that the impact of events and people may not be apparent until years later. For instance, SAS leader Ray Brown explained that because he was a child when the Supreme Court decided on the *Brown v. Board of Education* case, he felt a special obligation not only to integrate traditionally white institutions, but to use the knowledge and power he gained from the institutions to help his race and community.[4] In a similar vein, students chose to confront the buildup of the military-industrial complex about which President Eisenhower (former president of Columbia) had admonished the country. They chose to do so on campus. Then, the influence of the Civil Rights and Black Power movements showed in the manner in which many of the students conducted themselves in the face of what they considered immoral authority. It was apparent that the Columbia protests did not occur in a vacuum, and because of that, the events on the Heights should be placed in line with other major events of the 1960s. As the scars of early construction on the gym in Morningside Park are still physically visible, the memories of the events of 1968–69 will continue to show in the minds of all those who witnessed the rebellions of citizens—young and old, black and white—on the campus of Columbia University in the City of New York.

Epilogue

Where Are They Now?

Whenever one reads a history about the 1960s, one wonders what those activists and militants from yesteryear are doing now. One also wonders whether the agitators still feel the same way about the issues that they did in their younger years. Finally, one wonders if those demonstrators from the 1960s are still active in their struggles against racism, war, and poverty. The answer in the case of the Columbia rebels is overwhelmingly affirmative. The following is an attempt to locate some of the demonstrators in the four decades after the rebellions of the late 1960s.

In April 2008 nearly four hundred Columbia demonstrators and supporters came back to the Morningside Heights campus for a commemoration of their activities forty years earlier. Over the course of the commemoration, there were scholarly panels that analyzed the lasting impacts of the Columbia controversy. The topics that the panels covered included the Vietnam War and the current wars in the Middle East; current issues of race on Columbia's campus; feminism in larger society; campus activism. Although the scene was reminiscent of a college reunion at times, the event was very telling. For the very first time since 1968, Columbia University officially recognized and hosted an event commemorating the activities of the student rebels. Just as the current president, Lee Bollinger (who came to Columbia as a student in the fall of 1968), acknowledged that fact, an older, long-haired man stood up and shouted: "Bollinger is overseeing the expansion project of West Harlem . . . in Manhattanville! Shame on him!" While the long-haired man, who was not an alumnus of Columbia, was shouting, some of the crowd booed and hissed the president. Others in the audience, however, attempted to shout down the man who interrupted the president. That scene was replayed at several different events where the president made an appearance. Ironically, many of Columbia's 1968 agitators grew flustered and upset with the community people who kept raising the issue of Manhattanville and the potential loss of homes that may occur with the university's current acquisition of many acres of land in West Harlem. In this way, some of the 1960s demonstrators had become counterdemonstrators. Perhaps the former protesters understood the frustration of those who sat in the audience in 1968 when Rudd seized the microphone at the King memorial or of those who did not approve of the demonstrators who took over buildings.

Still, the politics of many of the Columbia rebels seem not to have changed. Most of the demonstrators oppose the current war in Iraq as they did that in Vietnam during the 1960s. Mark Rudd, who currently lives in New Mexico, considers himself still active. After having gone "underground" in 1969, Rudd resurfaced in 1977 and participated in political struggles regarding Nicaragua and Native Americans. At the time of the commemoration, he was revising his memoirs. Ron Carver, who was a member of SDS in 1968, has gone on to do union work with the Teamsters. While in 1964 and 1965 he worked with people like Julian Bond in Atlanta and Mississippi, Carver currently works with groups like the NAACP to ensure fairness in hiring and promotion at large companies. Laura Pinsky, who also occupied a building during the demonstrations, is a counselor at Columbia and an AIDS-awareness activist. Bob Feldman, who was a community activist and SDS member while at Columbia, continues to vigorously protest war and U.S. foreign policy today.

Many of the demonstrators have entered the halls of the academy. Lewis Cole, recently deceased, taught at Columbia, where he won teaching awards. Hilton Obenzinger, also an SDS member, teaches at Stanford University. Other educators who were members of or followed SDS include Josh De Wind (Hunter College), Les Gottesman (Golden Gate University), Michael Klare (Hampshire College), Mark Naison (Fordham University), and Michael Wallace (City University of New York). Frances Fox Piven, who was not a member of SDS but who entered Low Library with her daughter, also teaches at the City University of New York.

Several of the members or followers of SAS have also become educators. Bill Sales of SAS teaches at Seton Hall University. The late Henry Jackson of SAS taught at Hunter College. Some black women who were in Hamilton have gone on to educate as well. Cheryl Leggon teaches at Georgia Tech University, while Christine Clark-Evans teaches at Penn State University.

More than a few activists from the time have become authors and artists. SDS supporters like Paul Spike, David Shapiro, James Kunen, Mary Gordon,

Sharon Olds, Jonah Raskin, and Paul Auster have all contributed pieces of literature. Thulani Davis, one of the black women in Hamilton, has become a prolific writer and teaches at New York University; and black alumna Ntozake Shange wrote the award-winning play *For Colored Girls Who Have Considered Suicide When the Rainbow is Enuf* that has recently appeared in film. James "Plunky" Branch, of SAS and the Soul Syndicate, plays and produces music. Robert Friedman, who was at one time editor of the *Spectator*, is a renowned journalist and editor at Bloomberg News. SDSer Tom Hurwitz, who has won awards as a cinematographer, produces movies, as does Sherri Ann Suttles. So too did the late St. Clair Bourne, who occupied Hamilton Hall and became a documentary filmmaker. Juan Gonzalez, who helped take over Low Memorial Library in 1968, went on to join the Young Lords, a Puerto Rican organization based in Harlem that demonstrated for better hospital facilities, education, and housing for Harlem residents. He writes for the *New York Daily News* and cohosts the television program *Democracy Now!*

Some of the activists used the knowledge that they gained from being arrested, arraigned, and tried to become litigators themselves. At least two demonstrators became judges: Omega Psi Phi and SAS member Alford Dempsey and SDS member Gustin Reinbach. Ray Brown of SAS became an attorney, as did Arnim Johnson Jr. of SAS. Incidentally, Arnim Johnson's father, Arnim Johnson Sr., was one of the several attorneys who represented the black students from Hamilton Hall. SDS members or followers like Nancy Biberman, Art Leaderman, William Martin, Andrew Newton, and John Shils became lawyers as well. Biberman also works with a nonprofit organization to build housing complexes for low-income residents.

Others have maintained ties to the community through their vocations. Cicero Wilson of SAS currently operates a company that redevelops neighborhoods for affordable housing in New York City. John Herbert of SAS and Omega Psi Phi is a physician at Harlem Hospital. Carmen Martinez, who attended Barnard, also works at Harlem Hospital as a pediatrician.

Several demonstrators have entered the business world. Leon Denmark of SAS is an executive of Primerica, a subsidiary of Citigroup. The late Stephanie Skurdy, who also occupied Hamilton Hall, was an executive with the McDonald's Corporation. Steve Halliwell of SDS became an investment banker.

When looking back upon their experiences at Columbia, many of the black students who were in Hamilton Hall or who protested for black studies have mixed feelings. Most appreciate what they were able to achieve with a degree from Columbia. In fact, several of the black students went on to Harvard or other Ivy League universities for advanced degrees. Some of the other students, however, were traumatized by their experiences. Al Dempsey, who was a football player and member of Omega Psi Phi, left the university after the demonstration to "keep his sanity," he remembered. Other demonstrators like Cicero Wilson and James "Plunky" Branch claimed to have blocked many of their Columbia memories out of their mind. Wilson, at the fortieth commemoration, even expressed that he still felt uneasy on Columbia's campus. One SAS member asserted that the culture of Columbia in the 1960s was not much different from that of the segregated American South.

Some of the demonstrators saw Columbia in 1968 as a defining moment for them. The definitions of those moments, however, differ. Some remember the events of the Columbia rebellion in a light-hearted way. Some of the building occupants regaled the "sex, drugs, and rock 'n' roll" aspects of the demonstrations and the 1960s in general. They recall the humor and sense of satisfaction that were associated with dissenting.

Many of the black students who were in Hamilton Hall do not remember the events as light-heartedly. Some black students bristle at the image of the Columbia demonstrations that media sources often invoke. Some are dismayed at the representation of the rebellion as one where raucous white youth defied their parents and authority by taking over buildings. Many of the SAS-led students do not remember the situation as "sex, drugs, and rock 'n' roll," but rather as the "scariest time" of their lives, as a time when black students answered the call of the community to help in the fight against an intrusive white institution. Although many of the Hamilton demonstrators acknowledged the gravity of their actions, they did forge a bond among themselves. As one SAS member noted, "I forged life-long friendships in Hamilton Hall."[1]

Unfortunately, some of the participants of the 1968 and 1969 demonstrations can no longer tell of their experiences. Some of the black students and community members who occupied Hamilton Hall are deceased. These include:

Bruce Bailey, West Harlem Tenants Association
Robert Belt, former head of SAS
Deborah Billingsley, SAS and Barnard College
St. Clair Bourne, SAS
Denise Carty, SAS and Barnard College
Coco Bozman Dempsey (wife of Alford Dempsey)
Llewelyn Harrison, friend of SAS
C. Diane Howell
Henry F. Jackson, SAS
Arnim Johnson Sr., legal representative
Rick Johnson

Charles Kyoshi Jones, SAS and Omega Psi Phi
Joy Lewis, SAS and Barnard College
Bob McKay, West Harlem Community Organization
Charles McKinney, legal representative
Fred Samuels, City Council
Stephanie Skurdy, SAS and Barnard College
Frank Stimley, SAS
Reggie Thompkins
Kwame Ture (Stokely Carmichael), SNCC and BPP
Al Waller, SAS

Some of the members, followers, and supporters of SDS have since passed as well. Those include:

Stew Albert
Tara Avery
Martin Balin
William Banks
Joe Barthel
Robert Bernstein
Faris Bouhafa
Homer Brown
Robert Campbell
Lewis Cole
Vernon Dibble
Andrea Eagan
Sarah Eisenstein
Erich Fromm
Jerry Garcia, on campus
    performing
Ted Gold
Lev Gorkin
Fred Grab
Anya Gromadska
Isabel Grossner
Daniel Grutzendler
Marvin Harris
Abbie Hoffman, Yippies,
    on campus
Leo Hurwitz, on campus

John Jacobs
Richard Keithline
William Moses Kunstler,
    on campus
Dwight MacDonald, on
    campus
Norman Mailer, on campus
Billy Margolis
Melvin Margolis
Kevin Martin
Sam Melville, on campus
Sidney Morganbesser
J. Michael Nichols
Richard Nilsen
Phil Ochs
Gretchen Grossner Older
Robert Raterman
William Redfield
Jack Rohan
Jerry Rubin, on campus
Mario Savio, on campus
William Schulte
Jeff Shaman
Sam Steinberg, on campus
Sidney Von Luther
Fred Wilson

City officials as well as members of the faculty and administration of Columbia have also passed away. They include:

George Collins, Professor
Grayson Kirk, President
Serge Lang, Professor
Mayor John Lindsay
Margaret Mead, Barnard Professor
Seymour Melman, Professor
William Reinmuth, MD
Edward Said, Professor
James Shenton, Professor
Eliot Skinner, Professor (one of the first
    black professors at Columbia)
David Truman, Vice President[2]

Although many of the participants have since passed on, the issues at Columbia seem to linger. An activist from the Harlem Tenants Council, Nellie Bailey, continues to denounce Columbia for its expansion. At the fortieth commemoration, she passed out a flyer that read: "They Can Buy The Politicians, but They Still Have the Community to Deal With." The flyer ostensibly referred to the fact that city officials finally approved Columbia's expansion project in Manhattanville, just north and east of the university. According to the flyer, "Columbia Spent $2.3 million last year (2007) to lobby for its West Harlem eviction plan." The Coalition to Preserve Community vowed to stand against Columbia's plan. It observed that "it's been 40 years since Columbia students and community residents stopped the CU gym in Morningside Park. Let's show CU that Harlem is still not for sale." Neither the university nor the community can forget when concerned Harlem and Morningside Heights citizens and students used their power to check Columbia University in the City of New York. As a permanent reminder, on April 27, 2008, the current parks commissioner Adrian Benepe, Harlem community activist Suki Ports, and former SAS member and Harlem resident Samuel White planted a tree in Morningside Park, where there is no gym.

Notes

Introduction

1. "Columbia University, the Arrogant Giant."

2. Cruse, *The Crisis of the Negro Intellectual*, 13.

3. Olmsted Jr. and Kimball, *Frederick Law Olmsted, Landscape Architect, 1822–1903*; Sutton, *Civilizing American Cities*.

4. Morgan, *American Slavery, American Freedom*, 217–25; Holton, *Forced Founders*.

5. Foner, *Reconstruction*, 603–4; Foner, *Nothing but Freedom*, 55–56, 82–86, 107–8; McPherson, *Ordeal by Fire*, 505–6, 573; Du Bois, *The Souls of Black Folk*, 14–16.

6. Oliver and Shapiro, *Black Wealth/White Wealth*, x, 3, 58–60; Massey and Denton, *American Apartheid*, 7–9.

7. Wesley, "The Negro in the Organization of Abolition," in *Blacks in the Abolitionist Movement*, ed. Bracey, Meier, and Rudwick, 55–61.

8. Meier and Rudwick, "The Role of Blacks in the Abolitionist Movement," in *Blacks in the Abolitionist Movement*, ed. Bracey, Meier, and Rudwick, 116–18.

9. Ibid., 118.

10. Malcolm X, speech given in New York, New York, 1964, in Shabazz, *Malcolm X Speaks Out*.

11. Ibid., 257–59.

12. Eskew, *But for Birmingham*.

13. Frazier, ed., *Afro-American History*, 436–37.

14. Van DeBurg, ed., *Modern Black Nationalism*, 119.

15. Ibid., 123–24.

16. Incidentally, while occupying Hamilton Hall, the black student demonstrators referred to themselves as "The Black Students of Hamilton Hall." As the SAS provided

much of the leadership throughout the demonstration, this work will henceforth refer to the Black Students of Hamilton Hall as SAS.

17. Kahn, *The Battle for Morningside Heights*, 93.

18. Anderson, *The Movement and the Sixties*, 192.

19. Morgan, *American Slavery, American Freedom*, 266–67.

20. MacLean, *Behind the Mask of Chivalry*, 52–53.

21. O'Reilly, *Nixon's Piano*, 6–8, 279–329.

22. See Frazier, *Black Bourgeoisie.*

23. Edward Rubenstein, "College Seeks Negro Applicants," *Columbia Daily Spectator*, October 15, 1963, 1.

24. Ibid.

25. Kahn, *The Battle for Morningside Heights*, 118.

26. Edward Rubenstein, "CU Gets Few Negro Applications," *Columbia Daily Spectator*, October 17, 1963, 1.

27. Ibid., 3.

28. Avorn, *Up against the Ivy Wall*, 20–21.

29. "Negro Students Fighting Apathy," *New York Times*, December 20, 1964, 53.

30. Ibid.

31. *Crisis at Columbia: Report of the Fact-Finding Commission Appointed to Investigate the Disturbances at Columbia University in April and May 1968*, 17. Hereafter, *Crisis at Columbia.*

32. Professor Wallerstein based his scholarly work on the continent of Africa. In doing so, he was able to make a connection with the black student protesters in 1968–69. Some of Wallerstein's works at the time of the demonstrations were *Africa, the Politics of Independence* and *Africa, the Politics of Unity: An Analysis of a Contemporary Social Movement.*

33. Immanuel Wallerstein, interview by Robert Friedman and Andrew Crane, mid-June 1968, manuscript, Oral History Collection, Columbia University, New York, NY.

34. Donadio, "Columbia: Seven Interviews," 376.

35. *Crisis at Columbia*, 14.

36. Bennett Jr., "Confrontation on Campus," 27.

37. See the campus map in the illustrations.

38. Starr, "The Case of the Columbia Gym," 105.

39. Thomas L. Kennedy, interview by author, March 8, 1997, Pullman, Washington.

40. Avorn, *Up against the Ivy Wall*, 29.

41. Adelson, *SDS*, 3.

42. Liebert, *Radical and Militant Youth*, 75.

43. Adelson, *SDS*, 7.

44. Ibid., 206.

45. Donadio, "Columbia: Seven Interviews," 374.

46. Ibid., 372. Another source claims that a similar decision was made at a national SDS convention at the University of Indiana. "The Debacle at Columbia," 663. One member of Columbia's SDS at the time discounts that such a decision was ever made in a national setting. See http://www.bfeldman68.blogspot.com.

47. Sherry, *The Rise of American Air Power*; Pierpaoli, *Truman and Korea*.

48. Kahn, *The Battle for Morningside Heights*, 18.

49. Avorn, *Up against the Ivy Wall*, 4–8.

50. Liebert, *Radical and Militant Youth*, xv.

51. Bell and Kristol, eds., *Confrontation*, 96.

52. Grant, *Confrontation on Campus*, x.

53. Meyer, "Columbia's Ruddite Rebellion," 16.

54. Donadio, "Columbia: Seven Interviews," 377.

Chapter 1. Why I Hate You: Community Resentment of Columbia

1. Reverend Samuel N. Brown, interview by author, November 22, 1997, New York.

2. See the campus map in the illustrations.

3. Nash, *The University and the City*, 95.

4. Joel Griffiths and Lester Nafzger, "Sports: The Gym-in-the-Park Controversy" (Revisited), *New York Free Press*, February 20, 1969.

5. Olmsted and Vaux, *Preliminary Study of a Design for the Laying Out of Morningside Park*, 334–35; Olmsted and Fein, eds., *Landscape into Cityscape*, 334.

6. Handlin, *The Newcomers*, 35.

7. Ibid., 48.

8. Henri, *Black Migration*; Marks, *Farewell*; Thomas, *Life for Us Is What We Make It*; Osofsky, *Harlem*.

9. Handlin, *The Newcomers*, 48.

10. Roediger, *The Wages of Whiteness and the Making of the American Working Class*, 14; Nelson, *Divided We Stand*.

11. Jackson, *The Ku Klux Klan in the City, 1915–1930*.

12. Frieden and Morris, eds., *Urban Planning and Social Policy*, 67.

13. Leinwald, ed., *The Negro in the City*, 45.

14. Huggins, *Harlem Renaissance*; Martin, *Literary Garveyism*.

15. Frieden and Morris, eds., *Urban Planning and Social Policy*, 18.

16. Clarke, *Harlem*, 3.

17. Palmer, *Passageways*, 234.

18. Franklin, *From Slavery to Freedom*, 433–34.

19. Ibid.; Palmer, *Passageways*, 207–9.

20. Takaki, *Double Victory*, 55–57.

21. Marc Rauch, Bob Feldman, and Art Leaderman, *Columbia and the Community: Past Policy and New Directions*, A Report of the Columbia College Citizenship

Council Committee for Research (1968), 6, Collins Collection, Schomburg Center, New York Public Library, New York.

22. Samuels, "A Walk along 'the Worst Block,'" 18.

23. "Many Gains Noted by Puerto Ricans," *New York Times,* March 2, 1964, 18.

24. Ibid.

25. Brown, *Manchild in the Promised Land,* 192.

26. Massey and Denton, *American Apartheid,* 174.

27. "Columbia University in the City of New York—An Old Partnership," Collins Collection, box 5, folder 9, Schomburg Center for Research in Black Culture, New York Public Library, New York.

28. Bell and Kristol, eds., *Confrontation,* 110.

29. Rauch et al., *Columbia and the Community,* 11.

30. "President's Committee on Urban-Minority Problems, Report," 1967, Protest and Activism Collection, Series 1, RC1/14a, Columbiana Collection, Columbia University Archives, New York.

31. Nash, *The University and the City,* 97.

32. "Morningside Tenants Protest Renewal at City Hall Hearing," *New York Times,* March 12, 1965, 17.

33. Ibid.

34. Roediger, *Wages of Whiteness,* 14 and 19; Roediger, *Colored White.*

35. Kahn, *The Battle for Morningside Heights,* 82–83.

36. Peter Millones, "Gym Controversy Began in Late 50's," *New York Times,* April 25, 1968, 50.

37. Rauch et al., *Columbia and the Community,* 8. Liebert, *Radical and Militant Youth,* 36.

38. *Worker* (New York), May 17, 1968.

39. Ibid.; Massey and Denton, *American Apartheid,* 187; Frieden and Morris, eds., *Urban Planning and Social Policy;* Schwartz, *We Are Talking about Homes.*

40. Kahn, *The Battle for Morningside Heights,* 86.

41. Ibid.

42. Rauch et al., *Columbia and the Community,* 10.

43. *Columbia Daily Spectator,* October 30, 1964.

44. Frieden and Morris, eds., *Urban Planning and Social Policy,* 321.

45. Starr, "The Case of the Columbia Gym," 105.

46. Kahn, *The Battle for Morningside Heights,* 86.

47. Ibid.

48. Douglas Davidove, Assadour Tavitian, Teymour Darkhosh, and Michael Stama te Latos, "What Do the Tenants of the Occupied Buildings Say?" May 17, 1968, Columbiana Collection, Columbia University Archives, New York.

49. "Rights Group Asks CU to End Large-Scale Tenant Removal," *Columbia Daily Spectator,* January 5, 1965, 1.

50. *Columbia Daily Spectator,* February 25, 1965, 1.

51. *Columbia Daily Spectator,* December 22, 1966, 1, Columbiana Collection, Columbia University Archives, New York; "Columbia," *New York Amsterdam News,* December 17, 1966, 39.

52. *New York Amsterdam News,* February 15, 1967, Columbiana Collection, Columbia University Archives, New York.

53. James Booker, "Panther Party vs. Numbers," *New York Amsterdam News,* November 12, 1966, 9.

54. "50 Picket Kirk Home to Mourn Buildings 'Killed' by Columbia," Collins Collection, Schomburg Center, New York Public Library, New York.

55. Testimony of Harold McGuire, *Cox Commission Columbia University. Fact-Finding Commission Proceedings,* 428.

56. *Crisis at Columbia,* 39.

57. Testimony of Harold McGuire, *Cox Commission Columbia University,* 433.

58. *Crisis at Columbia,* 37–38.

59. Frieda Feldman to Mayor John Lindsay, January 1966, Collins Collection, Schomburg Center, New York Public Library, New York.

60. *Morningsiders United Newsletter,* September 1, 1964, 1, Collins Collection, Schomburg Center, New York Public Library, New York.

61. "Morningside Patrol: Law and Order?," *Columbia Daily Spectator,* April 30, 1970, 1.

62. Rauch et al., *Columbia and the Community,* 5.

63. "Morningside Area General Neighborhood Renewal Plan," City of New York City Planning Commission, January 20, 1965, New York.

64. George Weiser, "Heights Sellout," *West Side News and Morningsider,* May 20, 1965.

65. *Morningsiders United Newsletter,* September 1, 1964.

66. Frank Patton Jr., "Institutional Expansion," *Morningside Citizen,* May 6, 1966, 2.

67. Michael Drosnin, *Columbia Daily Spectator,* March 11, 1965, 1.

68. George Weiser, *Morningside Sentinel,* no. 2 (July 22, 1966), 1.

69. Ibid.

70. "Columbia Expands into 609 W. 115th Street," *Morningside Sentinel,* no. 3 (September 6, 1966), 1.

71. Cathy Aldridge, "The Confused Situation at Harlem Hospital," *New York Amsterdam News,* January 14, 1966, 1.

72. Blyden Jackson, "Building Harlem Down," *New York Free Press,* March 28, 1968, 3.

73. Ibid.

74. Priscilla Tucker, "Poor People's Plan," 265, Collins Collection, Schomburg Center, New York Public Library, New York.

75. Ibid.

76. "Urban Planners Get Harlem Aid," *New York Times,* April 16, 1967.

77. Ibid.

78. "ARCH's Political Role," 110.

79. James Booker, "Hush, Hush Meetings," *New York Amsterdam News,* January 14, 1967, 13.

80. "President's Committee on Urban-Minority Problems, 1967," Columbiana Collection, Columbia University Archives, New York.

81. "Columbia Picks Faculty Group to Work on Harlem Problems," *New York Amsterdam News,* December 17, 1966.

82. "Columbia U. Opens Account at Carver," *New York Amsterdam News,* November 16, 1966, 1.

Chapter 2. Gym Crow: Recreational Segregation in Morningside Park

1. Thomas L. Kennedy, interview by author, March 8, 1997, Pullman, Washington.

2. Avorn, *Up against the Ivy Wall,* 20.

3. Louis and Mary Lusky, "Columbia 1968," 196.

4. George Nash and Cynthia Epstein, "Harlem Views Columbia," *New York Magazine,* July 8, 1968, 58–59.

5. Parsons, ed., *Memories of Samuel Parsons, Landscape Architect of the Department of Public Parks, New York,* 59–65.

6. Ibid., 65.

7. *Morningsider,* March 19, 1964, 2.

8. "Condition of the Park," *Morningside Citizen,* March 20, 1964, 1.

9. Ira Silverman, "Arrest Thirteen Harlem Youths in 'Wolfpack' Mugging of Professor," *Morningsider,* May 28, 1964, 1.

10. Starr, "The Case of the Columbia Gym," 107.

11. The name "Bobby Smith" was an alias used in the story to protect the identity of the actual participant. The publication gave no justification for the use of an alias. *Partners in the Park* (New York), March 1968, Columbiana Collection, Columbia University Archives, New York.

12. Bell and Kristol, eds., *Confrontation,* 114.

13. *Partners in the Park* (New York), March 1968.

14. Testimony of Harold McGuire, *Cox Commission Columbia University,* 402.

15. Ibid., 401.

16. Dwight C. Smith, "Letter to the Editor," *New York Times,* May 20, 1966, 46.

17. Kahn, *The Battle for Morningside Heights,* 92.

18. See the campus map in the illustrations.

19. Wm. Theodore de Bary, interview by author, November 21, 1997, New York.

20. "New Gym Annex," *Columbia Alumni News,* date not indicated, Collins Collection, Schomburg Center for Research in Black Culture, New York Public Library, New York.

21. Grayson Kirk, "Within the Family," *Columbia College Today,* vol. 11, no. 1 (Fall 1963), 3.

22. Ibid., 17.

23. Bell and Kristol, eds., *Confrontation*, 111–12.

24. "New Gym Annex," *Columbia Alumni News*, date not indicated, Collins Collection, Schomburg Center, New York Public Library, New York.

25. Ibid.

26. Columbia Gymnasium Committee, "The New Columbia Gymnasium," Columbiana Collection, Columbia University Archives, New York.

27. McGuire testified that it was important that the "mayor and city council . . . send a home rule message to the state legislature for authorizing the carrying out of this project [the gym]." He also made it clear that the legislature should approve of the measure by two-thirds vote, the governor should concur, and so should all "cognizant municipal departments." Testimony of Harold McGuire, *Cox Commission Columbia University*, 407.

28. "Six Weeks That Shook Morningside: A Special Report," 31.

29. Bell and Kristol, eds., *Confrontation*, 118.

30. "Six Weeks That Shook Morningside," 31.

31. Kahn, *The Battle for Morningside Heights*, 93.

32. "Six Weeks That Shook Morningside," 31.

33. "Chain Link Citadel on M'side Heights," *Westside News*, February 22, 1968, 1.

34. Griffiths and Nafzger, "Sports," *New York Free Press*, February 20, 1969.

35. Frieden and Morris, eds., *Urban Planning and Social Policy*, 185.

36. Bell and Kristol, eds., *Confrontation*, 118.

37. "Undergraduate Group to Run Student Gym Collection Drive," *Columbia Daily Spectator*, October 23, 1963, 1.

38. Powledge, *Free At Last?*, 199–200.

39. Rust Gilbert, "Northern Student Movement to Debate New Right's Tack," *Columbia Daily Spectator*, October 24, 1963, 1, 3.

40. Rust Gilbert, "Northern Student Movement Seeks to End Negro Slums," *Columbia Daily Spectator*, October 25, 1963, 3.

41. Rust Gilbert, "NSM Praised at Conference by Delegates," *Columbia Daily Spectator*, October 29, 1963, 1.

42. Hampton and Fayer, eds., *Voices of Freedom*, 256–57, 261–62.

43. Shabazz, *Malcolm X Speaks Out*.

44. Reverend William Starr, "Spring Report, 1968," Columbiana Collection, Columbia University Archives, New York.

45. Ture and Hamilton, *Black Power*, 34–39.

46. Miller, *On Our Own*, 142.

47. Terry, *Bloods*, xiii.

48. Ibid., xiv.

49. Kahn, *The Battle for Morningside Heights*, 93.

50. Ibid., 94.

51. Starr, "The Case of the Columbia Gym," 116.

52. Hoving, "Thinking Big about Small Parks," 72.

53. Thomas Hoving to George Collins, November 16, 1966, Collins Collection, Schomburg Center, New York Public Library, New York.

54. Ibid.

55. Hoving, "Thinking Big about Small Parks," 12.

56. Bell and Kristol, eds., *Confrontation,* 120.

57. Richard Hatch, "Letter to the Editor," *New York Times,* February 1, 1966, 34.

58. "M. M. Graff to the Editor of the *New York Times,*" April 25, 1968, unpublished, Collins Collection, Schomburg Center, New York Public Library, New York.

59. Ibid.

60. Daniel Douglas, interview by author, November 22, 1997, New York.

61. Reverend Samuel N. Brown, interview by author, November 22, 1997, New York.

62. "Politicians Would Prevent Construction in Morningside Park," *New York Times,* May 17, 1966, 49.

63. Starr, "The Case of the Columbia Gym," 116.

64. "Politicians Would Prevent Construction in Morningside Park."

65. Griffiths and Nafzger, "Sports," *New York Free Press,* February 20, 1969.

66. "Slap in the Face," *New York Amsterdam News,* January 29, 1966, 14.

67. Ibid.

68. "Does Anyone Care?" *New York Amsterdam News,* March 19, 1966, 12.

69. "Being Robbed," *New York Amsterdam News,* March 19, 1966, 12.

70. "Citizens Protest," *Morningside Citizen,* May 6, 1966, 1–2.

71. Ibid.

72. Ibid., 2–3.

73. "Administration Version of Events File," 1968, Columbiana Collection, Columbia University Archives, New York.

74. "Columbia to Begin Gym Next October," *New York Times,* February 24, 1966, 21.

75. Fred M. Hechinger, "Columbia Starts 3-Year Campaign for $200 Million," *New York Times,* November 1, 1966, 1.

76. Ibid.

77. Gitlin, *The Sixties,* 234.

78. Ibid.

79. *Crisis at Columbia,* 95.

80. A borough is a ward or precinct that receives representation in state affairs. New York City consists of five boroughs: Queens, the Bronx, Staten Island, Brooklyn, and Manhattan. Harlem is located in Manhattan.

81. Stanley Salmen, October 14, 1966, Collins Collection, Schomburg Center, New York Public Library, New York. There is no indication as to whom Salmen actually

sent this letter; however, he carbon-copied the letter to a Dr. Chamberlain (Lawrence), who at one point was vice president of the university. Chamberlain suggested that the university assist the tenants evicted from its properties. A Dick Wolfe found a file copy of the letter in 1970 and sent it to Christiane Collins, who with her husband vehemently opposed the gym. Wolfe wrote to Mrs. Collins that "I think I should not tell you how I got them [the documents], though it was perfectly honest. . . . [T]hey were in University files[;] they are legitimate."

82. Ibid.

83. Ibid.

84. Ibid.

85. "M. A. Harris to the Editor of the *New York Free Press*," March 28, 1968, Collins Collection, Schomburg Center for Research in Black Culture, New York Public Library, New York.

86. Lusky, "Columbia 1968," 198.

87. Sara Slack, "Columbia Students in Siege," *New York Amsterdam News*, April 27, 1968, 37.

88. Avorn, *Up against the Ivy Wall*, 20.

89. "Protest against the Gym," Collins Collection, Schomburg Center, New York Public Library, New York.

90. "Harlem v/s Columbia Univ.," Collins Collection, Schomburg Center, New York Public Library, New York.

91. "West Harlem against Columbia University's Segregated Gymnasium" and "Did You Give Columbia Permission . . . ," Collins Collection, Schomburg Center, New York Public Library, New York.

92. "Stop Columbia University," Collins Collection, Schomburg Center, New York Public Library, New York.

93. "Schoolchildren Picket for Park," *Columbia Owl*, November 15, 1967.

94. Kahn, *The Battle for Morningside Heights*, 96.

95. Charles Skoro, "Twelve Arrested in Protest at Gym Construction Site," *Columbia Daily Spectator*, February 21, 1968, 1.

96. "Chain Link Citadel on M'side Heights," *Westside News*, February 22, 1968, 1.

97. Dearing Carpenter, "Thirteen Arrested While 150 Protest Gym Construction," *Columbia Daily Spectator*, February 29, 1968, 1; "Jim Crow Gym?," *Westside News*, March 7, 1968, 1.

98. "The Gymnasium," *Columbia Owl*, March 6, 1968, 4.

99. "Jim Crow Gym?," 1.

100. Ibid.

101. Ibid.

102. "Expansion: Gymnastic, Religious," *New York Free Press*, March 28, 1968.

103. "Night Faces," *Westside News*, March 28, 1968, 1.

104. "Columbia Is Giving It to Us in Morningside Park," *New York Free Press*, March 28, 1968, 12.

105. "Gym Crow," Collins Collection, Schomburg Center, New York Public Library, New York.

106. Griffiths and Nafzger, "Sports," *New York Free Press*, February 20, 1969.

107. Starr, "The Case of the Columbia Gym," 118.

Chapter 3. Up against the Wall: Columbia's Integrated Protest Effort

1. Avorn, *Up against the Ivy Wall*, 27, 292.

2. Ibid.

3. Miller, *On Our Own*, 191–93.

4. Ibid.

5. Bell and Kristol, eds., *Confrontation*, ix.

6. Ibid.

7. Ibid., vii.

8. Several students from Columbia had traveled to the South to work with SNCC in the 1960s. One Columbia student, Ron Carver, worked with SNCC in Mississippi and Georgia in the summers of 1964 and 1965 and subsequently returned to Morningside Heights to continue his efforts to change society with SDS.

9. Zinn, *SNCC*, 8.

10. Miller, *On Our Own*, 191.

11. Bell and Kristol, eds., *Confrontation*, 71.

12. Ibid.

13. Ibid.

14. *Crisis at Columbia*, 83.

15. Kahn, *The Battle for Morningside Heights*, 108.

16. Larry Frazier, "What Happened?," Columbia 1968 and the World Conference, Columbia University, April 24–27, 2008. For more information regarding the Howard University demonstrations, see McDowell et al., "Howard University Protest Movement."

17. William Sales, telephone interview by author, March 25, 1999, Columbia, Missouri.

18. Fraser, *1968*, 171–72.

19. Orest Ranum, "Columbia Crisis," 1970, Office of Oral History Research, Columbia University, New York.

20. As Bill Sales remembers the rally on campus, Rudd, in spite of Truman's efforts, was supposed to lead the protesters into Low Library but did not do so at that time. Sales claimed that Rudd "punked out." Sales interview.

21. On the Columbia campus, the conservative SFC was the main opponent to the tactics of SDS. Avorn, *Up against the Ivy Wall*, 40–41.

22. Ibid., 44–45.

23. *Crisis at Columbia*, 101.

24. Bill Sales, "What Happened?" Columbia 1968 and the World Conference, Columbia University, April 24–27, 2008.

25. Kahn, *The Battle for Morningside Heights,* 124–25.
26. Ranum interview.
27. Reverend William Starr, "Spring Report, 1968," Columbiana Collection, Columbia University Archives, New York.
28. Sales interview.
29. Avorn, *Up against the Ivy Wall,* 47.
30. Kahn, *The Battle for Morningside Heights,* 126.
31. Erikson, *Identity,* 128–35, 155–58.
32. Avorn, *Up against the Ivy Wall,* 47–48.
33. Adelson, *SDS,* 207; Miller, *Democracy in the Streets.*
34. *Crisis at Columbia,* 103.
35. Avorn, *Up against the Ivy Wall,* 49; Sales interview.
36. Kahn, *The Battle for Morningside Heights,* 127.
37. Avorn, *Up against the Ivy Wall,* 51.
38. Ibid., 33–34.
39. Kahn, *The Battle for Morningside Heights,* 134.
40. Quoted in Liebert, *Radical and Militant Youth,* 63.
41. Ibid.
42. Avorn, *Up against the Ivy Wall,* 41.
43. Grayson Kirk, interviewed by John Wooter, October 3, 1968, Oral History Collection, Columbia University, New York, NY.
44. Ranum interview.

Chapter 4. On Our Own: SAS's Self-Imposed Separation

1. Avorn, *Up against the Ivy Wall,* 58.
2. Ibid.
3. *Crisis at Columbia,* 107.
4. Donadio, "Columbia: Seven Interviews," 377–78.
5. Ibid.
6. Fraser, *1968,* 172.
7. Sales interview. The university reported as much to the public two days later. John Hasting, Office of Public Information, April 25, 1968.
8. Silberman, *The Civil Rights Movement,* 140.
9. Ibid.
10. Sales interview.
11. Thulani Davis, "What Happened?," Columbia 1968 and the World Conference, Columbia University, April 24–27, 2008.
12. Christine Clark-Evans, interview by author, April 26, 2008, New York; Cheryl Leggon, interview by author, April 26, 2008, New York.
13. Some of the members of Omega Psi Phi who demonstrated in Hamilton Hall were Robert Godfrey, Darryl Pittman, Nathania Jones, Cicero Wilson, Larry Frazier, Zachary Husser, Ernst Perodin, Charles Jones, and Marvin (Kelly) Sin.

14. *Columbia Revolt,* produced and directed by the students of Columbia University, 60 min., Third World Newsreel, 1968, videocassette.

15. Ibid.

16. Bell and Kristol, eds., *Confrontation,* 53.

17. Miller, *The Civil Rights Movement,* 144.

18. Sales interview.

19. Donadio, "Columbia: Seven Interviews," 377.

20. Frazier, *Black Bourgeoisie.*

21. Reverend Samuel N. Brown, interview by author, November 22, 1997, New York.

22. Kahn, *The Battle for Morningside Heights,* 140.

23. Liebert, *Radical and Militant Youth,* 50–79.

24. Arnim Johnson Jr., telephone interview by author, May 15, 2008, Alton, Illinois.

25. Liebert, *Radical and Militant Youth,* 73.

26. Ibid., 59–77.

27. Zach Husser, interview by author, April 26, 2008, New York.

28. Liebert, *Radical and Militant Youth,* 76–77; Keniston, *The Young Radicals.*

29. See chapter 3 for the original list of demands.

30. Donadio, "Columbia: Seven Interviews," 377.

31. Wallerstein interview.

32. Sales interview.

33. Liebert, *Radical and Militant Youth,* 108.

34. Ibid.

35. Michael Stern, "Students Arrested in Park Due to Violent Protest," *Columbia Daily Spectator,* April 24, 1968, 1–2; Kenneth Barry, "Challenge to Administration Strongest in School's History," *Columbia Daily Spectator,* April 24, 1968, 1–3.

36. David Bird, "300 Protesting Columbia Students Barricade Office of College Dean," *New York Times,* April 24, 1968, 1, 30.

37. Les Matthews, "Rally Blasts Columbia," *New York Amsterdam News,* April 27, 1968, 37.

38. Kennedy interview.

39. Eric Foner, interview by author, November 21, 1997, New York.

40. Wm. Theodore de Bary, interview by author, November 19, 1997, New York.

41. Liebert, *Radical and Militant Youth,* 55–61.

42. Ibid., 61–62.

43. James Shenton, "Columbia Crisis," 1970, Oral History Research Office, Columbia University, New York.

44. Juan Gonzalez and Thomas Hurwitz, "What Happened?," Columbia 1968 and the World Conference, Columbia University, April 24–27, 2008.

45. *Columbia Revolt* video.

46. Mark Jaffe, "Protesters Roam Offices in Low," *Columbia Daily Spectator,* April 25, 1968, 1.

47. Baker, *Police on Campus,* 19.

48. *Columbia Revolt* video; Avorn, *Up against the Ivy Wall,* 122.

49. Kirk interview.

50. Kahn, *The Battle for Morningside Heights,* 140.

51. From Vicki to Mr. and Mrs. SLS, circa April 25, 1968, Columbiana Collection, Columbia University Archives, New York.

52. *Columbia Revolt* video.

53. Sales interview. Graduate student Eric Foner had a similar recollection of Kirk, remembering him as a "very aloof figure." Foner interview.

54. Kirk interview.

55. "Columbia Crisis," Protest and Activism Collection, Oral History Research Office, 1970, Columbia University, New York.

56. Ibid.

57. Beichman, "Letter from Columbia," 25.

58. *Columbia Revolt* video.

59. Grant, *Confrontation on Campus,* 77.

60. Schoener, ed., *Harlem on My Mind,* 238.

61. Robert Stulberg, "Protesters Occupy New Buildings," *Columbia Daily Spectator,* April 25, 1968, 1–2.

62. *Crisis at Columbia,* 107.

63. Wallerstein interview.

64. Kirk interview.

65. David Truman, interview by John Wooter, October 4, 1968, Oral History Collection, Columbia University, New York.

66. Radio TV Reports, Inc., WCBS-TV, CBS News, April 25, 1968, New York, TV program.

67. "Schoolhouse on the Hill," *New York Amsterdam News,* May 4, 1968, 14.

68. *New York Amsterdam News,* May 11, 1968, 18.

69. Radio TV Reports, Inc., WCBS-TV, CBS News, April 25, 1968, New York, TV program.

70. Cicero Wilson, interview by author, April 26, 2008, New York.

71. "Siege on Morningside Heights," *Time,* May 3, 1968, 49.

72. Radio TV Reports, Inc., WOR, WOR News, April 26, 1968, radio program, New York.

73. *New York Amsterdam News,* May 11, 1968, 18; "Columbia's Ruddite Rebellion," *Triumph,* vol. 3 (June 1, 1968), 18; Radio TV Reports, Inc., WNBC, Assignment New York, April 26, 1968, radio program.

74. Arthur Kokot, "Black Leaders Support Strikers," *Columbia Daily Spectator,* April 27, 1968, 1.

75. Radio TV Reports, Inc., WOR, WOR News, April 26, 1968, radio program, New York.

76. Sara Slack, "Harlem Backed Columbia Students," *New York Amsterdam News,* May 4, 1968, 1.

77. Sales interview.

78. Ibid.

79. "Brown Speaks before 500 at Hamilton Rally," *Columbia Daily Spectator,* April 27, 1968, 4.

80. Ibid.

81. Radio TV Reports, Inc., WOR, WOR News, April 26, 1968, radio program, New York.

82. Kahn, *The Battle for Morningside Heights,* 168.

83. "Statement of Faculty," Columbiana Collection, Columbia University Archives, New York.

84. Dearing Carpenter, "Negotiations Are Begun on Discipline of Students after Use of Police Postponed by Administration; Gym Construction Is Halted; University Closed," *Columbia Daily Spectator,* April 26, 1968, 1.

85. Radio TV Reports, Inc., WABC-TV, ABC, 11 O'clock News, April 27, 1968, TV program, New York.

86. Ibid.

87. From Percy Sutton, Manfred Ohrenstein, Charles Rangel, Mark Southall, and Theodore Weiss to John Lindsay, April 27, 1968, Columbiana Collection, Columbia University Archives, New York.

88. Radio TV Reports, Inc., WCBS-TV, CBS, Evening Report, April 27, 1968, TV program, New York.

89. Ibid.

Chapter 5. Supporting the Cause: SDS, Protest, and the "Bust"

1. Radio TV Reports, Inc., WNBC-TV, NBC News, April 30, 1968, TV program, New York.

2. Avorn, *Up against the Ivy Wall,* 187–89.

3. Reverend William Starr, "Spring Report, 1968," Columbiana Collection, Columbia University Archives, New York.

4. Avorn, *Up against the Ivy Wall,* 189.

5. Stephen Cole and Hannelore Adamsons, "Professional Status and Faculty Support of Student Demonstrations," 3, Columbiana Collection, Columbia University Archives, New York.

6. "Lifting the Siege—And Rethinking a Future," 78; *Cox Commission Columbia University. Fact-Finding Commission Proceedings,* 783.

7. Cicero Wilson, interview by author, April 26, 2008, New York.

8. Starr, "Spring Report, 1968."

9. Testimony of Rabbi A. Bruce Goldman, *Cox Commission Columbia University. Fact-Finding Commission Proceedings,* 1039.

10. Radio TV Reports, Inc., WABC-TV, 11 O'clock News, April 30, 1968, TV program, New York.

11. Although the students did not resist the arrests by violence, they did so by linking arms and letting their bodies go limp. "Six Weeks That Shook Morningside," 65–66.

12. Ibid., 66–67.

13. Radio TV Reports, Inc., WABC-TV, ABC News, April 30, 1968, TV program, New York.

14. "Six Weeks That Shook Morningside," 67.

15. Eric Foner, interview by author, November 21, 1997, New York.

16. Ibid.

17. "Six Weeks That Shook Morningside," 68.

18. Foner interview.

19. Radio TV Reports, Inc., WABC-TV, 11 O'clock News, April 30, 1968, New York, TV program.

20. Ibid.

21. Sylvan Fox, "1,000 Police Act to Oust Students from Five Buildings at Columbia; Move in at University's Request," *New York Times,* April 30, 1968, 1.

22. Liebert, *Radical and Militant Youth,* 76.

23. Ibid.

24. "Cops' Side of Columbia Story," Columbiana Collection, Columbia University Archives, New York.

25. Ibid.

26. Fox, "1,000 Police Act to Oust Students from Five Buildings at Columbia."

27. Radio TV Reports, Inc., WCBS-TV, CBS Mid-day News, April 30, 1968, TV program, New York.

28. A. M. Rosenthal, "Combat and Compassion at Columbia," *New York Times,* May 1, 1968, 34.

29. Ibid.

30. Arthur Kokot, "The Ultimate Responsibility," *Columbia Daily Spectator,* May 2, 1968, 4.

31. Oren Root Jr., "Brutality on Tuesday Denied, Police Praised by Trustees," *Columbia Daily Spectator,* May 2, 1968, 1.

32. Ibid., 3.

33. Sylvan Fox, "Faculty Is Split on Strike Issue," *New York Times,* May 1, 1968, 34.

34. Ibid.

35. Ibid.

36. Radio TV Reports, Inc., WNEW-TV, 10 O'clock News, May 1, 1968, TV program, New York.

37. Radio TV Reports, Inc., WNBC-TV, 6 O'clock News, May 1, 1968, TV program, New York.

38. Arnim Johnson Jr. interview.

39. Sylvan Fox, "Columbia Group Warns Strikers to Keep Peace," *New York Times,* May 9, 1968, 40.

40. "Trustees Express Willingness to Consider Change," *Columbia Daily Spectator,* May 2, 1968, 1.

41. Sylvan Fox, "Kirk Points to Gains," *New York Times,* May 9, 1968, 2.

42. Michael Stern, "Support for Student Strike Gains Momentum," *Columbia Daily Spectator,* May 2, 1968, 2.

43. Eric Foner interview.

44. Stern, "Support for Student Strike Gains Momentum."

45. Avorn, *Up against the Ivy Wall,* 206.

46. Donadio, "Columbia: Seven Interviews," 390.

47. Avorn, *Up against the Ivy Wall,* 217.

48. Ibid.

49. Michael Stern, "College Faculty Approves Pass-Fail Option," *Columbia Daily Spectator,* May 4, 1968, 4.

50. Ibid.

51. Donadio, "Columbia: Seven Interviews," 390.

52. Avorn, *Up against the Ivy Wall,* 246.

53. Ibid., 248.

54. *Columbia Revolt* video.

55. Fox, "Faculty Is Split on Strike Issue," *New York Times,* May 1, 1968, 34.

56. Fox, "Columbia Group Warns Strikers to Keep Peace," *New York Times,* May 9, 1968, 40.

57. Avorn, *Up against the Ivy Wall,* 249.

58. Ibid., 251.

59. Ibid.

60. "SAS Statement," May 2, 1968, Columbiana Collection, Columbia University Archives, New York.

61. Ibid.

62. Avorn, *Up against the Ivy Wall,* 194.

63. Ibid., 72.

64. Herring, *America's Longest War,* 17, 24, 26, 128, 299, 310; LaFeber, *America, Russia, and the Cold War, 1945–1996,* 37–38, 76–77, 166, 219, 231, and 280–81; Paterson, *On Every Front.*

65. "Nixon Bids Columbia Oust 'Anarchic' Students," *New York Times,* May 16, 1968, 22.

66. "Text of the Community Telegram to the President of Columbia University," September 25, 1968, Collins Collection, Schomburg Center, New York Public Library, New York.

67. "Letter from the Community," Columbiana Collection, Columbia University Archives, New York.

68. Kahn, *The Battle for Morningside Heights.*

69. George Collins to James Biddle, October 1968, Collins Collection, Schomburg Center, New York Public Library, New York.

70. Radio TV Reports, Inc., WNDT-TV, May 3, 1968, TV program, New York.

71. Text of telegram from University of Washington SDS to Columbia SDS, Columbiana Collection, Columbia University Archives, New York.

72. "Support for Student Strike," Columbiana Collection, Columbia University Archives, New York.

73. "The Debacle at Columbia," 662.

74. Roberts, "The Debacle at Columbia," 287.

Chapter 6. Black Student Power: The Struggle for Black Studies

1. Kahn, *The Battle for Morningside Heights,* 218.

2. Ibid.

3. Office of Public Information, September 18, 1968, Columbiana Collection, Columbia University Archives, New York.

4. Ture and Hamilton, *Black Power,* 34–39.

5. King, "The Early Years of Three Major Professional Black Studies Organizations," 116.

6. Ibid., 120.

7. Ibid., 121.

8. Orrick, *Shut It Down!,* 115–24; Hine, Hine, and Harrold, *The African-American Odyssey,* 551.

9. Sara Slack, "Columbia U Has No Courses on Negroes," *New York Amsterdam News,* April 2, 1966, 1.

10. Ibid.

11. "SAS Presents Plans for Autonomous Black Institute," *Columbia Daily Spectator,* February 28, 1969, 1.

12. Ibid.

13. *Columbia Daily Spectator,* November 25, 1969, 3.

14. Ibid.

15. Eichel et al., *Strike,* 277–78.

16. "The Guns Come to Cornell," 25.

17. Ruth Hochberger, "Blacks at Barnard Make Ten Demands," *Columbia Daily Spectator,* February 25, 1969, 1.

18. *Black and Latin at Columbia,* Sherry Ann Suttles Papers, Barnard College Archives, New York.

19. William Sales, telephone interview by author, March 25, 1999, Columbia, Missouri.

20. Ray Brown, telephone interview by author, November 24, 1999, Columbia, Missouri.

21. Ture and Hamilton, *Black Power,* 34.

22. Ray Brown interview.

23. Ibid.

24. "SAS Presents Plan for Autonomous Black Institute," *Columbia Daily Spectator,* February 28, 1969, 2.

25. Frankel, *Education and the Barricades,* 30.

26. Ibid., 33.

27. Eric Foner, interview by author, April 3, 2002, New York.

28. Frankel, *Education and the Barricades,* 31–35.

29. "SAS Presents Plan for Autonomous for Black Institute," *Columbia Daily Spectator,* February 28, 1969, 2.

30. Ibid.

31. Ibid.

32. "Statement of the Faculty Civil Rights Group," January 20, 1969, Columbiana Collection, Columbia University Archives, New York; "SAS Presents Plan for Autonomous Black Institute," *Columbia Daily Spectator,* February 28, 1969, 3.

33. "Employees for March 25th," Columbiana Collection, Columbia University Archives, New York.

34. Robert Friedman, "Autonomous Black Studies," *Columbia Daily Spectator,* March 5, 1969, 4.

35. "On Separatism," *Columbia Daily Spectator,* March 7, 1969, 2.

36. Ibid.

37. Roediger, *The Wages of Whiteness;* Omi and Winant, *Racial Formation in the United States from the 1960s to the 1990s;* Lipsitz, *The Possessive Investment in Whiteness;* Kincheloe et al., eds., *White Reign;* Helfand and Lippin, *Understanding Whiteness.*

38. Walter James People, "Letter to the Editor," *Columbia Daily Spectator,* February 26, 1969, 5.

39. Ibid.

40. SDS, "Letter to the Editor," *Columbia Daily Spectator,* March 11, 1969, 4.

41. Ibid.

42. Ibid.

43. Oliver Henry, "A Negro Student's Observation of Blacks," *Columbia Daily Spectator,* March 11, 1969, c1.

44. Ibid., c7.

45. Ibid.

46. George Schuyler, "Teaching Negro History Is Questionable," *Globe Democrat,* August 13, 1968, 6A.

47. Ibid.

48. "Black Studies Boom: Colleges Race to Start Afro-American Classes," Eric Foner Papers, Columbia University, New York.

49. William Sales, "Response to a Negro Negative," *Columbia Daily Spectator,* March 14, 1969, 5.

50. Ture and Hamilton, *Black Power,* 37.

51. Ray Brown interview.

52. William Sales, "Response to a Negro Negative," *Columbia Daily Spectator,* March 14, 1969, 5.

53. Sara Slack, "Columbia Black Sit-Ins Walk Calmly Out of Hall," *New York Amsterdam News,* April 19, 1969, 1.

54. Sylvan Fox, "20 Negroes Stage a Columbia Sit-In," *New York Times,* April 15, 1969, 33.

55. Ibid.

56. Ture and Hamilton, *Black Power,* 39.

57. "Black Students Occupy Admissions Office," *Columbia Daily Spectator,* April 15, 1969, 3.

58. Ibid.

59. Michael Stern, "Black Protest: Touch of *Déjà vu*" *Columbia Daily Spectator,* April 16, 1969, 4.

60. Incidentally, Clark's son, Hilton, graduated from Columbia in 1966 and was one of the original founders of SAS. Fox, "20 Negroes Stage a Columbia Sit-In."

61. Ibid.

62. "SDS Is Supporting the Demand of High School Students for Open Admissions to Columbia and Barnard," Eric Foner Papers, Columbia University, New York.

63. "Sit-In by 15 Negro Students Is Ended at Columbia," *New York Times,* April 16, 1969, 50.

64. "Black Students Leave Hamilton after Two Days under Threat of Temporary Restraining Order," *Columbia Daily Spectator,* April 16, 1969, 1.

65. "Sit-In by 15 Negro Students Is Ended at Columbia."

66. Les Matthews, "Rally Blasts Columbia," *New York Amsterdam News,* April 27, 1968, 37.

67. Sara Slack, "Columbia Black Sit-Ins Walk Calmly Out of Hall," *New York Amsterdam News,* April 19, 1969, 34.

68. "Columbia," *New York Amsterdam News,* April 26, 1969, 34.

69. Radio TV Reports, Inc., WNDT-TV, Channel 13 News, May 3, 1968, TV program, New York.

70. Thomas A. Johnson, "Take-Over Ignored by Negro Students," *New York Times,* April 18, 1969, 28.

71. Ture and Hamilton, *Black Power,* 72.

72. Ibid.

73. Ibid., 81.

74. Thirman L. Milner, "Letter to the Editor," *New York Amsterdam News,* May 3, 1969, 36.

75. *Village Voice,* April 24, 1969, 57.

76. Ibid.

77. Louis Dolinar, "Demand for Board Is Non-Negotiable," *Columbia Daily Spectator,* April 18, 1969, 1.

78. "The Students' Afro-American Society Calls for an Evacuation!!," Eric Foner Papers, Columbia University, New York.

79. "Exchange on Interim Board," *Columbia Daily Spectator,* April 22, 1969, 1.

80. Ibid.

81. Eichel et al., *Strike,* 277–78.

82. John Brecher, "Black Admissions Board Denied," *Columbia Daily Spectator,* October 6, 1969, 6.

83. Office of Public Information, April 15, 1969, Columbiana Collection, Columbia University Archives, New York.

84. Juris Kaza, "Study Asks Increase in Minority Students," *Columbia Daily Spectator,* December 15, 1969, 3.

85. Office of Public Information, April 15, 1969, Columbiana Collection, Columbia University Archives, New York.

86. Office of Public Information, April 29, 1969, Collins Collection, Schomburg Center, New York Public Library, New York.

87. *Columbia University Newsletter,* April 28, 1960, Collins Collection, Schomburg Center, New York Public Library, New York.

88. "Black Studies: Quietly Unresolved," *Columbia Daily Spectator,* October 10, 1969, 4.

89. Naftali Bendavid, "CC Needs to Focus More on Black Studies, Critics Say," *Columbia Daily Spectator,* April 26, 1984, 1.

90. Ibid.

91. Ibid.

92. http://www.columbia.edu/cu/iraas/htm/iraas_history.htm.

93. David Goldberg, "CU Top in Number of Black Profs.," *Columbia Daily Spectator,* March 24, 2000, 11.

94. "No Black Humor," Collins Collection, Schomburg Center of Research in Black Culture, New York Public Library, New York.

95. *Black Forum,* vol. 1, no. 1 (October 8, 1969), 2–4, Sherry Ann Suttles Papers, Barnard College Archives, New York.

96. Ray Brown interview.

Chapter 7. Striking Similarities: Columbia, the Ivy League, and Black People

1. A good source regarding the recruitment and admission of African Americans to Ivy League universities is Karabel, *The Chosen.*

2. Morrison, *The Founding of Harvard College,* 182–83.

3. Parsons, "A Truce in the War between Universities and Cities," 9.

4. *Cambridge Chronicle,* May 17, 1962, 1–2.

5. Christopher Jencks, "Urban Renewal Tries to End Danger of Local Blight," *Harvard Crimson,* February 25, 1956, 3.

6. *Cambridge Chronicle,* February 9, 1961, 1.

7. Bill Cunningham, *Which People's Republic?,* http://www.rwinters.com/docs/which_peoples_republic.htm.

8. Eichel et al., *Strike,* 23–24.

9. Ibid., 68–69.

10. Ibid.

11. E.W. Kenworthy, "Harvard Students Vote New Demands and Extend Strike," *New York Times,* April 15, 1969, 30.

12. Eichel et al., *Strike,* 277–78.

13. "Statement by Harvard Corporation on Strike Issues," *New York Times,* April 16, 1969, 50.

14. "The Campus Spring Offensive," *Newsweek,* April 28, 1969, 66–67.

15. "Vote at Harvard Suspends Strike," *New York Times,* April 19, 1969, 19.

16. "Harvard's Negro Students Win Voice in Selecting Professors," *New York Times,* April 23, 1969, 1.

17. Ibid., 28.

18. Sollors, Titcomb, and Underwood, eds., *Blacks at Harvard,* 394, 398.

19. Bell and Kristol, eds., *Confrontation,* 141–42.

20. Kalman, *Yale Law School and the Sixties,* 167–70.

21. "City Police Charge Seale in Murder," *Yale Daily News,* September 18, 1969, 1.

22. Kalman, *Yale Law School and the Sixties,* 169.

23. Letter to Kingman Brewster, May 8, 1970, Kingman Brewster Jr., Presidential Records, Yale University Archives, New Haven.

24. Ibid.

25. "Proposal for an Emergency Fund for Black Organizations, February 1969," Kingman Brewster Jr., Presidential Records, Yale University Archives, New Haven.

26. News Release of the Black Coalition of New Haven, October 29, 1970, Kingman Brewster Jr., Presidential Records, Yale University Archives, New Haven.

27. Stephen Marmon, "SAAS Denounces University for Handling of Discrimination Case," *Daily Pennsylvanian,* April 30, 1968, 1–2; Glasker, *Black Students in the Ivory Tower,* 40–42.

28. Glasker, *Black Students in the Ivory Tower,* 47–49.

29. Ibid., 49–53.

30. Downs, *Cornell '69,* 4.

31. Ibid., 311.

32. Homer Bigart, "Cornell Faculty Votes Down Pact Ending Take-Over," *New York Times,* April 22, 1969, 1.

33. Ibid., 34.

34. Ibid.

35. Downs, *Cornell '69*, 8.

36. Ibid., 3–4.

37. "As Guns Are Added to Campus Revolts," 30.

38. Van DeBurg, *A New Day in Babylon*, 26–27; Joseph, *Waiting 'til the Midnight Hour*, 73.

39. "The Agony of Cornell," *Time*, May 2, 1969, 37.

40. Ibid.

41. Bell and Kristol, eds., *Confrontation*, 139–41; Downs, *Cornell '69*, 68–69.

42. Downs, *Cornell '69*, 68–72.

43. Ibid., 310.

44. Ibid., 78.

45. "It Can't Happen Here—Can It?," *Newsweek*, May 5, 1969, 27.

46. "Task Force Committee on Racism," Protests—Willard Straight Takeover, Cornell Clippings File, Cornell University Archives, Carl A. Kroch Library, Ithaca.

47. Homer Bigart, "Cornell Faculty Votes Down Pact Ending Take-Over," *New York Times*, April 22, 1969, 1.

48. Charisse Kannady, News Release, April 21, 1969, Protests—Willard Straight Takeover, Cornell Clippings File, Cornell University Archives, Carl A. Kroch Library, Ithaca.

49. "Task Force Committee on Racism," Protests—Willard Straight Takeover, Cornell Clippings File, Cornell University Archives, Carl A. Kroch Library, Ithaca.

50. Ibid.; Seale, *Seize the Time*, 393–403.

51. Gutman, *The Black Family in Slavery and Freedom, 1750–1925*; Whites, *The Civil War as a Crisis in Gender*; Scott, *The Southern Lady*; Oakes, *The Ruling Race*; Wyatt-Brown, *Honor and Violence in the Old South*; Williamson, *A Rage for Order*; Gilmore, *Gender and Jim Crow*; Foner, *The New American History*.

52. Homer Bigart, "Cornell Faculty Votes Down Pact Ending Take-Over," *New York Times*, April 22, 1969, 1.

53. "Task Force Committee on Racism," Protests—Willard Straight Takeover, Cornell Clippings File, Cornell University Archives, Carl A. Kroch Library, Ithaca.

54. John Kifner, "Cornell Negroes Seize a Building," *New York Times*, April 20, 1969, 1.

55. "It Can't Happen Here—Can it?," *Newsweek*, May 5, 1969, 27.

56. Downs, *Cornell '69*, 182–83.

57. John Kifner, "Armed Negroes End Seizure; Cornell Yields," *New York Times*, April 21, 1969, 1.

58. Ibid.

59. "Task Force Committee on Racism," Protests—Willard Straight Takeover, Cornell Clippings File, Cornell University Archives, Carl A. Kroch Library, Ithaca.

60. Kifner, "Armed Negroes End Seizure," 1.

61. Ibid., 35.

62. Zinn, *The Twentieth Century,* 204.

63. Downs, *Cornell '69,* 317.

64. Sylvan Fox, "Columbia Group Warns Strikers to Keep Peace," *New York Times,* May 9, 1968, 1.

65. "Students," *Time,* May 9, 1968, 50.

Chapter 8. Is It Over Yet? The Results of Student and Community Protest

1. Aniko Bodroghkozy, "After the Revolution: A Talk with Mark Rudd," *Broadway* (New York), November 25, 1986, 1.

2. *Columbia University Newsletter,* February 17, 1969, Columbiana Collection, Columbia University Archives, New York.

3. "Students and University in Our Age of Social Action," Columbiana Collection, Columbia University Archives, New York.

4. Office of Public Information, May 7, 1968, Columbiana Collection, Columbia University Archives, New York.

5. Ibid.

6. Ibid.

7. Fraser, *1968,* 11.

8. Ibid., 203, 261.

9. Guy Wright, "A Tardy Alarm," *San Francisco Examiner,* June 30, 1968.

10. Bledstein, *The Middling Sorts;* Baritz, *The Good Life;* Hunt, *Ideology and U.S. Foreign Policy.*

11. Keith Moore, "Only Make-Believe Says Student Rebel," *New York Daily News,* April 22, 1988, 1.

12. CIA cable, 236A CIA 7, box 113, August 28, 1967, Lyndon Baines Johnson Presidential Library, NSF.

13. William Sales, "Views on the '68 Protest," *Columbia Daily Spectator,* April 28, 1988, 1.

14. Ibid., 6.

15. *Kerner Report,* 369; Gitlin, *The Whole World Is Watching,* 9.

16. Barry Gottehrer, "The Mayor's Man," *New York Post Daily,* date unknown, Columbiana Collection, Columbia University Archives, New York.

17. Miller, *On Our Own,* 195.

18. Sanford Garelik, "Violence Almost Achieved Respectability," *New York Newsday,* April 24, 1988, 6.

19. Eskew, *But for Birmingham,* 85–121, 259–99.

20. *Kerner Report,* 204–5.

21. See Carson, *In Struggle;* Salmond, *"My Mind Set on Freedom";* Eskew, *But for Birmingham;* O'Reilly, *Racial Matters;* Garrow, *The FBI and Martin Luther King, Jr.* for comprehensive discussion on national, state, and city officials' racial brutality and misuse of the law.

22. "17 Campus Whites Express Their Views," *New York Times,* January 12, 1970, 64, Columbiana Collection, Columbia University Archives, New York.

23. Ibid.

24. Gottehrer, "The Mayor's Man."

25. *New York Times,* May 17, 1968, 1.

26. Ibid.

27. Keppel, *The Work of Democracy;* Kovic, *Born on the Fourth of July.*

28. Pintzuk, *Reds, Racial Justice and Civil Liberties.*

29. O'Reilly, *Racial Matters.*

30. Peter Johnson, "FBI Ran '68 Anti-Left Campaign on Campus," *Columbia Daily Spectator,* September 22, 1980, 1, Columbiana Collection, Columbia University Archives, New York.

31. Ibid.

32. Davis, *Assault on the Left,* 46.

33. Unger, *FBI,* 232.

34. Davis, *Assault on the Left,* 43.

35. FBI Memorandum, C. D. Brennan to W. C. Sullivan, May 9, 1968, National Security Archives, Washington, D.C.

36. Department of Defense, Cable, Confidential, September 11, 1986, National Security Archives, Washington, D.C.

37. FBI Memorandum, Headquarters to New York Field Office, July 3, 1968, National Security Archives, Washington, D.C.

38. FBI Memorandum, Headquarters to Field Offices, July 6, 1968, National Security Archives, Washington, D.C.

39. Johnson, "FBI Ran '68 Anti-Left Campaign on Campus," *Columbia Daily Spectator,* September 22, 1980, 2.

40. Ibid.

41. Office of Security Memorandum, Director of Security to Director of CIA, February 16, 1968, National Security Archives, Washington, D.C.

42. Ibid.

43. Fraser, *1968,* 10.

44. Wm. Theodore de Bary, interview by author, November 21, 1997, New York.

45. Carl Hovde, "No One Will Forget the Shock," *New York Newsday,* April 24, 1988, 4.

46. Ibid., 4–5.

47. William Sales, "The Struggle for Black Liberation," *New York Newsday,* April 24, 1988, 5.

48. Edwards, *Revolt of the Black Athlete,* 103–8.

49. Ibid., ix–xii.

50. Pinkney, *The Myth of Black Progress.*

51. Spearman, "Federal Roles and Responsibilities Relative to the Higher Education of Blacks since 1967."

52. Edwards, *Revolt of the Black Athlete,* 4–21; Sammons, "Race and Sport"; Marcello, "The Integration of Intercollegiate Athletics in Texas."

53. Edwards, *Revolt of the Black Athlete,* 10–11.

54. Ibid., 16.

55. Ibid., 179–82.

56. Richard Slovak, "Black Acceptances Drop 27 Percent from Last Year," *Columbia Daily Spectator,* April 19, 1973, 1, 3.

57. Kit Stolz, "Black Applications Increase at Three Ivy Colleges," *Columbia Daily Spectator,* September 30, 1976, 1.

58. Ibid., 2.

59. Ibid.

60. Sylvia Hurtado, "The Campus Racial Climate."

61. Ibid., 540.

62. Ibid., 542.

63. Cross, "Why the *Hopwood* Ruling Would Remove Most African Americans from the Nation's Most Selective Universities."

64. Aguirre Jr. and Baker, *Sources,* 88.

65. *Regents of the University of California v. Bakke,* 438 U.S. 265, 311-3122 (1978).

66. Bell, *And We Are Not Saved,* 140–62.

67. Ibid., 144.

68. Ibid., 156.

69. Marable, "Beyond the Race Dilemma," 428, 431.

70. Ibid.

71. Bell et al., "Race-Sensitive Admissions in Higher Education," 97.

72. Cross, "Why the *Hopwood* Ruling Would Remove Most African Americans from the Nation's Most Selective Universities," 66.

73. Ibid., 67.

74. Ibid.

75. Middleton, "Black Studies Professors Say Hard Times."

76. "Black College Students Overwhelmingly Pursue Business Degrees."

77. Fanon, *Wretched of the Earth,* 30.

78. Ibid.

79. *Kerner Report,* 35, 206.

80. Miller, *Democracy in the Streets;* Graham and Gurr, eds., *Violence in America;* Hofstadter and Wallace, eds., *American Violence;* Horne, *Fire This Time.*

81. Rhodes, *Voices of Violence,* 2.

82. Cohen and Murphy, *Burn, Baby, Burn!,* 23.

83. Ibid.

84. Sales, "The Struggle for Black Liberation," *New York Newsday,* April 24, 1988, 5.

85. Morris Dickstein, "Columbia Recovered," *New York Times Magazine,* May 15, 1988, 35.

86. Kors and Silvergate, *Shadow University*, 4.

87. Ibid., 11.

88. Hacker, *Two Nations,* 129; Slater, "The First Black Tenured Faculty at the Nation's Highest-Ranked Universities," 106.

89. "The Progress of Black Student Matriculations at the Nation's Highest-Ranked Colleges and Universities"; Pinkney, *Myth of Black Progress,* 157–58.

90. Morris Dickstein, "Columbia Recovered," *New York Times Magazine,* May 15, 1988, 68.

91. Ibid.

92. Ibid., 66.

93. *Columbia Daily Spectator,* April 25, 1983, 4.

94. See *Columbia Daily Spectator,* March–October 1983.

95. Sylvan Fox, "The Uprising Had Little Lasting Impact," *New York Newsday,* April 24, 1988, 7.

96. Ibid.

97. Bodroghkozy, "After the Revolution," *Broadway* (New York), November 25, 1986, 5.

98. Ibid., 6.

99. Mark Rudd, "'68 Still Echoes at Columbia," *New York Newsday,* April 24, 1988, 4.

100. Keith Moore, "Columbia Takes a Look Back," *New York Daily News,* April 22, 1988, J2.

101. Ibid.

102. Rudd, "'68 Still Echoes at Columbia," 32.

103. http://www.temple.edu/tempress/authors/1532_qa.html; Naison, *White Boy;* Naison, "A White Scholar in the Early Days of Black Studies."

104. McGirr, *Suburban Warriors.*

105. "Somebody's Trying to Hurt Us Both—Columbia and Harlem," *New York Amsterdam News,* June 1, 1968, Columbiana Collection, Columbia University Archives, New York.

106. Ibid.

107. Letter from Edith Pennamon to Members of West Harlem Community Organization, May 26, 1969, "Morningside Park Including Relationship with Columbia University, 1960–1970," Collins Collection, Schomburg Center, New York Public Library, New York.

108. "West Harlem Community Organization, Inc. Annual Report November 1, 1970–October 31, 1971," Collins Collection, Schomburg Center, New York Public Library, New York.

109. "Institutional Arrogance," *Washington Post,* November 21, 1971, C3.

110. "I. M. Pei Resigns as CU Planner," and "McGill Calls Columbia Overextended," *Columbia Daily Spectator,* September 16, 1970, 1.

111. "Institutional Arrogance," C3.

112. Ibid.

113. Stephen Isaacs, "The Battle of Morningside Heights (Continued)," *Washington Post,* November 21, 1971, C1.

114. "West Harlem Community Organization, Inc., 1968–1971," Collins Collection, Schomburg Center, New York Public Library, New York.

115. School of Architecture and Environmental Studies, City College of New York, "Master Plan of St. Nicholas, Colonial, and Morningside Parks for the Parks, Recreation and Cultural Affairs Administration of the City of New York, 1972," Collins Collection, Schomburg Center, New York Public Library, New York.

116. Bob McKay to Mrs. George Collins, June 16, 1969, Collins Collection, Schomburg Center, New York Public Library, New York.

117. "6 Years after Furor, Columbia Will Get New Gymnasium," *New York Times,* September 23, 1974, 37, 58.

118. Ibid.

119. "Reunion for Rudd and Other Rebels," *New York Times,* April 22, 1988, B4.

120. Ibid.

121. *Partners in the Park* (New York), March 1968, Columbiana Collection, Columbia University Archives, New York.

122. "Reunion for Rudd and Other Rebels."

123. Ibid.

124. Schwartz, *We Are Talking about Homes,* 174.

125. Ibid., 81.

126. "Columbia's Expansion into Manhattanville in West Harlem," Info for Our Neighbors, Columbia University. Available at http://www.neighbors.columbia.edu/pages/manplanning/index.html.

127. Lee Bollinger, "Manhattanville Project," May 14, 2004. Available at http://www.campus-watch.org/article/id/1174; Jamal Watson, "Columbia University Expansion," August 15, 2004. Available at http://www.able2know.com/forums/about31336.html.

128. http://www.neighbors.columbia.edu/pages/manplanning/jobs_economics/index.html.

129. Walter South, "Critique of Riverside Park Plaza," Collins Collection, Schomburg Center, New York Public Library, New York.

130. Jamal Watson, "Columbia University Expansion," August 15, 2004. Available at http://www.able2know.com/forums/about31336.html.

131. Jimmy Vielkind, "Battle over Eminent Domain Rages Around CU," October 4, 2004, *Columbia Daily Spectator,* online edition. Available at http://www.columbiaspectator.com/vnews/display.v/ART/2004/10/04/4160f515d15ea.

132. A log of events can be found at a blog operated by the CB9 chairman, Jordi Reyes-Montblanc, http://cb9m.blogspot.com.

133. Anna Phillips, "CB9 Rejects Manhattanville Rezoning," *Columbia Daily Spectator,* online edition, September 4, 2007. Available at http://www.columbiaspectator.com/node/26349.

134. Gitlin, *The Sixties,* 1–7.

135. Gottehrer, "The Mayor's Man."

136. William Sales, Transcript of National Public Radio Broadcast, April 21, 1988, Columbiana Collection, Columbia University Archives, New York.

Conclusion

1. Chinyelu, *Harlem Ain't Nothin' but a Third World Country,* 1–3.

2. Ibid., 105–21.

3. Reverend Samuel N. Brown interview.

4. Ray Brown interview.

Epilogue. Where Are They Now?

1. Arnim Johnson Jr., telephone interview by author, May 15, 2008, Alton, Illinois.

2. Thulani Davis supplied the lists of deceased participants and supporters.

Bibliography

Adelson, Alan. *SDS*. New York: Charles Scribner's Sons, 1972.

Aguirre, Adalberto, Jr., and David Baker. *Sources: Notable Selection in Race and Ethnicity*. Guilford: Dushkin/McGraw Hill, 1998.

Aldridge, Delores P., and Carlene Young, eds. *Out of the Revolution: The Development of Africana Studies*. Lanham, Md.: Lexington Books, 2000.

Anderson, Terry. *The Movement and the Sixties*. New York: Oxford University Press, 1995.

"ARCH's Political Role." *Advocacy Planning*, September 1968.

"As Guns Are Added to Campus Revolts." *US News and World Report*, May 5, 1969.

Astin, Helen. *Themes and Events of Campus Unrest in Twenty-Two Colleges and Universities*. Washington, D.C.: Bureau of Social Science Research, 1969.

Avorn, Jerry L. *Up against the Ivy Wall: A History of the Columbia Crisis*. New York: Atheneum, 1969.

Baker, Michael A. *Police on Campus: The Mass Police Action at Columbia University Spring 1968*. New York: Temco Press, 1969.

Baritz, Loren. *The Good Life: The Meaning of Success for the American Middle Class*. New York: HarperCollins, 1990.

Barnard College Archives. Sherry Ann Suttles Papers. Barnard College, New York.

Barnard Electronic Archive and Teaching Laboratory.

Becker, Howard, ed. *Campus Power Struggle*. 2nd ed. New Brunswick: Transaction Books, 1973.

Beichman, Arnold. "Letter from Columbia: The Progress of Putsch." *Encounter*, vol. 32 (May 5, 1969).

Bell, Daniel, and Irvin Kristol, eds. *Confrontation: The Student Rebellion and the Universities*. New York: Basic Books, 1968.

Bell, Derrick. *And We Are Not Saved: The Elusive Quest for Racial Justice*. New York: Basic Books, 1987.

Bell, Derrick. *Faces at the Bottom of the Well: The Permanence of Racism.* New York: Basic Books, 1992.

Bell, Derrick, Richard Kahlenber, Michael Dorf, Mark Tushnet, Richard Delgado, and Jean Stefancic. "Race-Sensitive Admissions in Higher Education: Commentary on How the Supreme Court Is Likely to Rule." *Journal of Blacks in Higher Education,* vol. 0, no. 26 (Winter 1999–2000), 97–101.

Bennett, Lerone, Jr. "Confrontation on Campus." *Ebony* (May 1968).

"Black College Students Overwhelmingly Pursue Business Degrees." *Journal of Blacks in Higher Education,* no. 13 (Autumn 1996), 22–23.

Bledstein, Burton. *The Middling Sorts: Exploration in the History of the American Middle Class.* New York: Routledge, 2000.

Boyd, William. *Desegregating America's Colleges: A Nationwide Survey of Black Students, 1972–1973.* New York: Praeger, 1974.

Bracey, John H., Jr., August Meier, and Elliott Rudwick, eds. *Blacks in the Abolitionist Movement.* Belmont, Calif.: Wadsworth, 1971.

Branch, Taylor. *Parting the Waters: America in the King Years.* New York: Simon and Schuster, 1988.

Brewster, Kingman, Jr. Kingman Brewster Jr., Presidential Records. Yale University Archives, New Haven.

Broadway (New York), November 25, 1986, 5.

Brown, Claude. *Manchild in the Promised Land.* New York: Signet Books, 1965.

Brown, Raymond, telephone interview with author, November 24, 1999, Columbia, Missouri.

Brown, Rev. Samuel N., interview with author, November 22, 1997, New York.

Buckley, William. *The Unmaking of a Mayor.* New York: Viking Press, 1965.

Cambridge Chronicle, 1961–1969.

Carson, Clayborne. *In Struggle: SNCC and the Black Awakening of the 1960s.* Cambridge: Harvard University Press, 1981.

Chinyelu, Mamadou. *Harlem Ain't Nothin' but a Third World Country: The Global Economy, Empowerment Zones, and the Colonial Status of Africans in America.* New York: Mustard Seed Press, 1999.

CIA cable, August 28, 1967. Johnson Library, NSF.

Citron, Casper. *John V. Lindsay and the Silk Stocking Story.* New York: Fleet, 1965.

Clark, Kenneth. *Dark Ghetto: Dilemmas of Social Power.* New York: Harper and Row, 1967.

Clarke, John Henrik. *Harlem: A Community in Transition.* New York: Citadel Press, 1964.

Clark-Evans, Christine, interview with author, April 26, 2008, New York.

Cohen, Jerry, and William Murphy. *Burn, Baby, Burn! The Watts Riot.* New York: Avon Books, 1966.

Collins Collection. Archives, Schomburg Center for Research in Black Culture, New York Public Library, New York.

Columbia College Today, 1963–1968.

Columbia Daily Spectator (New York), 1963–2000.

Columbiana Collection. Archives, Columbia University Library, New York.

Columbia Owl, 1967–1968.

Columbia University Newsletter, 1968–1969.

"Columbia University, the Arrogant Giant." *Liberator,* vol. 8, no. 6 (June 1968).

Cornell Daily Sun, 1967–1969.

Cox Commission Columbia University. Fact-Finding Commission Proceedings, Archibald Cox, chairman (University Microfilms, A Xerox Company, Ann Arbor: 1972), text-microfilm.

Crisis at Columbia: An Inside Report on the Rebellion at Columbia from the Pages of the Columbia Daily Spectator. New York: Columbia University, 1968.

Crisis at Columbia: Report of the Fact-Finding Commission Appointed to Investigate the Disturbances at Columbia University in April and May 1968. New York: Random House, 1968.

Cross, Theodore. "Why the *Hopwood* Ruling Would Remove Most African Americans from the Nation's Most Selective Universities." *Journal of Blacks in Higher Education,* volume 0, issue 11 (Spring 1996).

Cruse, Harold. *The Crisis of the Negro Intellectual: From Its Origins to the Present.* New York: William Morrow, 1967.

Davis, James Kirkpatrick. *Assault on the Left: The FBI and the Sixties Antiwar Movement.* Westport: Praeger, 1997.

"The Debacle at Columbia." *America,* vol. 118 (January–June 1968).

de Bary, Wm. Theodore, interview with author, November 21, 1997, New York.

Department of Defense, Cable, Confidential, September 11, 1986.

Divale, William. *I Lived inside the Campus Revolution.* New York: Cowles, 1970.

Donadio, Stephen. "Columbia: Seven Interviews." *Partisan Review,* vol. 35, no. 3 (1968), 367–81.

Douglas, Daniel, interview with author, November 22, 1997, Harlem, New York.

Downs, Donald. *Cornell '69: Liberalism and the Crisis of the American University.* Ithaca: Cornell University Press, 1999.

Du Bois, W.E.B. *The Souls of Black Folk.* New York: Dover, 1994.

Dudley, William, ed. *The Civil Rights Movement: Opposing Viewpoints.* San Diego: Greenhaven Press, 1996.

Dupee, F. W. "The Uprising at Columbia." *New York Times Magazine,* September 26, 1968.

Edwards, Harry. *Black Students.* New York: Free Press, 1970.

———. *The Revolt of the Black Athlete.* New York: Free Press, 1970.

Eichel, Lawrence, et al. *Strike: The Harvard Strike.* Boston: Houghton Mifflin, 1970.

Eric Foner Papers, Columbia University, New York.

Ericson, Edward. *Radicals in the University.* Stanford: Hoover Institution Press, 1975.

Erikson, Erik. *Identity: Youth and Crisis.* New York: W. W. Norton, 1994.

Eskew, Glenn. *But for Birmingham: The Local and National Movements in the Civil Rights Struggle.* Chapel Hill: University of North Carolina Press, 1997.

Exum, William. *Paradoxes of Protest: Black Student Activism in a White University.* Philadelphia: Temple University Press, 1985.

Fallaci, Oriana. *The Egoist; Sixteen Surprising Interviews.* Chicago: H. Regnery, 1968.

Fanon, Frantz. *The Wretched of the Earth.* New York: Grove Press, 1963.

FBI Memorandum, C. D. Brennan to W. C. Sullivan, May 9, 1968.

———. Headquarters to Field Offices, July 6, 1968.

———. Headquarters to New York Field Office, July 3, 1968.

Foner, Eric, interview with author, November 19, 1997, New York.

———. Interview with author, April 3, 2002, New York.

———. *The New American History,* rev. and exp. ed. Philadelphia: Temple University Press, 1997.

———. *Nothing but Freedom: Emancipation and Its Legacy.* Baton Rouge: Louisiana State University Press, 1983.

———. *Reconstruction: America's Unfinished Revolution.* New York: Harper and Row, 1988.

Foner, Philip Sheldon. *The Black Panthers Speak.* Philadelphia: Lippincott, 1970.

Forman, James. *The Making of Black Revolutionaries.* New York: Macmillan, 1972.

Foster, Julian, and Durward Long. *Protest! Student Activism in America.* New York: William Morrow, 1970.

Frankel, Charles. *Education and the Barricades.* New York: W. W. Norton, 1968.

Franklin, John Hope. *From Slavery to Freedom: A History of African Americans.* 7th ed. New York: McGraw Hill, 1994.

Fraser, Ronald. *1968: A Student Generation in Revolt.* London: Chatto and Windus, 1988.

Frazier, E. Franklin. *Black Bourgeoisie: The Rise of a New Middle Class.* New York: Free Press, 1957.

Frazier, Thomas, ed. *Afro-American History: Primary Sources.* Chicago: Dorsey Press, 1988.

Frieden, Bernard, and Robert Morris, eds. *Urban Planning and Social Policy.* New York: Basic Books, 1968.

Garrow, David. *The FBI and Martin Luther King, Jr.* New York: W. W. Norton, 1981.

———. *Bearing the Cross: Martin Luther King, Jr. and the Southern Christian Leadership Conference.* New York: William Morrow, 1986.

Gilmore, Glenda Elizabeth. *Gender and Jim Crow: Women and the Politics of White Supremacy in North Carolina, 1896–1920.* Chapel Hill: University of North Carolina Press, 1996.

Gitlin, Todd. *The Sixties: Years of Hope, Days of Rage.* Toronto: Bantham Books, 1987.

———. *The Whole World Is Watching: Mass Media in the Making and Unmaking of the New Left.* Berkeley: University of California Press, 1980.

Glasker, Wayne. *Black Students in the Ivory Tower: African American Student Activism at the University of Pennsylvania, 1967–1990.* Amherst: University of Massachusetts Press, 2002.

Graham, Hugh, and Ted Gurr, eds. *Violence in America: Historical and Comparative Perspectives.* Beverly Hills: Sage Publications, 1979.

Grant, Joanne, ed. *Black Protest: History, Documents, and Analyses, 1619 to the Present.* New York: Fawcett World Library, 1968.

———. *Confrontation on Campus: The Columbia Pattern for the New Protest.* New York: Signet Books, 1969.

"The Guns Come to Cornell." *Life*, May 2, 1969.

Gutman, Herbert. *The Black Family in Slavery and Freedom, 1750–1925.* New York: Pantheon, 1976.

Hacker, Andrew. *Two Nations: Black and White, Separate, Hostile, Unequal.* New York: Ballantine Books, 1995.

Hampton, Henry, and Steven Fayer, eds. *Voices of Freedom: An Oral History of the Civil Rights Movement from the 1950s through the 1980s.* New York: Bantam Books, 1991.

Handlin, Oscar. *The Newcomers: Negroes and Puerto Ricans in a Changing Metropolis.* Cambridge: Harvard University Press, 1959.

Harvard Crimson, 1968–1969.

Helfand, Judy, and Laurie Lippin. *Understanding Whiteness: Unraveling Racism.* New York: Thomas Learning Custom Publishing, 2001.

Henri, Florette. *Black Migration: Movement North, 1900–1920.* Garden City: Anchor Doubleday, 1975.

Herring, George C. *America's Longest War: The United States and Vietnam, 1950–1975.* New York: McGraw Hill, 1996.

Hine, Darlene Clark, William C. Hine, and Stanley Harrold. *The African-American Odyssey.* Upper Saddle River, N.J.: Prentice Hall, 2000.

Hofstadter, Richard, and Michael Wallace, eds. *American Violence: A Documentary History.* New York: Vintage Books, 1971.

Holton, Woody. *Forced Founders: Indians, Debtors, Slaves and the Making of the American Revolution in Virginia.* Chapel Hill: University of North Carolina Press, 1999.

Horne, Gerald. *Fire This Time: The Watts Uprising and the 1960s.* Charlottesville: University of Virginia Press, 1995.

Hoving, Thomas. "Thinking Big about Small Parks." *New York Times Magazine*, April 10, 1966, 72.

Huggins, Nathaniel. *Harlem Renaissance.* New York: Oxford University Press, 1971.

Hunt, Michael. *Ideology and U.S. Foreign Policy.* New Haven: Yale University Press, 1987.

Hurtado, Sylvia. "The Campus Racial Climate: Context of Conflict." *Journal of Higher Education*, vol. 63, no. 5 (September–October 1992), 539–69.

Husser, Zach, interview with author, April 26, 2008, New York.

"It Can't Happen Here—Can It?" *Newsweek*, May 5, 1969.

Jackson, Kenneth. *The Ku Klux Klan in the City, 1915–1930.* New York: Oxford University Press, 1967.

Johnson, Arnim, Jr., interview with author, May 15, 2008, Alton, Illinois.

Joseph, Peniel. *Waiting 'til the Midnight Hour: A Narrative History of Black Power in America.* New York: Henry Holt, 2006.

Kahn, Roger. *The Battle for Morningside Heights.* New York: William Morrow, 1970.

Kalman, Laura. *Yale Law School and the Sixties: Revolt and Reverberations.* Chapel Hill: University of North Carolina Press, 2005.

Karabel, Jerome. *The Chosen: The Hidden History of Admission and Exclusion at Harvard, Yale, and Princeton.* Boston: Houghton Mifflin, 2005.

Kelley, Robin. *Race Rebels: Culture, Politics, and the Black Working Class.* New York: Free Press, 1996.

Keniston, Kenneth. *The Young Radicals.* New York: Harcourt, Brace and World, 1968.

Kennedy, Thomas, interview with author, March 8, 1997, Pullman, Washington.

Keppel, Ben. *The Work of Democracy: Ralph Bunche, Kenneth Clark, Lorraine Hansberry, and the Cultural Politics of Race.* Cambridge: Harvard University Press, 1995.

The Kerner Report: Report of the National Advisory Commission on Civil Disorders. New York: Bantam Books, 1968.

Kincheloe, Joe, Shirley Nelson Rodriguez, and Ronald Chennault, eds. *White Reign: Deploying Whiteness in America.* New York: St. Martin's Griffin, 2000.

King, William M. "The Early Years of Three Major Professional Black Studies Organizations." In *Out of the Revolution: The Development of Africana Studies,* ed. Aldridge and Young.

Klein, Woody. *Lindsay's Promise: The Dream That Failed.* New York: Macmillan, 1970.

Kors, Alan, and Harvey Silvergate. *The Shadow University: The Betrayal of Liberty on America's Campuses.* New York: Harper Perennial, 1999.

Kovic, Ron. *Born on the Fourth of July.* New York: Pocket Books, 1976.

Kunen, James. *The Strawberry Statement: Notes of a College Revolutionary.* New York: Avon Books, 1968.

LaFeber, Walter. *America, Russia, and the Cold War, 1945–1996.* New York: McGraw Hill, 1997.

Leggon, Cheryl, interview with author, April 26, 2008, New York.

Leinwald, Gerald, ed. *The Negro in the City.* New York: Pocket Books, 1968.

Liebert, Robert, *Radical and Militant Youth: A Psychoanalytic Inquiry.* New York: Praeger, 1971.

"Lifting the Siege—And Rethinking a Future." *Time,* May 10, 1968.

Lindsay, John. *The City.* New York: W. W. Norton, 1970.

Lipsitz, George. *The Possessive Investment in Whiteness: How White People Profit from Identity Politics.* Philadelphia: Temple University Press, 1998.

Lusky, Louis and Mary. "Columbia 1968: The Wound Unhealed." *Political Science Quarterly,* vol. 84, no. 2 (June 1969), 169–288.

MacLean, Nancy. *Behind the Mask of Chivalry: The Making of the Second Ku Klux Klan.* Oxford: Oxford University Press, 1994.

Marable, Manning. "Beyond the Race Dilemma." *Nation,* April 11, 1968.

Marcello, Ronald. "The Integration of Intercollegiate Athletics in Texas: North Texas State College as a Test Case, 1956." *Journal of Sport History,* no. 3 (1987), 286–316.

Marks, Carole. *Farewell: We're Good and Gone: The Black Migration.* Bloomington: Indiana University Press, 1989.

Martin, Tony. *Literary Garveyism: Garvey, Black Arts, and the Harlem Renaissance.* Dover: Majority Press, 1983.

Massey, Douglas, and Nancy Denton. *American Apartheid: Segregation and the Making of the Underclass.* Cambridge: Harvard University Press, 1993.

McCaughey, Robert, interview with author, April 2, 1997, New York.

McDowell, Sophia F., et al. "Howard University Protest Movement." *Public Opinion Quarterly,* vol. 34, no. 3 (Autumn 1970), 383–88.

McEvoy, James, and Abraham Miller, eds. *Black Power and Student Rebellion.* Belmont, Calif.: Wadsworth, 1989.

McGirr, Lisa. *Suburban Warriors: The Origins of the New American Right.* Princeton: Princeton University Press, 2002.

McPherson, James. *Ordeal by Fire: The Civil War and Reconstruction.* New York: McGraw Hill, 1992.

Meier, August, and Elliott Rudwick. *CORE: A Study in the Civil Rights Movement, 1942–1968.* New York: Oxford University Press, 1973.

———. "The Role of Blacks in the Abolitionist Movement." In *Blacks in the Abolitionist Movement,* ed. Bracey, Meier, and Rudwick.

Meyer, John C. "Columbia's Ruddite Rebellion." *Triumph,* June 1, 1968.

Middleton, Lorenzo. "Black Studies Professors Say Hard Times." *Chronicle of Higher Education,* March 6, 1981, 1–6.

Miller, Douglas T. *On Our Own: Americans in the Sixties.* Lexington: D. C. Heath, 1996.

Miller, James. *Democracy in the Streets: From Port Huron to the Siege of Chicago.* New York: Simon and Schuster, 1987.

Miller, Loren. "White Liberals Should Play a Limited Role in the Civil Rights Movement." In *The Civil Rights Movement: Opposing Viewpoints,* ed. Willaim Dudley. San Diego: Greenhaven Press, 1996.

Morgan, Edmund S. *American Slavery, American Freedom: The Ordeal of Colonial Virginia.* New York: W. W. Norton, 1975.

Morningside Citizen, 1966–1970.

Morningsider, 1964–1969.

Morningsiders United Newsletter, 1964–1968.

Morningside Sentinel, 1966–1969.

Morrison, Samuel Eliot. *The Founding of Harvard College.* Cambridge: Harvard University Press, 1935.

Naison, Mark. *White Boy: A Memoir.* Philadelphia: Temple University Press, 2001.

Naison, Mark. "A White Scholar in the Early Days of Black Studies." *Journal of Blacks in Higher Education,* no. 37 (Autumn 2002), 119–23.

Nash, George. *The University and the City: Eight Cases of Involvement (A Report Prepared for The Carnegie Commission on Higher Education).* New York: McGraw-Hill, 1973.

Nash, George, and Cynthia Epstein. "Harlem Views Columbia." *New York Magazine,* July 8, 1968, 58–59.

Nelson, Bruce. *Divided We Stand: American Workers and the Struggle for Equality.* Princeton: Princeton University Press, 2001.

New York Amsterdam News (New York) 1965–1969.

New York Daily News, April 22, 1988, 12.

New York Free Press, February 1969.

New York Newsday, April 24, 1988, 5.

New York Post Daily, 1968–1988.

New York Times, 1960–1969.

New York Times Magazine, 1966–1988.

1969 Harvard Student Strike Collection. Harvard University Archives, Cambridge.

Oakes, James. *The Ruling Race: A History of American Slaveholders.* New York: Vintage Books, 1983.

Office of Security Memorandum, Director of Security to Director of CIA, February 16, 1968.

Oliver, Melvin, and Thomas Shapiro. *Black Wealth/White Wealth: A New Perspective on Racial Inequality.* New York: Routledge, 1997.

Olmsted, Frederick Law, and Albert Fein, eds. *Landscape into Cityscape.* Ithaca: Cornell University Press, 1968.

Olmsted, Frederick Law, Jr., and Theodore Kimball. *Frederick Law Olmsted, Landscape Architect, 1822–1903.* New York: G. P. Putnam, 1922.

Olmsted, Frederick Law, Jr., and Calvert Vaux. *Preliminary Study of a Design for the Laying Out of Morningside Park.* New York: Board of the Department of Public Parks, Document 50, October 11, 1873.

Omi, Michael, and Howard Winant. *Racial Formation in the United States from the 1960s to the 1990s.* New York: Routledge, 1994.

Oral History Collection. Rare Books and Manuscripts, Columbia University Library, New York.

———. Kirk, Grayson, interview with John Wooter, October 3, 1968, New York.

———. Ranum, Orest, Office of Oral History Research, 1970.

———. Rudd, Mark, interview with Ronald Grele, March 30, 1987, New York.

———. Shenton, James, "Columbia Crisis of 1968," Office of Oral History Research, 1970.

———. Truman, David, interview with John Wooter, October 4, 1968, New York.

———. Wallerstein, Immanuel, interview with Robert Friedman and Andrew Crane, June 1968, New York.

O'Reilly, Kenneth. *Nixon's Piano: Presidents and Racial Politics from Washington to Clinton.* New York: Free Press, 1995.

———. *Racial Matters: The FBI's Secret File on Black America, 1960–1972.* New York: Free Press, 1989.

Orrick, William. *Shut It Down! A College in Crisis,* Report to the National Commission on the Causes and Prevention of Violence. Washington, D.C., June 1969.

Orum, Anthony. *Black Students in Protest: A Study of the Origins of the Black Student Movement.* Washington, D.C.: American Sociological Association, 1972.

Osofsky, Gilbert. *Harlem: The Making of a Ghetto.* New York: Harper and Row, 1968.

Palmer, Colin. *Passageways: An Interpretive History of Black America,* volume 2: *1863–1965.* Fort Worth: Harcourt Brace College Publishers, 1998.

Parsons, Kermit. "A Truce in the War between Universities and Cities: A Prologue to the Study of City-University Renewal." *Journal of Higher Education,* vol. 34, no. 1 (January 1963), 205–16.

Parsons, Mabel, ed. *Memories of Samuel Parsons, Landscape Architect of the Department of Public Parks, New York.* New York: G. P. Putnam's Sons, 1926.

Paterson, Thomas. *On Every Front: The Making and Unmaking of the Cold War.* New York: W. W. Norton, 1992.

Pierpaoli, Paul. *Truman and Korea: The Political Culture of the Early Cold War.* Columbia: University of Missouri Press, 1999.

Pilat, Oliver. *Lindsay's Campaign: A Behind the Scenes Diary.* Boston: Beacon Press, 1968.

Pinkney, Alphonso. *The Myth of Black Progress.* Cambridge: Cambridge University Press, 1984.

Pintzuk, Edward. *Reds, Racial Justice and Civil Liberties: Michigan Communists during the Cold War.* Minneapolis: MEP, 1997.

Powledge, Fred. *Free At Last?: The Civil Rights Movement and the People Who Made It.* New York: Harper Perennial, 1991.

"The Progress of Black Student Matriculations at the Nation's Highest-Ranked Colleges and Universities." *Journal of Blacks in Higher Education,* vol. 0, issue 21 (Autumn 1998), 8–14.

Regents of the University of California v. Bakke, 438 U.S. 265, 311-3122 (1978).

The Report of the President's Commission on Campus Unrest. New York: Arno Press, 1970.

Rhodes, Joel. *The Voices of Violence: Performative Violence as Protest in the Vietnam Era.* Westport: Praeger, 2001.

Roberts, Steven. "The Debacle at Columbia." *Commonweal,* May 18, 1968.

Roediger, David. *Colored White: Transcending the Racial Past.* Berkeley: University of California Press, 2002.

———. *The Wages of Whiteness and the Making of the American Working Class.* New York: Routledge, Chapman, and Hall, 1991.

Rojas, Fabio. *From Black Power to Black Studies: How a Radical Social Movement Became an Academic Discipline.* Baltimore: Johns Hopkins University Press, 2007.

Sale, Kirkpatrick. *SDS.* New York: Random House, 1973.

Sales, William. *From Civil Rights to Black Liberation: Malcolm X and the Organization of Afro-American Unity.* Cambridge, Mass.: South End Press, 1994.

——. Telephone interview with author, March 25, 1999, Columbia, Missouri.

Salmond, John. *"My Mind Set on Freedom": A History of the Civil Rights Movement, 1954–1968.* Chicago: Ivan R. Dee, 1997.

Sammons, Jeffrey. "Race and Sport: A Critical, Historical Examination." *Journal of Sport History,* vol. 21, no. 3 (1994), 203–78.

Samuels, Gertrude. "A Walk along 'the Worst Block.'" *Time Magazine,* September 30, 1962.

San Francisco Examiner, 1968.

Schoener, Allon, ed. *Harlem on My Mind: Cultural Capital of Black America, 1900–1968.* New York: Random House, 1968.

Schuyler, George. "Teaching Negro History Is Questionable." *Globe Democrat,* August 13, 1968.

Schwartz, Lynne. *We Are Talking about Homes: A Great University against Its Neighbors.* New York: Harper and Row, 1985.

Scott, Anne Firor. *The Southern Lady: From Pedestal to Politics, 1830–1930.* Charlottesville: University Press of Virginia, 1995.

Seale, Bobby. *Seize the Time: The Story of the Black Panther Party and Huey P. Newton.* Baltimore: Black Classic Press, 1991.

Sellers, Cleveland. *The River of No Return: The Autobiography of a Black Militant and the Life and Death of SNCC.* New York: William Morrow, 1973.

Shabazz, Betty. *Malcolm X Speaks Out.* Indianapolis: Curtis Management, 1992.

Sherry, Michael. *The Rise of American Air Power: The Creation of Armageddon.* New Haven: Yale University Press, 1987.

Silberman, Charles. "Different Goals." In *The Civil Rights Movement: Opposing Viewpoints,* ed. William Dudley. San Diego: Greenhaven Press, 1996.

"Six Weeks That Shook Morningside: A Special Report." *Columbia College Today* (Spring 1968).

Skolnick, Jerome. *The Politics of Protest, Violent Aspects of Protest and Confrontation: A Staff Report to the National Commission on the Causes and Prevention of Violence.* Washington, D.C.: U.S. Government Printing Office, 1969.

Slater, Robert. "The First Black Tenured Faculty at the Nation's Highest-Ranked Universities." *Journal of Blacks in Higher Education,* vol. 0, issue 22 (Winter 1998–99), 97–106.

Sollors, Werner, Caldwell Titcomb, and Thomas Underwood, eds. *Blacks at Harvard: A Documentary History of African-American Experience at Harvard and Radcliffe.* New York: New York University Press, 1993.

Spearman, Leonard. "Federal Roles and Responsibilities Relative to the Higher Education of Blacks since 1967." *Journal of Negro Education,* vol. 50, no. 3 (Summer 1981), 285–98.

Starr, Roger. "The Case of the Columbia Gym." *The Public Interest* (May 1968), 102–21.

Strout, Cushing, and David Grossvogel, eds. *Divided We Stand: Reflections of the Crisis at Cornell.* Garden City: Doubleday, 1970.

"Students." *Time,* May 9, 1968.

Students of Columbia University, directors and producers. *Columbia Revolt.* Third World Newsreel, 1968, video cassette.

Sutton, S. B. *Civilizing American Cities: A Selection of Frederick Law Olmsted's Writings on City Landscapes.* Cambridge: MIT Press, 1971.

Takaki, Ronald. *Double Victory: A Multicultural History of America in World War II.* Boston: Little, Brown, 2000.

Terry, Wallace. *Bloods: An Oral History of the Vietnam War by Black Veterans.* New York: Random House, 1984.

Thomas, Richard. *Life for Us Is What We Make It: Building Black Community in Detroit, 1915–1945.* Bloomington: Indiana University Press, 1992.

Trimberger, E. K. "Why a Rebellion at Columbia Was Inevitable." *Trans-Action* (September 1968), 28–38.

Ture, Kwame [Stokely Carmichael], and Charles Hamilton. *Black Power: The Politics of Liberation in America.* New York: Vintage Books, 1992.

Unger, Sanford. *FBI: An Uncensored Look Behind the Walls.* Boston: Little, Brown, 1975.

U.S. Senate. Assembly. Senator Basil Paterson and Assemblyman Charles Rangel Reading for the Committee on City of New York. S. 2262 and A. 2952, January 24, 1968.

Van DeBurg, William, ed. *Modern Black Nationalism: From Marcus Garvey to Louis Farrakhan.* New York: New York University Press, 1997.

———. *A New Day in Babylon: The Black Power Movement and American Culture, 1965–1975.* Chicago: University of Chicago Press, 1992.

Village Voice (New York), April 24, 1969.

WABC-TV, April 16, 1968, New York.

WABC-TV, April 27, 1968, New York.

WABC-TV, April 30, 1968, New York.

Wallerstein, Immanuel. *Africa, the Politics of Independence.* New York: Vintage Press, 1961.

———. *Africa, the Politics of Unity: An Analysis of a Contemporary Social Movement.* New York: Vintage Press, 1961.

Washington Post, 1968–1971.

WBAI-FM, April 26, 1968, New York.

WBAI-FM, April 30, 1968, New York.

WCBS-TV, April 25, 1968, New York.

WCBS-TV, April 27, 1968, New York.

WCBS-TV, April 30, 1968, New York.

Wesley, Charles. "The Negro in the Organization of Abolition." In *Blacks in the Abolitionist Movement,* ed. Bracey, Meier, and Rudwick.

West, Cornel. *Race Matters.* New York: Vintage Books, 1994.

Westside News, 1965–1969.

Whalen, Jack, and Richard Flacks. *Beyond the Barricades: The Sixties Generation Grows Up.* Philadelphia: Temple University Press, 1989.

Whites, LeeAnn. *The Civil War as a Crisis in Gender: Augusta, Georgia, 1860–1890.* Athens: University of Georgia Press, 1995.

"Why Columbia Happened." *Newsweek,* October 14, 1968.

Willard Straight Takeover Collection. Cornell University Archives, Ithaca.

Williamson, Joel. *A Rage for Order: Black and White Relations in the American South since Emancipation.* Oxford: Oxford University Press, 1986.

"Will Toughness Halt Student Uprisings?" *US News,* June 3, 1968.

Wilson, Cicero, interview with author, April 26, 2008, New York.

Witcover, Jules. *The Year the Dream Died: Revisiting 1968 in America.* New York: Warner Books, 1997.

WMCA, April 26, 1968, New York.

WNBC, April 26, 1968, New York.

WNBC, April 29, 1968, New York.

WNBC-TV, May 1, 1968, New York.

WNEW-TV, April 29, 1968, New York.

WNEW-TV, May 1, 1968, New York.

Worker (New York), May 17, 1968.

WOR-TV, April 25, 1968, New York.

WOR-TV, April 26, 1968, New York.

WOR-TV, April 29, 1968, New York.

WTOP Radio, May 1, 1968, New York.

Wyatt-Brown, Bertram. *Honor and Violence in the Old South.* Oxford: Oxford University Press, 1986.

Yale Daily News, 1968–1970.

Zinn, Howard. *SNCC: Snick, Student Nonviolent Coordinating Committee, the New Abolitionists.* Boston: Beacon Press, 1965.

———. *The Twentieth Century: A People's History.* New York: HarperPerennial, 1998.

Index

STEFAN M. BRADLEY is an assistant
professor in the Department of History/
African American
Studies at St. Louis University
in St. Louis, Missouri.

The University of Illinois Press
is a founding member of the
Association of American University Presses.

———————————————————————

University of Illinois Press
1325 South Oak Street
Champaign, IL 61820-6903
www.press.uillinois.edu